FRIEDRICH HÖLDERLIN
An Early Modern

Hölderlin in 1823
From a pencil sketch by
Johann Georg Schreiner and Rudolph Lohbauer

FRIEDRICH HÖLDERLIN

An Early Modern

Hölderlin Bicentennial Symposium

Edited by
Emery E. George

Ann Arbor
THE UNIVERSITY OF MICHIGAN PRESS

Permissions

Oxford University Press, New York

David Gascoyne, "Tenebrae," from David Gascoyne, *Collected Poems*, edited by Robin Skelton. Copyright © 1965 by Oxford University Press.

Edwin Muir, "Hölderlin's Journey." From *Collected Poems* by Edwin Muir. Copyright © 1960 by Willa Muir. Reprinted by permission of Oxford University Press, Inc.

Pantheon Books, a Division of Random House, Inc.

Passages of prose and verse from *The True Voice of Feeling: Studies in English Romantic Poetry*, by Herbert Read. Copyright 1953 by Herbert Read.

Random House, Inc.

Stephen Spender, "Hoelderlin's Old Age," from *Collected Poems, 1928-1953*, by Stephen Spender.

Schiller-Nationalmuseum

Inked silhouette of Hölderlin, probably from 1797, in Hölderlin's personal copy of *Hyperion*. The original is preserved at the Schiller-Nationalmuseum. Reproduced as jacket illustration by kind permission of the Director, Schiller-Nationalmuseum, Marbach am Neckar.

Pencil drawing of Hölderlin, dated July 27, 1823, by Johann Georg Schreiner and Rudolf Lohbauer. The original is preserved at the Schiller-Nationalmuseum. Reproduced as frontispiece by kind permission of the Director, Schiller-Nationalmuseum, Marbach am Neckar.

Stephen Tonsor and *Modern Age*

Stephen Tonsor, "Hölderlin and the Modern Sensibility," first published in *Modern Age*, Spring 1971.

The University of Michigan Press

Passages of verse in English translation from Friedrich Hölderlin, *Poems and Fragments*, translated by Michael Hamburger. Copyright © 1967 by Michael Hamburger.

Introduction

Twelve of the fourteen signed contributions gathered in this
volume—all with the exception of the opening anthology by
Michael Hamburger and the group of three translations by
Christopher Middleton—were originally presented at the Hölderlin Bicentennial Symposium held on the Ann Arbor campus of The
University of Michigan, November 5-7, 1970. When the Symposium
was first planned, each prospective contributor was asked to
submit a paper that would touch, in one form or another, on the
Symposium's general theme "In What Sense Is Hölderlin an Early
Modern?" The rather considerable variety of response that the
resulting essays represent may be explained first of all by the
interdisciplinary design of the Symposium. Those who spoke as
official participants represent six fields, two of them outside
the literary disciplines: classics, comparative literature,
English, German, history, and psychiatry. The variety of response
noted was made possible also by the equally important, if more
general, consideration that no two of us think exactly alike on
any given question, and the Symposium did try to bring together
scholars in an unusual, possibly even improbable, pattern. But
the general wording of the title of the conference itself, as I
well knew from the beginning, was of a leading nature. Logically,
it asks two questions: (1) *Is* Hölderlin an early modern? and
(2) Once we have agreed that he is one, *in what sense* may this

be said to hold true? The intention behind asking a leading
question was to assure not only variety, but also fruitful
controversy. The practical results were gratifying. In a few
of the essays the palpable response is either: "I cannot think
of a single respect in which Hölderlin is an early modern," or:
"I prefer to see him as something other than an early modern."
The papers by Lawrence Ryan and Wilfried Malsch incorporate some
of both views. Malsch argues directly that early modernity must
be denied a poet of Hölderlin's historical situation, while Ryan,
initially at least, has simply chosen another topic. While some
prospective participants demurred (and in the two or three sever-
est cases the person approached declined to participate), the
results do show an amazing degree of harmonious collaboration
on such a complex problem.

The issue of modernity is not merely one of zeitgeist. We
may justly feel that this is one of the fundamental questions
that art can pose. It strikes at the validity of aesthetic
phenomena with an intensity matched only by questions concerning
the poet's vision, or a poem's structure and form. Like the
latter issues, modernity has its proper methodological fields
of inquiry--the historical, the interpretive, the evaluative.
The historical field, at least in a special sense of the word
history, seems closest to Hölderlin's own understanding of his
own modernity, and to this I shall come presently. In the interpretive and evaluative fields the critic is, relatively speaking,
on his own. The well-known Heideggerian hermeneutical circle,
so successfully adapted by Emil Staiger to the study of literary
genres, appears as one, none-too-distant point of reference in
method when we argue that Hölderlin is an early modern because
we, out of our historical situation, discover how very much like
us he is. This is one subject-oriented version of what, for
Lawrence Ryan, becomes an object-oriented "method of integral
understanding"--a method of interpreting Hölderlin *"durch Hölderlin und auf Hölderlin hin"* (through Hölderlin and toward

Hölderlin).[1] But modernity as a critical concept has a naïve as
well as a sophisticated aspect, and here is where the evaluative
task of analysis must ally itself with the interpretive. I hope
it will seem clear that no one in this volume argues totally on
the naïve side; no one says that an early modern is that, solely
because he strikes *us moderns* as one. I suspect that the super-
ficiality of such statements has to do with their exclusive concentration on etymology. As *Webster's Third New International
Dictionary* tells us, the word *modern* is ultimately derived from
the Latin adverb *modo* "just now," and connotes ideas of the
fashionable, modish, ephemeral, and even sensationalistic.
Modernity in its sophisticated aspect transcends etymology. In
this sense it implies a marriage of two disparate views, namely
that progress in art is possible, and that preservation of supratemporal values is a cultural and aesthetic imperative. The
result is an orientation toward a present and a future that make
the best of what they inherit from the past.

  As illustrations of acknowledged modernity in each of the
two senses, the sophisticated and the naïve, let me counterpoise
the current fate of Hölderlin with that of Hermann Hesse. These
two writers considered together can be regarded as a pair of
very nearly ideal test cases. Despite the disparity in chronology, some similarities are amazing. Each writer was a Swabian
with a strong Pietist background; each was a rebel against the
bureaucratic and religious establishment of his day; each looked
to the East for spiritual sustenance. In his recent, highly
revealing, and disarmingly personal essay "Hermann Hesse, the
American Youth Movement, and Problems of Literary Evaluation,"
Egon Schwarz quotes the critic Stephen Koch, who in the June 13,
1968, issue of *The New Republic* states that, ever since Timothy
Leary pronounced *Steppenwolf* his favorite work of literature,
"Hesse has been standard psychedelic equipment, along with water
pipes, day-glow art, the Maharishi, Jim Morrison and the I Ching."[2]
Whether such adulation, or if you will, abuse, can be taken as

an indication of Hesse's or any other writer's actual literary
worth in any sense, negative *or* positive, is one of the seminal
questions that Professor Schwarz's very persuasive article raises.
Hölderlin's claim to standard modernity on the contemporary scene
is of a very different order. Hesse's zenith of popularity in
this country is matched by a corresponding nadir in his native
land; for Hölderlin, informed public acclaim in Germany could
not be higher, while in America we have hardly as yet begun to
understand him. (The 1967 publication of Michael Hamburger's
definitive translations of Hölderlin's poetry by The University
of Michigan Press was certainly a major step in the right direction.) Analogous imbalances on the international scene aside,
Hölderlin and Hesse are moderns in two very different senses of
the word. Hölderlin's works do not stand a very good chance of
ever becoming "standard psychedelic equipment." But while Hölderlin now appears to be a reasonably model example of a fad-
resistant writer, we will do well to reflect that this has not
always seemed so obvious. In order to appreciate the change
that has taken place in our image of the poet, one need but recall the various misunderstandings his late poetry aroused during the nineteenth century, or indeed the Third Reich's prosti-
tution of all that Hölderlin's name stands for. Pierre Bertaux's
recent identification of Hölderlin with the Swabian Jacobins
makes us wonder about the possibility of such excesses even in
our own time.[3]

  And yet this very sense of our now having, by and large, a
sophisticated grasp of the ways in which Hölderlin addresses the
human spirit ought to make us doubly wary of the dangers of too
snug a feeling of intellectual security. I am not referring to
the unattractive, although inevitable, metaphor of the "literary
stock market" where, from time to time, we are told that "Schiller
is low" while "Novalis is high" in critical favor, or that "the
thing to do now is to study Büchner," while "nobody looks at
Hebbel any more." As Professor Schwarz reflects, wisely: *"Habent*

sua fata libelli. These crooked paths, these ups and downs have
their reasons, no doubt, and in some instances they are even
discoverable. What is needed here is a phenomenology of fame."[4]
True; but such fluctuations are, in my opinion, no cause for
serious concern. One suspects that every low will bring another
high, that Schiller and Hebbel will never really be out altogether. What I would like to stress is the danger inherent in
the extent to which Hölderlin, with the rapid publication of the
Stuttgarter Hölderlin-Ausgabe and the increase in the number of
studies on his works, has risen in stature to a veritable international literary institution. The bicentenary in whose wake we
now find ourselves is as good a time as any to consider that
unqualified acceptance can very easily lead to total neglect of
important areas of criticism and method. Idolatrous acclaim can
give us the feeling that we understand a writer, while in reality
we either misunderstand him or fail to take into account important aspects of his practice, theory, and total spiritual being.
Such caveats can make our centennial and multicentennial observances in honor of great poets times for sober reflection as
well as for exhilaration. On such rare occasions for celebration, it seems proper to join forces to the ends of a thoughtful
reassessment of (1) our present image of an artist, and (2) the
best ways in which we can keep alive our latter-day conversation
with an early modern like Hölderlin.[5]

In what sense, then, *is* Hölderlin an early modern? In just
the sense, we may suggest, in which we are able to bring him
the best of our spiritual strength out of our particular situation in space as in time. This double qualification--in space
and in time--seems important for understanding how, in Hölderlin's own spiritual existence, the term *modern* ceases to imply
a temporal opposition exclusively. In my welcoming remarks at
the opening session of the Symposium I suggested that if Hölderlin is to be one of our early moderns it is because he is a
latter-day ancient as well. True modernity joins hands with

the past as it does with the future; only in this way can it
create that sense of time-bound timelessness out of which T. S.
Eliot spoke of an "ideal order" among the existing monuments of
literature. We know that this ideal order, in its axiom that
Sophokles is as modern as Anouilh, Anouilh as ancient as Sophokles, and Hölderlin as ancient-modern as either, has nothing
to do with acceptances and rejections as recorded by the best-
seller lists. In my remarks I also suggested that the concept
of modernity itself becomes free to move into dimensions other
than that of time and that the authority for an American Hölderlin celebration comes from the poet himself. I quote, as I
did on that bright Thursday morning, a passage from a manuscript
variant to the late elegy "Brod und Wein" (2:608):

> *Nämlich zu Haus ist der Geist*
> *Nicht am Anfang, nicht an der Quell. Ihn zehret die Heimat,*
> *Kolonie liebt, und tapfer Vergessen der Geist.*

> (For, see, the mind is at home
> Not at the outset, not at its source. Home makes it restless.
> Colony is what the mind craves. Courageous forgetting.)

The dangers of quoting for purposes of establishing spiritual authority are here, I believe, minimal. The above passage
is only the most famous from among the mass of material--poetic,
theoretical, epistolary, documentary--that is time and again
drawn upon by critics preoccupied with Hölderlin's curious and
highly original *"Abendländische Wendung"* (Occidental turn of
heart) toward the end of his lucid career. While this is not
the place to examine this phenomenon in detail (scholars have
puzzled over it ever since Wilhelm Michel coined the two phrases
"Abendländische Wendung" and *"Vaterländische Umkehr"* a full
fifty years ago), it may be useful to point out that this turn
toward the concerns of his fatherland is the very illumination
that clinches Hölderlin's unified time-space concept of modernity,
as it sets the poet's preoccupation with the Greeks apart from

the preoccupations of others of his age. And it is just this
difference, as Stephen Tonsor's paper so aptly points out, that
made Goethe and Schiller suspicious of Hölderlin's seemingly
private brand of classicism. The younger poet's classicism is
not, of course, private in the sense of being incommunicable.
On the contrary, it was in the most personal form of written
communication, the letter, that he expressed his thoughts on
how his individual approach to the Greeks was different from
any other approach on record up to and including his time. In
an important fragment of a letter to an acquaintance, Christian
Gottfried Schütz, Professor of Classics at Jena, Hölderlin writes
(6:381; No. 203):

Das innigere Studium der Griechen hat mir dabei geholfen und
mir statt Freundesumgang gedient, in der Einsamkeit meiner Be-
trachtungen nicht zu sicher, noch zu ungewiss zu werden. Übrigens
sind die Resultate dieses Studiums, die ich gewonnen habe, ziem-
lich von andern, die ich kenne, verschieden. Man hat, wie Ihnen
bekannt ist, die Strenge, womit die hohen Alten die verschie-
denen Arten ihrer Dichtung unterschieden, häufig ganz und gar
misskannt, oder doch nur an das Äusserliche derselben sich
gehalten, überhaupt ihre Kunst viel mehr für wohlberechnetes
Vergnügen gehalten als für eine heilige Schicklichkeit, womit
sie in göttlichen Dingen verfahren mussten. Das Geistigste
musste ihnen zugleich das höchste Charakteristische *sein. So*
auch die Darstellung *desselben. Daher die Strenge und Schärfe*
der Form in ihren Dichtungen, ...

(A rather thorough study of the Greeks has helped me, and
served me as an alternative to conversations with friends, in
becoming neither too self-assured nor too uncertain in the
solitude of my thoughts. Incidentally, the results I have obtained from this study are quite different from others known
to me. As you well know, people have often completely misunderstood the severity with which the sublime ancients differentiated among the various genres of their literature. Or
indeed, critics have paid attention only to externals of the
latter, and have in general considered the art of the Greeks
to be a well-calculated pleasure rather than a sacred propri-
ety by means of which they had to treat of divine matters.
For the Greeks, the most intellectual had at the same time
to be the most highly *characteristic*. This also had to hold
for its *representation*. Hence the severity and sharpness of
form in their literary productions, ...)

The difference between Hölderlin's vision of the Greeks and the
vision of his countrymen resides in Hölderlin's recognition that,
in Greek art and poetry, the most spiritual aspects of inspiration lent themselves to artistic rendition best. This paradox,
in Hölderlin's estimation, is the secret of the unique clarity
of vision and line which Greek art attained. Although the exact
date of the fragment is unknown, it is thought to have been
written in the beginning months of 1800; during the summer of
that year he was to write the elegy "Brod und Wein," the source
of the variant quoted earlier, and Hölderlin's most eloquent
statement on his vision of the reconciliation between Greek and
Christian religious experience.

    The year 1800 was important to the Germans in many respects,
and was exciting as the year, par excellence, of *deutsche Klassik*.
In Weimar Goethe and Schiller were doing some of their finest
work. But it was also a year in which growing dissent from
classicism began to make itself heard, and from other than
strictly romantic quarters. Herder's last great project, the
journal *Adrastea* (1801-1804, completed by his widow and eldest
son), was motivated, as Robert T. Clark, Jr., writes, at least
in part by "Herder's desire to take up arms against Goethe and
Schiller, ... Although himself an admirer of Greek culture,
he remained a relativist, and was therefore unable to understand
Schiller's naïve--and uninformed--worship of Greek beauty, with
which Goethe apparently concurred."[6] Certainly in its essays
at least, the *Adrastea* completes the program, begun in Herder's
Ideen zur Philosophie der Geschichte der Menschheit (1784-91),
of demonstrating the essential equivalence of cultures, and of
reminding the Germans that they would do well to look for their
inspiration in periods and civilizations other than the Greek.
Without perhaps meaning to in a conscious way, Hölderlin takes
up the torch approximately where his spiritual mentor Herder
puts it down. In the letter quoted earlier the younger man
expresses his realization of just how shallow much of the helle-

nizing of his countrymen had been. He is beginning to say, in
effect: "If you want to be Greek, the way to go about it is not
to dress up in Greek costume, to sing in Greek meters (half-
heartedly, and often badly), and to allude to Greek (or pseudo-
Greek) taste in any number of other areas (in architecture and
interior decorating, in typography and bookmaking)." To do this,
and this only, is to vie with a level of cultural frustration
matched on the contemporary scene perhaps only by French chinoi-
serie. In order to become Greek one must follow the *example* of
the Greeks, who after all had no Greeks of their own to look
back upon. The issue, in other words, is one that pits imitation against originality. The Greeks created their inimitable
world out of nothing; they were great because they were themselves.

Precisely so, Hölderlin must become himself. This is the
tone and preoccupation of a letter from the poet to his friend,
Casimir Ulrich Böhlendorff, dated December 4, 1801. It is the
eve of Hölderlin's departure for France, and many critics have
said France is the closest Hölderlin ever came to Greece. Even
at such a critical moment he takes time to advise his friend,
who had sent him a comedy of his own to read, and to praise the
younger man for having, apparently since the play's last-seen
draft, *"an Präzision und tüchtiger Gelenksamkeit so sehr gewonnen und nichts an Wärme verloren"* (gained so strongly on the
counts of precision and controlled flexibility and lost none of
its warmth). And the lesson Hölderlin offers to the young
author of the now-forgotten *Fernando oder die Kunstweihe* is a
chapter in Western poetics second to none (6:425-26; No. 236):

*Wir lernen nichts schwerer als das Nationelle frei gebrauchen.
Und wie ich glaube, ist gerade die Klarheit der Darstellung
uns ursprünglich so natürlich wie den Griechen das Feuer vom
Himmel. Eben deswegen werden diese eher in schöner Leidenschaft, die Du Dir auch erhalten hast, als in jener homeri-
schen Geistesgegenwart und Darstellungsgabe zu übertreffen sein.
   Es klingt paradox. Aber ich behaupt es noch einmal, und stelle*

es Deiner Prüfung und Deinem Gebrauche frei: das eigentliche
Nationelle wird im Fortschritt der Bildung immer der geringere
Vorzug werden. Deswegen sind die Griechen des heiligen Pathos
weniger Meister, weil es ihnen angeboren war, hingegen sind sie
vorzüglich in Darstellungsgabe, von Homer an, weil dieser ausser-
ordentliche Mensch seelenvoll genug war, um die abendländische
Junonische Nüchternheit *für sein Apollonsreich zu erbeuten, und*
so wahrhaft das fremde sich anzueignen.

Bei uns ists umgekehrt. Deswegen ists auch so gefährlich, sich
die Kunstregeln einzig und allein von griechischer Vortefflich-
keit zu abstrahieren. Ich habe lange daran laboriert und weiss
nun, das ausser dem, was bei den Griechen und uns das Höchste
sein muss, nämlich dem lebendigen Verhältnis und Geschick, wir
nicht wohl etwas gleich mit ihnen haben dürfen.

Aber das Eigene muss so gut gelernt sein, wie das Fremde.
Deswegen sind uns die Griechen unentbehrlich. Nur werden wir
ihnen gerade in unserm Eigenen, Nationellen nicht nachkommen,
weil, wie gesagt, der freie Gebrauch des Eigenen das schwerste
ist.

(Nothing is more difficult for us to learn than to use our
native gifts freely. And, as I believe, it is precisely clarity
of representation that is originally as natural to us as the
fire from heaven is to the Greeks. That is just why the latter
will have to be *surpassed* much sooner in agreeable passion,
which you have also preserved in yourself, than in that Homeric
presence of mind and penchant for artistic realization.

It sounds paradoxical. But I assert it once more and submit
it to your verification and use: in the progress of culture,
what is strictly native will always come to be the less preferred. The reason the Greeks are masters of holy pathos to a
lesser degree is that it was inborn in them. On the other hand,
they are excellent in the gift of representation from Homer on,
because this extraordinary man was sufficiently profound of soul
to acquire, for his Apollonian realm, Occidental *Junonian sobri-*
ety, and thus truly to make his own that which was once foreign
to him.

With us the reverse holds true. That is precisely why it is
so dangerous to abstract for oneself the rules of art purely
and solely from Greek standards of excellence. I have worked
at this for a long time and know now that, with the exception
of what must count highest both with the Greeks and with us,
namely living proportion and craftsmanship, there is not anything we can hold in common with them.

But what is inborn must be mastered just as thoroughly as what
lies outside one. That is why the Greeks are indispensable to us.
It is just that precisely in our native endowments we will not
come to equal them because, as I have said, the free use of
one's own gifts is the hardest.)

If you can be yourself, you can do anything; but being oneself is the most difficult task of all. The letter brings order into the chaotic subject of originality versus imitation and emulation, of intercultural tribute and borrowing. The poet may be bound to his time and place but, more important, he is bound to himself. Yet, paradoxically, it is himself he must find. The German artist cannot afford to rest content with being like the Greek artist in a material sense. That German *art* is akin to and feeds on Greek *nature* is axiomatic in the chiastic set of relationships Hölderlin explores. On the theorematic and programmatic levels of artistic growth the German artist must surpass in himself what is natural to the Greek temperament. It is from Homer's method rather than from his given materials that the Occidental poet must steal the heavenly fire that is the Greek artist's birthright. But colonizing the native fire of the Greeks is only the first of two steps toward self-realization. The statement that nothing is more difficult than to learn to use one's native gifts freely and naturally, lends fresh meaning to the "Brod und Wein" variant. Its home grounds make the mind restless: it yearns for a colony, for a kind of forgetting. Characteristically for Hölderlin's carefully thought-out theory, it is not mere forgetting the spirit wants, but rather what Hölderlin calls *"tapfer Vergessen"* (brave oblivion). The thought seems close to Goethe's concept of *Stirb und werde* (die and become), which is not mere dying, either, but rather dying in order to be reborn. What the spirit yearns for is an émigré condition in which it may achieve union with its counterpart so that, as a result, it may become the more aware of itself. While Hölderlin owed much to the Greeks in a substantial sphere, and paramountly to Plato, this argument need not be taken to refer to the myth in the *Timaios* in which the spirit is on a journey looking for its "lost better half." It is enough to remember that the story of the soul's withdrawal from and subsequent return to the realm of men is surely one of

the profoundest myths of the human consciousness. In the face
of frequent, at times sharp, disagreements among critics concerned with Hölderlin's "Occidental turn" in its various ramifications, I am tempted to think M. B. Benn is right in calling
Hölderlin's present preoccupation with the Greeks "historical
thinking." Benn writes:

> What is commonly referred to as Hölderlin's "abendländische
> Wendung" is just this increasingly clear realisation that if
> modern nations are to achieve anything at all comparable in
> value with the Greek achievement they must avoid imitating the
> Greeks and adapt their aims and methods to their own peculiar
> circumstances, their own unique historical situation. But it
> is not a "Wendung" in the sense that the Greeks cease to be
> important for Hölderlin or even that their importance for him
> is much reduced. For in the German and the Greek syntheses as
> conceived by Hölderlin the common factors ... are ... the
> means by which a people is enabled to form a worthy conception
> of the divine and to enter on a period of supreme religious
> fulfilment.[7]

Hölderlin's remarkable definition of artistic modernity spans
time and space, and unites within itself the spatial and the
temporal in an indissoluble bond. The new pattern that emerges
from the union (and one is tempted to think of Goethe's *Wahlver-
wandtschaften* principle) is one that counterpoises *here and now*
against *there and then*. But this is accomplished with a difference. It is clear from the letter to Böhlendorff that in the
modern writer's consciousness of the here and now the there and
then must be understood to live a vital inner life. Modernity
thus comes to imply, indeed mean, supratemporality. This implies
further that modernity cannot be thought of as an exclusive
characteristic of any particular age, but is a concept under-
going constant shift with reference to the way any given historical period regards its past and measures itself against a probable future.

How relative such historical thinking can be may be illustrated by reference to what we now call the Middle Ages, a period

of the world not ordinarily thought of as central to Hölderlin
studies, although it is one that can be shown to have been of
interest to the poet himself.[8] My present concern is not with
these details, but rather with the implications, for Hölderlin's
thought, of our introducing the medieval concept into the more
immediate ancient-modern continuum. It may be a telling circumstance that, in ways quite other than the purely factual, the
idea of being medieval was unknown to twelfth-century moderns
(at least, surely, the Scholastics of Paris or Limoges would
never have dreamed of calling themselves *medieval* either in the
objective or in the psychological sense!). We may be equally
resigned to the possibility that, to *moderns* five or six centuries hence, we ourselves may appear medieval in some respects.
Hölderlin who, in many places besides the Böhlendorff letter of
1801, demonstrates a theoretical understanding of the structure
of experience, was keenly aware that, in matters both spiritual
and historical, *les extrèmes se touchent*. A surprising set of
distinctions in the relation of historical periods begins to
emerge. We may well feel that *ancient* versus *modern* are the
congenial touching extremes, and that *medieval* versus *modern*
are the antagonistic ones; at least this seems to work for our
understanding of Hölderlin's poetic experience. I myself should
not mind too much if in the thirty-fifth century people were to
look back on our epoch as on ancient times. But medievaldom is
a condition to be overcome; the Middle Ages are middle in the
sense of a great intermediate age of the world characterized by
marking time, waiting for a better tomorrow that cannot come
just yet. Hölderlin has in his poetry a powerful caveat against
the age going medieval in quite this way. In the important
seventh stanza of the definitive version of "Brod und Wein" the
poet speaks of his (our) age as one from which the gods of classical Greece have departed, an era when anxious souls are ques-
tioning sacred truths, among others the validity of the poet's
vocation (2:93-94):

Aber Freund! wir kommen zu spät. Zwar leben die Götter,
   Aber über dem Haupt droben in anderer Welt.
Endlos wirken sie da und scheinens wenig zu achten,
   Ob wir leben, so sehr schonen die Himmlischen uns.
Denn nicht immer vermag ein schwaches Gefäss sie zu fassen,
   Nur zu Zeiten erträgt göttliche Fülle der Mensch.
. . . .
Donnernd kommen sie drauf. Indessen dünket mir öfters
   Besser zu schlafen, wie so ohne Genossen zu sein,
So zu harren, und was zu tun indes und zu sagen,
   Weiss ich nicht, und wozu Dichter in dürftiger Zeit.
Aber sie sind, sagst du, wie des Weingotts heilige Priester,
   Welche von Lande zu Land zogen in heiliger Nacht.

(But, my friend, we have come too late. Though the gods are
      living,
  Over our heads they live, up in a different world.
Endlessly there they act and, such is their kind wish to
      spare us,
  Little they seem to care whether we live or do not.
For not always a frail, a delicate vessel can hold them,
  Only at times can our kind bear the full impact of gods.
. . . .
Thundering then they come. But meanwhile too often I think it's
  Better to sleep than to be friendless as we are, alone,
Always waiting, and what to do or to say in the meantime
  I don't know, and who wants poets at all in lean years?
But they are, you say, like those holy ones, priests of the
      wine-god
  Who in holy Night roamed from one place to the next.)

The last two lines are a courageous and optimistic answer to
the despair contained in the preceding two. The overall shape
of the stanza, asserting as it does Hölderlin's persistently
recurring cyclic vision of history--mythical, personal, social--
hardly needs further elaborate comment. Hölderlin utters his
faith that our modern age can muster the intellectual forces
to overcome its local and temporary tendencies toward the vege-
tative medieval state. And within the context of the need to
overcome inertia of the spirit, the question *"Wozu Dichter in
dürftiger Zeit?"* (Who wants poets at all in lean years?) answers
itself. No age can do without its best poets who, in singing,
recall the past less than they will the future into being. In

terms of the historical specifics: there is a real reason for
the enduring freshness of the work of the best medieval poets,
from Prudentius through Chaucer. The secret of the early modernity of these poets (and I am intentionally stretching the term
in a plea for Hölderlin's universality) is that they sing not
on a semantic but on a truly spiritual plane, and in this sense
they sing *not their own times but us.* "*Siehe! wir sind es, wir;*
Frucht von Hesperien ists!" (Look, we are it, ourselves; fruit
of Hesperia it is!)--Hölderlin argues in the closing stanza of
"Brod und Wein" that the true subject of all the viable religious
prophecy, meaning song, of previous ages is the most recent age
that masters the tones of that body of song. This I understand
to be the substance of Wilfried Malsch's argument, which includes
the very cogent statement that Hölderlin is an early modern in
the same sense in which the second Isaiah was one.

As with modern song, so with modern criticism: the significance of Hölderlin's theoretical thought lies in its being so
highly poetic and practical at the same time. The notion of
native talent schooling itself on a tradition opposed to it in
nature is no more abstract than it is new. Deserving young
Americans go to Europe to study with as much anticipation of
finding themselves as their ancient Roman counterparts went to
Athens, and the strictures quoted in Herbert Barrows's essay
notwithstanding, translation is widely recognized as a good way
for sensitive young talents to learn what their language can do.
It is tempting to call these activities forms of temporary intellectual exile. Dante away from Florence, Goethe in his Persia
of the imagination, Heine in Paris--all united the act of leaving the native heritage with an enduring, if in some instances
painful, love for it. At the end of his first letter to Böhlendorff (which, not so incidentally, also contains Hölderlin's
finest tribute to Goethe) Hölderlin too could juxtapose the two
sentences: "... *sie können mich nicht brauchen. Deutsch will und*
muss ich übrigens bleiben, und wenn mich die Herzens- und die
Nahrungsnot nach Otaheiti triebe" (... they have no use for me.

German, incidentally, is what I shall and must remain, even if
personal and economic misery drive me all the way to Tahiti [6:
428]). We are again reminded of the second Isaiah's religion
of exile, a religion of *"tapfer Vergessen"*--not of oblivion,
but of transfigured renewal. For Hölderlin went to France,
came back, and wrote Böhlendorff once more (6:432; No. 240):

> *Das gewaltige Element, das Feuer des Himmels und die Stille
> der Menschen, ihr Leben in der Natur, und ihre Eingeschränkt-
> heit und Zufriedenheit, hat mich beständig ergriffen, und wie
> man Helden nachspricht, kann ich wohl sagen, dass mich Apollo
> geschlagen.*

> (The powerful element, the fire from heaven and the still-
> ness of people, their life in nature and their confinement and
> contentment, fascinated me constantly and, as is said of heroes,
> I can truly say Apollo has struck me.)

Many critics have taken this passage to be Hölderlin's declaration of his own insanity. But it was after this experience
that Hölderlin wrote most of the poetry that inspires us to
raise the question of his early modernity in the first place.

The arrangement of the ten essays in the second, central
part of this volume causes them to fall into two equal parts.
Five of the papers, those by Herbert Barrows, Stephen Tonsor,
Ingo Seidler, Theodore Fiedler, and Aleksis Rannit, account for
Hölderlin's claim to modernity directly. The following group
of five studies, by Gerald F. Else, Wilfried Malsch, Lawrence
O. Frye, Lawrence Ryan, and Helm Stierlin, either do justice to
Hölderlin's modern import indirectly or treat another topic.
Tellingly enough, some papers in this latter category counterpoise against the modern not the ancient or the medieval, but
the romantic. Romanticism, that protean and troublesome mystique,
can of course be very medieval in substance, while pointing ahead
to a great deal that we now recognize as modern, or congenial to
the tradition of modernism. Herbert Barrows makes an important
point in his essay by saying, in effect, that modern concerns
continually hark back to romantic ones; that Hölderlin "has

recently been claimed by many interests, and he does indeed seem
to have had something to say to surrealists, to existentialists,
to theologians, and to many who claim merely to be modern. But
behind it all there lies a participation in recognizable phases
of romanticism, ..." (p. 32). This new historical concept, logical and insistent as it seems for Hölderlin's literary-historical
situation, can encourage the reader to see the ten papers in Part
II in yet another configuration: five contributions (those by
Seidler, Fiedler, Rannit, Else, Stierlin) treat Hölderlin's early
modernity and with it, his classicism; five (by Barrows, Tonsor,
Malsch, Frye, Ryan) see the poet's achievement, not as modern,
but rather in the light of qualities and tendencies that argue
closer ties with the romantic program and temperament. Returning
to the original arrangement of five plus five papers, it is possible to say, finally, that the essays by Barrows through Rannit
(the first five) are concerned primarily with the modern *reception*
of Hölderlin, while the second group of five contributions (by
Else through Stierlin) are overwhelmingly of a *historical and
hermeneutical* orientation.

Whatever a reader's first attempt at classifying the ten
essays might be, I hope he will not miss certain inescapable
attitudes that tend to make each piece a highly individual and
independent contribution. Else's classical subject, Seidler's
and Rannit's concern with how Hölderlin has fared in our century,
are such clearly marked approaches. Equally individualistic are
Ryan's subject *(deutsche Romantik)* and the approaches of Malsch
(enlightenment) and Tonsor (irrationality). Increased complexity
in thought and method seems evidenced in two of the longest essays: the lead article by Herbert Barrows and the closing piece
by Helm Stierlin. The former study, by a scholar of English
literature, approaches the problem of "colonizing" Hölderlin
for English-speaking moderns, and finds, fascinatingly enough,
that it must accomplish this by stressing Hölderlin's affinities
with prime representatives of English romanticism--Wordsworth,
Shelley, Keats, and Byron. The latter investigation, by a psy-

chiatrist, approaches Hölderlin's oft-romanticized psychotic
condition and studies its reconciliation with self-healing powers
in poetic creativity. Thus Stierlin's argument tends toward
seeing the establishment of a classical balance in the poet's
psyche. Of interest also are the ways in which one paper seems
to answer another, whether in substance or by tacit response to
a key point or theory. Else argues that Hölderlin's modern
relevance may perhaps be sought in his taking Sophokles seriously
on a religious plane. Rannit, at the other end both of the
chronological and methodological spectra, nevertheless seems to
answer the classicist's plea by insisting that elevated Hölderlinian style rings clear and true in the practice of contemporary
moderns. Close substantial response is evidenced between the
papers by Seidler and Fiedler. Seidler's conclusion that we need
not have conscious poetic emulators of Hölderlin's practice in
order to experience his essential modernity is answered by Fiedler's insistence that, as Trakl's example shows, poetic disci-
pleship and independent creativity are not mutually exclusive
quantities.

No less interesting than the amiable substantial controversy are the most important disagreements in principle, and
the consequences of such disagreement. Ryan's contention that
Hyperion stands closer to Friedrich Schlegel's definition of
romanticism than does *Wilhelm Meisters Lehrjahre* comes to be
tantamount to saying that Hölderlin is a more satisfying modern
than Goethe (in the novel, at least), if we agree that the definition given in "Athenäums-Fragment" No. 116--*"Die romantische
Poesie ist eine progressive Universalpoesie"*--speaks of all
poetry, regardless of time or of place. Frye's initial point
of reference may be Plato (Kronian versus Zeusian time in the
Politikos), but the "festive dawn" at the end of *Hyperion* (Frye,
p. 117) cannot help referring us, in its way, to Hölderlin's
own hopes for the future of his people (Hyperion, after all, is
about to embark on a poetic career), and to that messianic religion of the future with which the paper by Malsch is also con-

cerned. The ultimate point of agreement in principle among the
ten studies overrides, it seems to me, their particular points
of disagreemnnt. All the contributors to this volume share a
serious concern with poetic language as a carrier of the meaning of early modernity as aesthetically significant timelessness.
One comes back to Hölderlin's fragment from around 1800, adopted
by Heidegger as the second of his *Leitworte* at the head of the
essay "Hölderlin und das Wesen der Dichtung": *"... und darum ist
... der Güter Gefährlichstes, die Sprache dem Menschen gegeben,
... damit er zeuge, was er sei"* (and that is why language, most
dangerous of possessions, has been given to man: in order that
he may affirm what he is [2:325]). One of the best recent commentaries on Hölderlin's position at this focal point is found
in the Princeton *Encyclopedia of Poetry and Poetics*, at the end
of the long article "Modern Poetics": "Because of their greater
proximity to language, poets reflect the fundamental tensions
of human existence more faithfully than even the greatest among
the metaphysicians. And the purest of them all, the poet who,
according to Heidegger, has been able to name the very essence
of poetry, Hölderlin, offers therefore an insight into Being
which is without antecedent in the history of human thought."[9]

A word should be said about the overall tripartite division
of the volume into contributions by poets, scholars, and translators. This practical orientation harks back to the fifth and
final session of the Symposium, which was a workshop organized
under the principle that efforts to understand Hölderlin's poetry
must be expended in the actual presence of the poetry. In addition to Cyrus Hamlin's translation of the elegy "Heimkunft" and
my version of the hymn "Patmos," both of which were read at the
workshop, I am happy to be able to include three new Hölderlin
translations by Christopher Middleton, the odes "Heidelberg"
and "Vulkan" and the third draft of the late hymnic fragment
"Griechenland." The workshop session also included the reading
of several poems on or to Hölderlin; these, for reasons having
mainly to do with length, could not be included here. But it

is in the spirit of this latter genre of work that the anthology
of English and American Hölderlin poems, gathered and introduced
by Michael Hamburger, is included as part I. As regards the
sequential relation between parts I and III, it may for a moment
seem a reversal of priorities to turn our attention first to
followers and only then to the poet himself. What is actually
being stressed is that poets should precede translators. The
work that poets do today as a response to their Hölderlin experience can (to register respectful disagreement with Seidler) be
taken as one index of the strength of our modern claim to the
earlier poet. Whether or not this actually seems so at any given
time depends on the quality of the work done. I think that by
this criterion there can be no doubts about the poems by Edwin
Muir, Stephen Spender, and others included in part I. I hope
that the work of the translators in part III will seem no less
interesting, especially since the five translated texts represent
three widely divergent viewpoints on the theory and practice of
translation. One also hopes that this closing group of offerings
of Hölderlin in English may be representative of a new beginning
in the translation of Hölderlin's poetry in the English-speaking
world.

   The sources of the English translations following the verse
or prose quotations from various languages--German, Greek, Italian, Russian--are of four categories:

1. For Hölderlin's poetry Michael Hamburger's translations are
   used wherever possible. This is duly mentioned in the permissions section preceding this introduction.
2. For works by authors other than Hölderlin, and for one late
   Hölderlin fragment, several contributors in part II use published sources. To this category belong the quotations of
   lines from the Fitts-Fitzgerald translation of the Sophoklean
   Antigone (Else), of the passage of the Skemp translation of
   Plato's *Politikos* (Frye), and of the Douglas Scott translation of Hölderlin's 1800 fragment on language, embedded in
   Herbert Read's essay (Barrows).

3. Several authors in part II, and the authors of the two commentaries in part III, prefer to use their own translations. In part II Tonsor translates the concluding stanza of "An die Parzen"; Seidler offers his own English for prose passages from the writings of Josef Weinheber; Else renders passages of Sophokles' *Antigone* at crucial points; Malsch offers his own translation of several passages; and Stierlin supplies his own translation of the letter by Hölderlin's mother to her son, dated October 29, 1805.

4. For "Patmos," "Friedensfeier," and for all examples of Hölderlin's poetry for which a translation by Hamburger or by a contributor is not available, I offer my own translation. For purposes of this volume these include: the Frankfurt epode "An Diotima" (*"Komm und siehe die Freude um uns ..."*), the rhymed "Diotima, Mittlere Fassung," "Der Tod fürs Vaterland," "Gesang des Deutschen," "Stutgard," and variants to "Natur und Kunst oder Saturn und Jupiter" and "Brod und Wein." My translations are also used for the rather numerous quotations from *Hyperion*, from Hölderlin's theoretical essays (including the "Anmerkungen zur Antigonae" and the collaborative "Das älteste Systemprogramm des deutschen Idealismus"), and from Hölderlin's letters, as well as for passages from Friedrich Schlegel, Novalis, Hegel, and for the series of shorter quotations from the works and letters of Trakl and other twentieth-century poets. I hope that the grotesqueness of Weinheber's so-called variation on Hölderlin's "An die Parzen" comes through in my equally garbled English verse; perhaps the latter may serve also as criticism by translation. I also hope that all the translations will seem accurate and helpful, and that they will increase the usefulness of this book to everyone interested in Hölderlin, to the scholar and the general reader alike.

A note of warm thanks goes out to everyone connected with and enthusiastic about this Hölderlin project from its very inception. My thanks are due first of all to all the participants

in the Hölderlin Bicentennial Symposium, to those who subsequently became contributors to this Symposium volume as well as
to those who did not; to the National Endowment for the Humani-
ties for a grant in partial support of the activities of the
Symposium; to the Office of the Vice-President for Academic
Affairs of The University of Michigan for generously providing
funds to cover expenses; to Professor Gerald F. Else, Director
of The University of Michigan's Center for Coördination of
Ancient and Modern Studies, for including the Hölderlin Symposium in the Center's busy schedule of conferences during the
year 1970-1971, as well as for providing funds; to Mrs. Dorothy
Warner, secretary of the Center, for invaluable assistance with
numerous details connected with the organization of the Symposium; to the Department of Germanic Languages and Literatures,
The University of Michigan, for its enthusiastic support of
the Symposium and for releasing time from regular teaching
duties to enable me to chair its activities. At the stages of
planning, editing, and producing the book, I express thanks
first to Professors Michael Hamburger and Christopher Middleton
for their generous and enthusiastic collaboration with poems
and translations; to the readers of the manuscript for their
dispatch, as for very helpful suggestions; to The University
of Michigan Press for friendly encouragement, and for its warm
interest in a volume commemorating the bicentenary of Friedrich
Hölderlin; to the Associate Director of the Press, Mr. J. Scott
Mabon, for the wisdom of his experience, and for counsel and
assistance in ways too numerous to list. Here too I thank
the publishers without whose sympathetic cooperation in grant-
ing needed permissions to reprint texts the book could not have
had the form it has. And finally, I thank my family: my mother
Mrs. Julianna George and my wife Mary, who understand what this
book means to me.

                                                    E. E. G.

Ann Arbor, Michigan
October 1971

Contents

Part III: Translators

PART I

Poets

English Hölderlin Poems

Collected by
Michael Hamburger

In the preface to the book of poems *Journeys and Places* (1937), which contains his poem on Hölderlin, Edwin Muir wrote: "The references in one of the new poems may need some explanation, for Hölderlin is little known in this country except as the name of a German poet. The journey of which I try to give an imaginary account is one which he made in the summer of 1805 [*sic*] ...." There follow further biographical elucidations. The first English poems on Hölderlin appeared before he was known to a large educated public, either through critical or biographical studies, or through translations.

True, Edwin Muir himself was among the first to translate Hölderlin into English. As early as February 1935, about the time he wrote his Hölderlin ballad, he published his essay on Hölderlin's "Patmos" in *The European Quarterly*. Parts of the early and late versions of the poem were also first quoted in English translation in this periodical. (In the essay, inci-

First published in *Hölderlin-Jahrbuch* 13 (1963-64): 80-102. English translation of introductory essay by the editor.

dentally, Muir gave the date of the journey to Bordeaux correctly as 1802; in the later preface his memory slipped.)

Edwin Muir (1887-1959) was born on an island of the Scottish Orkneys as a farmer's son. During his childhood the family had to move to Glasgow, where it gradually sank into and
withered in the urban proletariat. This root experience, connected also with the deaths of several brothers and sisters,
determined Muir's development as a poet. The early years on
the economically "backward" Orkneys, with their orally transmitted ballad poetry, became for Muir a lost paradise--a world
of primordial mythical images--which in his poems and in his
autobiography is time and again evoked in opposition to the
labyrinth of time. In his early poems the Scottish ballads
persistently figure among his stylistic models. "Hölderlin's
Journey" must be counted as such an early poem, as Muir's art
grew to full maturity and independence only in the forties of
the century. At the very end of his life he returned to this
beginning by planning a work on the transmitted and recorded
Scottish ballads, a project that his widow Willa Muir has since
brought to completion. "Hölderlin's Journey" also treats of
the labyrinth of time--of a terrible and tragic going astray
in this labyrinth. Only in the late poetry is the latter
reconciled with the timeless primordial world by virtue of a
religious transfiguration and redemption undergone by time
itself. In this poem the ballad-like treatment prevents a
complete fusion with the subject, Muir's sincere and deeply
rooted sympathy with the tragically lost Hölderlin notwithstanding. The elements of the landscape also are, as yet, of
a general nature and for that reason convey an effect of ab-
straction. But with this poem Hölderlin enters English poetry.

Together with Edwin Muir, *Stephen Spender* (born 1909) is
one of the few English poets of this century to whom, through
residence in German-speaking countries, German poetry has

become formative experience. Among the writers translated by Edwin Muir are Hauptmann, Kafka, and Broch. Spender has translated poems by Goethe, George, Hofmannsthal, and Rilke, and dramas by Schiller and Wedekind. Unlike the early poems of Muir, Spender's early poems show an essential—not merely thematic but also stylistic—influence of the German lyric. That his little Hölderlin poem "Hoelderlin's Old Age" is in part a free paraphrase of "Ehmals und jetzt," or that this ode by the twenty-seven-year-old is ascribed to the aged insane poet, demonstrates, to be sure, that Spender's encounter with Hölderlin was no more mediated by systematic literary study than was Muir's. But this circumstance detracts neither from the overall quality of the poem, nor from its genuine fusion of two styles and sensibilities. Spender's poem is richer in images but at the same time, paradoxically enough, is more rhetorical than the original; in this respect it reminds one of the metaphorical rhetoric of the late German expressionist poets—of Werfel, Becher, and their followers. In the thirties Spender was also an activist on the political left, but his best poems of that time—"Hoelderlin's Old Age" is taken from his 1939 collection *The Still Centre*, in which personal and metaphysical preoccupations had gained the upper hand—are at the most only indirectly related to the political and social events of the period between the two wars.

David Gascoyne (born 1916) published, in his early youth, the first volume of English poetry that bore Hölderlin's name. *Hölderlin's Madness*, which appeared in 1938, consists of a brief essay on Hölderlin, and of twenty-four English poems that either freely adapt poems and fragments of Hölderlin with the aid of the French translation by Pierre Jean Jouve, or else, like "Tenebrae," are connected with Gascoyne's own Hölderlin experience. In the preface he notes: "The entire offering represents something that could perhaps be regarded as a *persona*." That Gascoyne became acquainted with Hölderlin via a detour over France--he himself has scarcely any command of the German language--is indicative both of his own situation and of the cultural conditions of the time. In even earlier publications he had made himself a spokesman of French surrealism. His interest in Hölderlin, like that of the surrealists, was directed first and foremost at the poet's insanity. In the introduction to the book he designates madness in general as "the logical conclusion of romanticism," and places Hölderlin alongside Rimbaud as a seer whose poetry "is stronger than despair, and which reaches into the future, into the light." Gascoyne himself has suffered serious psychic disturbances and gave up writing poetry for more than a decade. "Tenebrae" is at the same time one of the purest of Gascoyne's early visionary poems and a witness to his encounter with Hölderlin. The images taken from late Hölderlin poems--the organ, the rivers, and the swans--do not in any way clash with the remaining components of the apocalyptic scene. Despite the prevailing iambic rhythm, the metrical freedom of the hymns and hymnic fragments has also carried over into Gascoyne's verse.

Sir Herbert Read (1893-1968) grew up on a farm, as did Edwin Muir. Read's poetic beginnings coincide with World War I, in which he distinguished himself as an officer. Distinction came to him also as an author of poems and prose works that did not in any way glorify the war. Like Muir, Read experienced the contradiction between the "innocent eye" of childhood and a corrupt civilization; he became a literary spokesman of the tiny Anarchist party in England, which carried on the intellectual tradition of a romanticism hostile to industrial development. As a poet he was close to the imagists, as well as to other avant-garde literary circles in the metropolis. In his late years his influence on a wider public was chiefly as an art critic and impresario of modern

art, unfortunately at the expense of his own poetic productivity. Some of his bitterness and sorrow over that fact may perhaps be traceable in his late poem of homage to Hölderlin,
taken from Read's volume *Moon's Farm and Poems Mostly Elegiac*
(1955). His collection of critical essays *The Sense of Glory*
(1929) bears a Hölderlin quotation as its motto. In a letter
to the author in 1961 Read mentioned Hölderlin as "the one poet
I return to again and again." For him Hölderlin figured among
the representatives of pure imagination, and of that fundamental principle of "organic form" on which Read's poetic work,
as well as his aesthetics and cultural criticism, was based.
True to his early alliance with imagism, the late poem also
excels by its free form and image progression, in preference
to arguments and logical connectives.

The Welsh poet *Vernon Watkins* (who wrote his poetry in
English as did his friend Dylan Thomas) was born in 1906 in
Maestag, South Wales, and died in Seattle, Washington, in 1967.
For a time Watkins studied modern languages, but then gave up
his studies, and after 1925 worked as a bank official in
Swansea. It was not until World War II that his first book of
poems appeared. It was followed by six further volumes of
verse, as well as by a translation of Heine's *Die Nordsee* and
many other translations of German and French poetry as yet
scattered in magazines and anthologies. Nor are his translations of numerous Hölderlin poems, especially of the late
hymns, as yet available in collected form. The poem cycle
"Hölderlin's Childhood" is printed in the volume *Affinities*
(1962), which contains several poems of homage to Hölderlin as
an exemplary poet. Watkins also belongs to the altogether
small rank of English poets--W. H. Auden is another--who have
been inspired by Hölderlin's ode forms to undertake experiments
of their own. Since the sixteenth century all classical meters
have in general been held to be incapable of reproduction in

English. Out of this belief there arises for the English translator of Hölderlin an almost insurmountable difficulty, since the dynamics of the Hölderlinian ode can be rendered in no other metrical medium. Despite this limitation it is precisely the translations that have proven at least the Alcaic ode to be a clear possibility in English. For Vernon Watkins, who categorically dissociated himself from any and all attempts to "industrialize" literature, as from all nonlyrical by-products of such attempts, lyrical poetry is timeless and supratemporal. Among his models are to be reckoned the English romantics and symbolists, quite paramountly the Irish poet W. B. Yeats.

The poem by *Delmore Schwartz* (1913-1966) is included here as the sole contribution by an American poet. Schwartz became known as a poet and dramatist shortly before World War II, and after 1943 gained renown as editor and contributing editor of the distinguished periodical *Partisan Review*, in which his Hölderlin poem was published in 1954. His first book *In Dreams Begin Responsibilities* (1938) contained, besides poems, a short story and a play. There followed the dramatic poems *Shenandoah* (1941), *Genesis* (1943), and the book of lyrics *Vaudeville for a Princess* (1951). Schwartz studied philosophy and taught philosophy and English literature at several American universities. As the title of the volume named last indicates, his poetic work shows an extraordinary tension between the poet's consciousness of his own position, in a certain setting, at a given point in time, and the archetypes of religion and myth. In one of his best-known poems the "naked bed" of one awakening daily turns into Plato's cave, swept across by the beams of automobile headlights. The consciousness of a similar dualism seems to be common to almost all of Hölderlin's English-speaking admirers.

The poems by Herbert Read, Vernon Watkins, and Delmore Schwartz were written in a later phase of awareness and recep-

tion of Hölderlin. Notably, it was only during the forties
that Hölderlin's significance and a portion of his oeuvre gradually penetrated to the consciousness of a general (though always limited) English and American public. An English-language
monograph on Hölderlin had been available to specialists since
1923; but, despite the slowly growing body of critical literature, which included especially Ronald Peacock's 1938 study of
Hölderlin, English schoolboys and university students of the
war years still had a portion of a Klopstock ode presented to
them as a poem by Hölderlin in *The Oxford Book of German Verse*.
(The author translated it as such when he was fifteen or six-
teen years old.) The Hölderlin translations by Frederic
Prokosch and those by Michael Hamburger appeared in 1943, those
by J. B. Leishman in the following year; the Hölderlin biography by Agnes Stansfield appeared in 1944, E. L. Stahl's
study of Hölderlin's symbolism in 1945. With the publication
of these books the legendary name of the thirties became a
historical figure and a body of work--although one still meets
educated Britons who confuse Hölderlin with Rilke (influential
in England since the twenties), or who think of Hölderlin as
Rilke's contemporary. In America too Hölderlin is now better
known than the sole poem that could be considered for the present collection would allow one to suppose. Thus, in "A Funeral
Poem for Rainer M. Gerhardt" by the American poet Charles Olson,
Hölderlin is mentioned thus:

> as Hölderlin on Patmos you
> trying to hold bay leaves
> on a cinder block!

(Donald Allen, ed., *The New American Poetry* [New York: Grove
Press, 1960], p. 17). A similar effect is conveyed by the
mention of Hölderlin in part 13 of the cycle "Poems from
Pictures of the Gone World" in Lawrence Ferlinghetti's

A Coney Island of the Mind. Here too Hölderlin is celebrated
as a poet-martyr, as a sacrificial scapegoat of civilization,
as one of many who in the "civilized thicket" have fallen vic-
tim to insanity. Homage is the function also of a translation
of the concluding section of the elegy "Menons Klagen um Diotima," spoken by the "Melpomene Mask" in the verse drama *The
Tree Witch* by the American poet and historian Peter Viereck.
(The dramatic poem was published in book form in New York in
1961.)

The monologue "Hölderlin" by *Michael Hamburger* (born
1924) is a poem of his youth, written in Oxford in the winter
of 1941, at the age of seventeen. Although, as a student and
translator, Hamburger was at that time already preoccupied
with Hölderlin, the actual inspiration for this monologue was
neither a specific poem by Hölderlin nor any literary event
at all, but rather a movement from a late string quartet by
Beethoven. Like Gascoyne's book and all the poems gathered
here, this monologue should be understood as a *persona,* and
not as a reconstruction of the historical Hölderlin. The
monologue was the first poem that Hamburger published (in
1942, in the anthology *Z: Oxford and Cambridge Writing;* later
it was included in his first volume of poems, *Flowering Cactus*
[1950]). The poem "Mad Lover, Dead Lady" first appeared in
the Fall 1969 issue of the American periodical *Sumac.*

Like the majority of English poets of this more recent
generation, *Christopher Middleton* (born 1926) and *Geoffrey Hill*
(born 1932) are active as university lecturers--Middleton in
German at Austin, Texas, Hill in English at Leeds. Both are
among the outstanding poets of the postwar period and distinguish themselves from many of their peers precisely in that
they have overcome a prevailing insularity and are receptive
to foreign influences. Middleton's cosmopolitanism is evident
from his translations of a selection of Hölderlin's letters

(The Poet's Vocation. Austin: University of Texas Press, 1967),
of prose pieces by Robert Walser, whom Middleton made known in
England through excellent translations and critical essays;
and of twentieth-century German poems which are now collected
in part in the bilingual anthology *Modern German Poetry 1910-
1960,* edited by him and by Michael Hamburger.

    For years now Middleton has been concerned with the symbol-
ism of mountains and hills and is preparing a comparative study
using materials ranging from the earliest religious and mythical
documents to modern poetry. In the poem "Thinking of Hölderlin" (written in 1960 in the loft of a house in Neckargemünd)
he opposes the mountains, mythically transfigured by Hölderlin,
to the real hills that were perhaps known to the latter, at
the same time comparing Hölderlin's visionary contemplation
with a newer, more soberly factual way of looking. Out of this
opposition arise the tension and the dialectic of the poem.
The first line assumes a tacit train of thought, namely the
poet's disappointment as he feels the "avarice" of the hills
and sees an impoverished landscape. The poem contains no judg-
ment on Hölderlin, although Middleton distinguishes his own way
of perceiving and feeling from Hölderlin's. Middleton has also
mentioned to the author that he was at the time engaged in reading poems by Pindar, in Lattimore's new American translation.

    A similar comparison, if a hidden one, with modern ways
of poetic seeing is contained in Geoffrey Hill's "Little Apocalypse." Hölderlin's exemplary purity is not praised with
conventional rhetoric, his heroism is only hinted at by means
of a concealed allusion to Icarus. The short, syntactically
chopped-off sentences stand in conscious contrast to the over-
flowing rhythms of Hölderlin's verse prior to his insanity,
similar to the way in which Middleton, through words and phrases
taken from colloquial speech, deliberately maintains a distance
from Hölderlin's vocabulary. Without such distance, a result

of the difference between one's own experience and manner of expression and that of the admired poet, praise would be presumption and homage a shameless act.

Christopher Salvesen (author of "Hölderlin at the Fountain") was born in Edinburgh in 1935 and lectures in English at the University of Reading. He has published a book on Wordsworth's poetry, *The Landscape of Memory,* and has contributed art criticism to *The New Statesman* and *The Listener.*

Hölderlin's Journey

When Hölderlin started from Bordeaux
  He was not mad but lost his mind,
For time and space had fled away
  With her he had to find.

"The morning bells rang over France
  From tower to tower. At noon I came
Into a maze of little hills,
  Head-high and every hill the same.

"A little world of emerald hills,
  And at their heart a faint bell tolled;
Wedding or burial, who could say?
  For death, unseen, is bold.

"Too small to climb, too tall to show
  More than themselves, the hills lay round.
Nearer to her, or farther? They
  Might have stretched to the world's bound.

"A shallow candour was their all,
  And the mean riddle, How to tally
Reality with such appearance,
  When in the nearest valley

"Perhaps already she I sought,
  She, sought and seeker, had gone by,
And each of us in turn was trapped
  By simple treachery.

"The evening brought a field, a wood.
  I left behind the hills of lies,
And watched beside a mouldering gate
  A deer with its rock-crystal eyes.

"On either pillar of the gate
  A deer's head watched within the stone.

The living deer with quiet look
  Seemed to be gazing on

"Its pictured death--and suddenly
  I knew, Diotima was dead,
As if a single thought had sprung
  From the cold and the living head.

"That image held me and I saw
  All moving things so still and sad,
But till I came into the mountains
  I know I was not mad.

"What made the change? The hills and towers
  Stood otherwise than they should stand,
And without fear the lawless roads
  Ran wrong through all the land.

"Upon the swarming towns of iron
  The bells hailed down their iron peals,
Above the iron bells the swallows
  Glided on iron wheels.

"And there I watched in one confounded
  The living and the unliving head.
Why should it be? For now I know
  Diotima was dead

"Before I left the starting place;
  Empty the course, the garland gone,
And all that race as motionless
  As these two heads of stone."

So Hölderlin mused for thirty years
  On a green hill by Tübingen,
Dragging in pain a broken mind
  And giving thanks to God and men.

                              Edwin Muir

Hölderlin's Old Age

When I was young I woke gladly in the morning
With the dew I grieved towards the close of day.
Now when I rise I curse the white cascade
That refreshes all roots, and I wish my eyelids
Were dead shutters pushed down by the endless weight
Of a mineral world. How strange it is that at evening
When prolonged shadows lie down like cut hay
In my mad age I rejoice and my soul sings
Burning vividly in the centre of a cold sky.

Stephen Spender

Tenebrae

Brown darkness on the gazing face
In the cavern of candlelight reflects
The passing of the immaterial world in the deep eyes.

The granite organ in the crypt
Resounds with rising thunder through the blood
With daylight song, unearthly song that floods
The brain with bursting suns:
Yet it is night.

It is the endless night, whose every star
Is in the spirit like the snow of dawn,
Whose meteors are the brilliance of summer,
And whose wind and rain
Are all the halcyon freshness of the valley rivers,
Where the swans,
White, white in the light of dream,
Still dip their heads.

Clear night!
He has no need of candles who can see
A longer, more celestial day than ours.

David Gascoyne

A Gift for Scardanelli

See: the field is empty ...
You came here by a curious detour
the hedges were trimmed but o-
ranges among the intricate thorns
glowed like torches. You expected to find
a temple of honey-coloured stone
and an old man crouched in the porch
listening to a marble-browed girl
that there discourses on the nature of love.

April und Mai und Junius sind ferne
Ich bin nichts mehr: ich lebe nicht mehr gerne ...

The clouds are unanchored: they might
fall from the sky to cover you
I have brought you a basket of figs
and some fine linen
but alas
no white goat to slaughter
and fingers have faltered
that should have played the flute.

Herbert Read

To Hölderlin

Poet of godlike stillness, anchorite,
Son of the world God made before man sinned,
Outcast of Hellas, aether's lonely friend,
Worshipper wounded at the shrine of light:
Children were no less glorious in your sight
Than those blessed genii whom you saw descend;
The sea held riches from the same first mind:
Love was to you as to the birds their flight.

You looked for constancy. Heroic power
Greece gave you. Deep was every breath you drew,
Deeper the sacrifice which overthrew
All with divinity; but then love's hour
Had broken Rousseau's consecrated flower,
The tragic splendour of the entirely true.

                         *

Harmonious Nature named you her happiest child,
Singer of Patmos and the golden islands.
Godlike, reborn of light's aethereal silence,
The Christian and the Greek were reconciled.
Your senses prayed, and on that happy field
Heaven's light, all-healing, bathed the enamoured lands.
You heard the stillness under which Christ stands.
In Diotima's eyes stood love revealed.

Over the castle hung with a kestrel's power
Her memory, rivers, mountains peaked with snow
Descending sheer, for shadows to devour.
Smooth on the flowering lake, swans plunged their eyes
Into a walled, a wintry world below,
Where light was cloistered, and became unwise.

Vernon Watkins

Hölderlin

Now as before do you not hear the nameless voices,
Serene in the midst of their rejoicing,
Chanting to those who have hopes and make choices,
Clear as the birds in the thick summer foliage:

> *It is! It is!*
> *We are! We are!*

Clearly, as if they were us and yet not us,
Hidden like the future, distant as the stars,
Having no more meaning than the fullness of music,
Chanting from the blue peaks where success,
Effort and desire are meaningless,
Surpassed at last in the joy of joy,
Chanting enchanted the blue's last vow:

> *It is! It is!*
> *This is eternity: eternity is now!*

Delmore Schwartz

Hölderlin

(Tubingen, December 1842)

Diotima is dead, and silent
the island's singing bird.
The temple I raised from ruin
fallen again.

Where is the flame I stoked from ashes
of the mind? Where are the heroes
and my pulsing song?
Nothing stirs on the lakes of time.
Give back my agony,
O stir the forest's sap,
sweep my slow blood.

And yet, no caged old panther I,
pacing my madness. These muttered words
are gates, not bars, where only I can pass.
This is my wisdom, where no flowers grow,
no weeds, this is my peace.

I am calm now, with the world
locked out, bowed to the door;
my meadow end is pensioned by the gods.
They did not hear,
O crippled Fate, the grimy idol's
golden teeth led them away.

I have no tears to mourn forsaken gods
or my lost voice.
This is my wisdom, where no laughter sounds,
no sighs, this is my peace.

Glory is gone, and the swimming clouds;
my dumb hand grips the frozen sky,
a black bare tree in the winter dusk.

Michael Hamburger

Mad Lover, Dead Lady

Oh, my Diotima.
Is it not my Diotima you are speaking of?
Thirteen sons she bore me, one of them is Pope,
Sultan the next, the third is the Czar of Russia.
And do you know how it went with her?
Crazy, that's what she went, crazy, crazy, crazy.

Thirteen funerals they gave me when I died.
But she was not there. Locked up in a tower.
That's how it goes; round the bend
Out of the garden where lovers meet,
Walking, talking together. Over the wall.
No one there. Till you visitors came:
Will the corpse write a poem today
About his mad lady?

But I'll tell you a secret: we meet.
Round the bend, on the other side of the wall
Our garden is always there,
Easy, with every season's flowers.
Each from a dark street we come
And the sun shines.
She laughs when I tell her
What it's like to be dead.
I laugh when she gives me
News of our crazy children
Who've made their way in the world.

No poem today, sir.
Go home. In a dream you'll see
How they remove themselves, your dead
Into madness. And seem to forget
Their loved ones, each in his own dark street.
How your mad loved ones
Seem to forget their dead.
That's how it goes. No one there.
Oh, my Diotima.
Waiting for me in the garden.

Michael Hamburger

Thinking of Hölderlin

(Hills Near Heidelberg)

Never mind avarice; the hills
squander at least a sprawl
of steep oak. Speak
of the moroccan green
pines that fetlock them; of rumps,
rutted by axes; of bristling stung flanks,
flushed by puffs of cloud--

for first and last
who saw them crammed the air
with hawk and temple;
and what fetched them avarice, in the interim,
cannot change their green
bulk and butts of sandstone,
let alone rot the wits, killing,

as hawk and temple, his, for the crime
of being put, by them, wise to the least thing.
No, not in his name
do I join these crooked words, lest I miss
for him, more than temple, his hawk,
now lofted by their hot gusts, now
plucking the crowded vermin from their folds.

Christopher Middleton

Little Apocalypse

Hölderlin: 1770-1843

Abrupt tempter; close enough to survive
The sun's primitive renewing fury;
Scorched vistas where crawl the injured and brave:
This man stands sealed against their injury:

Hermetic radiance of great suns kept in:
Man's common nature suddenly too rare:
See, for the brilliant coldness of his skin,
The god cast, perfected, among fire.

Geoffrey Hill

Hölderlin at the Fountain

(1802; the incident is reported in E. M.
Butler's "The Tyranny of Greece over Germany")

Once again water, source of many wanderings ...
Water ... He came once more upon his mind,
Who had stumbled stricken the summer through
Amongst the dust, the stony fields of France,
There where a marble fountain played and spilled,
With calm milky statues, the Gods of Greece,
Presiding round and mirrored in its pool,
There he knew at once innocence, a want.

Water--it washes, washes ... And he cries
"It should be clearer: for the gods are clarity."
It laps where dogs lap, the yellow leaves float,
Meaty breath ruffling where the images lie
Clean--shivering--muddied, their darkening close.
He drinks; and from the slope the household smiles.
"You are a Greek?" "Ach no, like you, a contrary.
But fountains like music call me home, falling, rising ...

And these--these, a people's immortal thoughts:
That is poetry--that is what abides."
"And you, are you immortal?" "No; but once ...
Nine years ago ... that was another I ...
Of the ancient world ... then I lay at the source ...
Bewildered now ... by river, sea ... set loose
To follow the years, the populous clouds,
The melodies migrant under the waters."

In the night he raved: at dawn, wandered, went.
The waters broke, giving mad birth, outbursting.
He dreamed of the innocent poet, pure sun:
He knew the inflamed contaminated gods.
He is driven: let him be calm again,
His peace lies beyond the liberty of parklands
Or politics. The lawns in a heaved-up country
Wither--his swirling mind waters a new land.

Christopher Salvesen

PART II

Scholars

Hölderlin and the
English-Speaking Reader

by Herbert Barrows

I

The city of Florence has had a certain importance in my life,
but from my first sight of it, on a dark winter afternoon in
the last year of World War II, only two recollections remain.
One has to do with coming suddenly out of the via Cavour,
unprepared for what lay at the end, and being shocked to a
standstill by the sheer mass of the Duomo, for all its pink
and green filigree a more impressive witness to the power of
human hands than any skyscraper has ever seemed to be. The
other memory, and no less vivid, is of the excitement with
which I came across a small secondhand volume of selections
from Hölderlin on the depleted wartime shelves of one of the
international bookshops on the via Tornabuoni.[1] I had not
read Hölderlin then, but I was sure that this was a book to
buy and to read, that Hölderlin was a poetic property of the
first importance, and as I look back, the reasons for this
confidence are not hard to discover. Ever since the late
thirties, one had been hearing about Hölderlin, in the little
magazines and elsewhere; sometimes only as a name in lists of
writers who were of lively interest to the new generation of

27

English poets (these lists often included Rilke and Baudelaire, but they were sure to include Rimbaud); sometimes because a few of Hölderlin's poems were offered in translation; sometimes because he--or more specifically, his tragic fate--was made the subject of poems, as for example Edwin Muir's "Hölderlin's Journey," or Stephen Spender's "Hoelderlin's Old Age."[2] Hölderlin had figured, perhaps noncommittally but in sanctified company, in the invocation at the end of W. H. Auden's "Epithalamion," celebrating the marriage of Giuseppe Antonio Borgese and Elizabeth Mann on November 23, 1939:

> Mozart with ironic breath
> Turning poverty to song,
> Goethe ignorant of sin
> Placing every human wrong,
> Blake the industrious visionary,
> Tolstoi the great animal,
> Hellas-loving Hoelderlin,
> Wagner who obeyed his gift
> Organised his wish for death
> Into a tremendous cry,
> Looking down upon us, all
>   Wish us joy.[3]

In 1938 there had been published Ronald Peacock's book on Hölderlin--certainly a model of what a detailed critical study of a great poet should be, with its resolute attention to strictly poetic questions, as opposed to indulgence in biography for its own sake. Yet, unjust as it may seem, the kind of attention drawn to Hölderlin by the new poets who mentioned him in their work was more important in winning new readers for Hölderlin than Peacock's permanently valuable book. Thus David Gascoyne's book of poems--some of them inspired by Hölderlin, others translations from him--entitled *Hölderlin's Madness*, and also published in London in 1938, had had its importance in fixing Hölderlin in the imagination of a generation. And this generation, which included members of the Auden-Spender-Isherwood

circle who had gone to Germany in the thirties and brought back
with them an immediately fruitful interest in certain German
writers, most notably Rilke, was the first generation of English writers to pay any attention to Hölderlin, not merely
as private readers or as critics but also as writers who in
their own poetry were inspired by one aspect or another of his
life or his work.

Today, Ronald Peacock's stricture about the kind of interest that is epitomized in the title of Gascoyne's book seems
entirely justified. Pointing out that the book contained "a
brief introduction about Hölderlin's life and his significance
as a 'romantic' poet for the present-day surrealists," Peacock
adds that "the title and the tendency indicate frankly that to
this way of thought Hölderlin's madness is more important than
his sanity."[4]

But the thirties and the early forties did *establish* Hölderlin for English readers, perhaps on erroneous terms, but at
least in a way and to an extent that many other German poets
never have been established. In 1943, the centenary year of
Hölderlin's death, Frederic Prokosch's book of translations
had been the occasion for reviews which talked not only about
the quality of the translations but also about such fundamental
questions as the nature of Hölderlin as a poet and his importance for the modern reader. J. B. Leishman's selection of
poems, with German text, translations, and a long biographical
and critical introduction, had been published in London by The
Hogarth Press in 1944, but that book I had not seen when I
bought *Hölderlins Leben in seinen Briefen und Gedichten* in
Florence. As I read the latter off and on during the winter
of 1944-45, it was against a background of the particular kind
of glamor that Hölderlin as a figure had had for a certain few
English poets of the years just past or just passing. From
this reading, I acquired the inevitable fondness for "Hyperions
Schicksalslied," about which I am unrepentant even in the face

of Peacock's willingness to see an admiration for this poem as
a strong indication of a reader's unfitness to read poetry at
all. There were other poems that stood out for me, particularly "Andenken," and some of them were more commendable to a
developed taste than the "Schicksalslied." As to the impressions of life and character which I gathered from the excerpts
from Hölderlin's letters included in the volume, today I am
vague, except that I recognize that I allowed nothing to disturb the notion picked up earlier that Hölderlin was chiefly
interesting by reason of his somehow emblematically tragic or
ironic fate. A notion, needless to say, which was eventually
to be very much disturbed by a careful reading of the letters
in the *Stuttgarter Ausgabe*.

In my present title I mean to refer to the reader, English
or American, whose native language is English (or American)
and whose first and most complete literary experience has been
with literature in English. Without prejudice to the existing
translations of Hölderlin into English, such a reader, like
any other, if he is to have any but the most limited acquaintance with Hölderlin, must be able to read him in German, for
reasons which, though less obvious today than they once seemed
to be, are still obvious. Professional students of German
literature will no doubt bring to the reading of Hölderlin a
familiarity with his language and a detailed knowledge of
German cultural history that will enable them to read him as
Germans read him. But here I am interested in the reader who
approaches Hölderlin today, not with any misguided wish to
assimilate him to an alien tradition, but nevertheless in the
presence of a likelihood that his response will be channeled
and conditioned--sometimes made easier, sometimes made more
difficult--by his experience of the poetry he knows best, the
poetry of his own language. Not only ideally but actually,
any reader, to get anything worth having from Hölderlin, must
learn to see in him what is there, not something that might

only seem to be there. But we proceed in our developing acquaintance with a foreign writer, I believe, on the basis of
initial response to elements in his own work which bear some
relation to the work of writers already known to us, and only
later do we learn to value the new writer exactly in proportion
as he is unlike *any* writer we have known before. Certainly the
likelihoods will be very different, in approaching Hölderlin,
for a reader whose first language is English and for a native
speaker of German, even though in the end the goals should be
the same: to see Hölderlin for what he permanently, uniquely,
and fully *is*, not as a temporary reflection of a passing interest or need or fashion. Ultimately, everything depends on our
learning to read the poems, and this means reading them over a
period of years.

My own interest in Hölderlin was given a new impetus a few
years ago when I read what Herbert Read had to say about him in
The True Voice of Feeling: Studies in English Romantic Poetry
(London: Faber and Faber, 1953). From this book I received, or
thought I received, encouragement to regard Hölderlin as a
romantic poet who, besides being Wordsworth's exact contemporary, also presented certain clear parallels with Wordsworth's
ideas about the function of the poet. It seemed to me, moreover,
as I went about the always difficult task of establishing a
dependable concept of what romanticism essentially stood for
in the cultural and aesthetic history of the past century and
a half, that a number of its characteristic patterns or tendencies could be illustrated by reference to Hölderlin.[5] I realize
that the present critical tendency is not this way. Lilian
R. Furst is allowing more room for difference of opinion than
many critics would do when, in the introduction to her recent
book *Romanticism in Perspective* she lists Hölderlin with a
number of other writers whom she does not intend to treat
because their relation to romanticism is only marginal.[6] Other
critics appear to find the relation nonexistent.

Now I have no wish to set up a narrow definition of
romanticism--even if that were possible--and then to circum-
scribe Hölderlin's achievement and effect within that definition. It is entirely true to say that as a poet Hölderlin is
unique, but even if it were less true, nothing would be gained
by pinning on him a label that would seem to say that in him
would be found exactly the same range of characteristics and
purposes that would be found in a number of other poets who
wore the same label. Miss Furst, in the book mentioned, is
concerned to point out something that is by no means hard to
accept: that in the three countries studied--England, France,
and Germany--the romantic movement made three very different
kinds of impact, depending on chronology and national history,
and produced, in those three countries, very different combina-
tions from all the possible array of habits of poetic life and
thought that, taken together, make up the complex of attitudes
known as romanticism. But one very important interest that
Hölderlin can have for us today is that he may be seen as yet
another exemplar, another individual patterning, of certain of
the forces that are central to European romanticism. He has
recently been claimed by many interests, and he does indeed
seem to have had something to say to surrealists, to existentialists, to theologians, and to many who claim merely to be
modern. But behind it all there lies a participation in recognizable phases of romanticism, and I believe the English or
American reader will be helped, on a first approach to Hölderlin, by seeing him in this light.

Not that Hölderlin emerges from a careful reading of his
letters as strongly resembling the commonly received notion of
what constitutes the romantic temperament, any more than he
emerges as what his modern fame as a "mad" poet might lead us
to expect. Admittedly letters do not tell us all the truth
about the man who wrote them, and sometimes what they do tell
us is not the truth at all. But if one wanted a single word

by which to characterize the mind and temperament encountered
in these letters, the word might quite well be "sanity," or
"balance," or "wisdom." (The question of the cost to Hölderlin
of maintaining the sanity, the balance, is of course crucial:
but they *were* maintained during the years in which he produced
the larger part of his work.) As a very young man, Hölderlin
is sometimes lonely and unhappy: from Maulbronn he writes that
nobody in the seminary likes him, that although his flute is
his only consolation, his friends would rather have an instrument missing than ask him to play with them; in the same letter
to Nast, he mentions that the girls from the *Direktion* had
spoken to him in passing: *"Du solltests gesehen haben--ich habe
mich gefreut wie ein Kind--dass mich auch nur jemand angeredt
hat--und das war doch keine so wichtige Sache zum Freuen"* (You
should have seen it--I was happy as a child--that even a single
person had talked to me--and after all, it was not such an
important matter to be happy about [6:8; No. 4]). This is a
real loneliness, unavoidable perhaps, not a romantically cultivated one, and Hölderlin sees it for exactly what it is and does
what he can to cope with it. Time and again, in the years that
follow, it is his strategy to cope with problems in the most
sensible way that is available to him, to see the given conditions, whether in his own life or in the lives of his half-
brother or of his friend Neuffer, and to do the best that can
be done under those conditions. There is an herb, Hölderlin
writes to his sister, that will make their brother forget all
bitterness: *"Beschäftigung des denkenden Geistes"* (preoccupation for the thinking mind [6:59; No. 37]). What makes for
a complete man is not *"der Stoff und die Lage, sondern die
Behandlung des Stoffs und der Lage"* (subject and situation,
but treatment of the subject and the situation [6:251; No.
145]). And there are many statements that *might* sound like
copybook maxims but that somehow don't sound so, such as that
"der ruhige Verstand ist die heilige Aegide, die im Kriege der

Welt das Herz vor giftigen Pfeilen bewahrt" (quiet of the understanding is the holy aegis that in the war of the world protects
the heart from poisoned arrows [6:302; No. 172]).

If we think of the romantic poet, at least in one range of
his manifestation, as luxuriating in his sorrow, making his
sensitivity to it one of the signs that distinguish him as a
superior being, we find virtually nothing in Hölderlin's letters
that would allow us to see him as romantic in this sense. (We
find nothing of the kind in Keats's letters, either.) When
Hölderlin describes the vivifying, expansive effects of love
the story is a bit different, and here it would be possible
to enlist him in the service of illustrating important romantic
doctrines. But in most of his life concerns, even those involved in the extremely difficult conflict between his deep
sense of a poetic vocation and the necessity of making a living
and following a recognizable career, his temperament is a cool
one. Not cold, not callous, but clear and essentially noble.
Anguish is often present, perhaps between the lines rather than
written in them, but anguish and difficulty are things that
must be controlled and overcome. And indeed the abiding sense
one has in reading Hölderlin's letters is that they present to
us a uniformly dignified, clear-sighted, coherent character, a
temperament of very great purity. If we are working with
labels, such a temper could be called classic far more readily
than it could be called romantic.

All the same, and whether Hölderlin may be called a romantic poet in any absolute sense, the English-speaking reader
will be likely to assimilate him, on quite specific grounds,
to romanticism as it is represented by the English romantic
poets. In reading Hölderlin we tend to be reminded of certain
strains, whether of doctrine or of practice, in the complex
array of phenomena that constitutes English romanticism, and
since there *are* such bases for comparison, we tend to take his
poetry back with us as a standard of comparison in reading the

English poets. Talking about Goethe's and Schiller's failure
to understand Hölderlin, Alessandro Pellegrini, in his book on
the history of Hölderlin criticism, points out that such incomprehension is understandable because while Hölderlin *"s'ispirava
da premesse communi ai maestri del classicismo tedesco, egli
era però iniziatore di una forma assolutamente nuova di poesia"*
(was imbued with premises common to the masters of German classicism, he was nevertheless the initiator of an absolutely new
form in poetry), and that it is therefore not possible to sub-
sume his oeuvre entirely within the orbit of classicism, or
even to talk in his case of a "romantic classicism." What is
necessary, in Pellegrini's view, is to avoid such attempts at
cultural schematization, which do little to illuminate poetic
problems, but instead to examine *"i rapporti fra la nuova
poesia di Hölderlin e l'opera di alcuni fra i maggiori poeti
del secolo XIX; e non si dovrà parlare d'influenze o di sugges-
tioni, ma di spontanee corrispondenze"* (the affinities between
the new poetry of Hölderlin and the work of certain of the
major poets of the nineteenth century; and one ought to speak
not of influences or of promptings, but of spontaneous correspondences).[7]

This, it would seem to me, is exactly what a modern reader
instinctively does as he builds up an acquaintance with Hölderlin: the reader maintains a willingness to recognize this
poet's uniqueness, at the same time that he sees that uniqueness as coming at the beginning of the line of intense poetic
development that begins with romanticism, runs through the
nineteenth century (sometimes running underground), and manifests itself with renewed vigor and somewhat altered linea-
ments in the various late nineteenth-century movements that
center in symbolism and in the literature of the modern period
which grows out of them. Some of Hölderlin's most salient
traits as a poet place him at the beginning of this continuum:
his great and sometimes opaque subtlety, his faithfulness to

a personally conceived vision which must be symbolically mediated, and his invention and development of highly personal approaches to style and form. At the moment, however, I should like to glance at some of the points at which he seems to represent romantic principles or practices, as we find them illustrated in the English romantic poets, *points de repère* which may help the English or American reader to "place" Hölderlin, to understand him in terms of things already familiar. To isolate such similarities, which are admittedly only parts in a very complex whole, should in the end have the effect of emphasizing Hölderlin's individuality, at the same time that doing this makes it easier for us to be aware of that individuality.

In *The True Voice of Feeling,* Sir Herbert Read makes one of the most important comparisons that it is possible to make between Hölderlin and an English romantic poet, comparing him with Wordsworth on the basis of a discovered resemblance between their theories on the function of the poet:

> By intense reflection on the nature of being, Wordsworth had arrived at certain convictions which he could oppose to the nihilism that already, at the opening of the nineteenth century, threatened European thought. He shared this achievement, not only with his friend Coleridge, but also with his exact contemporary, Friedrich Hölderlin, who retreated into madness about the same time that Wordsworth retreated into dullness. "But that which remains, is established by the poets"--this dictum of Hölderlin's, the concluding line of his poem "Andenken" (Remembrance), describes the function which both poets assigned to poetry, and themselves assumed. Hölderlin said that language, the most dangerous of possessions, had been given to man so that he might affirm what he is. This is exactly Wordsworth's conception of the function of the poet, and Book XIII of *The Prelude* is an inspired expression of this view--it explains the exalted and dedicated role which Wordsworth assigned to poets in general and to himself in particular.[8]

Pointing out that there are several passages in *The Prelude* in which the doctrine is expounded, Read quotes one of them:

> Dearest Friend,
> Forgive me if I say that I, who long
> Had harbour'd reverentially a thought
> That poets, even as prophets, each with each
> Connected in a mighty scheme of truth,
> Have each for his peculiar dower, a sense
> By which he is enabled to perceive
> Something unseen before; forgive me, Friend,
> If I, the meanest of this band, had hope
> That unto me had also been vouchsafed
> An influx, that in some sort I possess'd
> A privilege, and that a work of mine,
> Proceeding from the depth of untaught things,
> Enduring and creative, might become
> A power like one of Nature's.[9]

This passage, in which many a phrase illuminates some facet of
the romantic conception of the poet's uniquely creative role
as mediator between "the depth of untaught things" and the
mass of mankind for whose welfare the mighty scheme of truth
is to be revealed, can be matched in innumerable places in the
writings of the English romantic poets. In Wordsworth's
preface to *Lyrical Ballads*, for instance, where it is said
of the poet: "He is the rock of defence for human nature; an
upholder and preserver, carrying everywhere with him relationship and love." Or in Shelley's *Defence of Poetry*, where we
are asked to consider, among so many other things, what the
world would have been without its poets; or throughout Keats's
letters, and in the poems, where careful attention is always
given to the exact place occupied by the poet in the progression from immediate aesthetic or emotional experience to the
vision of truth--and nowhere in Keats more movingly and
directly than in one of the sonnets, "The Poet":

> To his sight
> The hush of natural objects opens quite
> To the core: and every secret essence there

    Reveals the elements of good and fair;
    Making him see, where learning hath no light.[10]

    With the passage from *The Prelude*, Sir Herbert compares
a brief passage which he had found quoted in Heidegger's essay
on "Hölderlin and the Essence of Poetry," and which he describes as a "fragmentary sketch for a poem":

*Aber in Hütten wohnet der Mensch, und hüllet sich ein ins
verschämte Gewand, denn inniger ist, achtsamer auch und dass
er bewahre den Geist, wie die Priesterin die himmlische
Flamme, dies ist sein Verstand. Und darum ist die Willkür
ihm und höhere Macht zu fehlen und zu vollbringen, dem
Götterähnlichen, der Güter Gefährlichstes, die Sprache, dem
Menschen gegeben, damit er schaffend, zerstörend, und
untergehend, und wiederkehrend zur ewiglebenden, zur
Meisterin und Mutter, damit er zeuge, was er sei, geerbet
zu haben, gelernt von ihr, ihr Göttlichstes, die allerhal-
tende Liebe.*

(But man dwells in huts and wraps himself in the bashful
garment, since he is more fervent and more attentive too
in watching over the spirit, as the priestess the divine
flame; this is his understanding. And therefore he has
been given arbitrariness, and to him, godlike, has been
given higher power to [fail] and to accomplish, and
therefore has language, most dangerous of possessions,
been given to man, so that creating, destroying and
perishing and returning to the ever-living, to the
mistress and the mother, he may affirm what he is--that
he has inherited, learned from thee, thy most divine
possession, all preserving love.)[11]

More matter-of-fact, perhaps, but nonetheless essentially in
accord with the romantic conception of the poet's place among
men are many passages in Hölderlin's letters. Poetry is not
play, he insists, quoting some verses from Klopstock who says
the same thing, and in the long letter to his brother that
extends over several days at the end of 1798 (Letter No. 172
in the *Stuttgarter Ausgabe*), and in which he points out what
the German people, in their sorry limitedness, have to learn

from philosophy (*"Kant ist der Moses unserer Nation ..."*) and political science, he distinguishes between the right and wrong uses of poetry (6:305):

> ... *es wäre zu wünschen, dass der grenzenlose Missverstand, einmal aufhörte, womit die Kunst, und besonders die Poesie, bei denen, die sie treiben, und denen, die sie geniessen wollen, herabgewürdigt wird. Man hat schon so viel gesagt über den Einfluss der schönen Künste auf die Bildung der Menschen, aber es kam immer heraus, als wär es keinem Ernst damit, und das war natürlich, denn sie dachten nicht, was die Kunst, und besonders die Poesie, ihrer Natur nach, ist. Man hielt sich bloss an ihre anspruch[s]lose Aussenseite, die freilich von ihrem Wesen unzertrennlich ist, aber nichts weniger als den ganzen Charakter derselben ausmacht; man nahm sie für Spiel, weil sie in der bescheidenen Gestalt des Spiels erscheint, und so konnte sich auch vernünftiger-weise keine andere Wirkung von ihr ergeben, als die des Spiels, nämlich Zerstreuung, beinahe das gerade Gegenteil von dem, was sie wirket, wo sie in ihrer wahren Natur vor-handen ist. Denn alsdann sammelt sich der Mensch bei ihr, und sie gibt ihm Ruhe, nicht die leere, sondern die leben-dige Ruhe, wo alle Kräfte regsam sind, und nur wegen ihrer innigen Harmonie nicht als tätig erkannt werden. Sie nähert die Menschen, und bringt sie zusammen, nicht wie das Spiel, wo sie nur dadurch vereiniget sind, dass jeder sich ver-gisst und die lebendige Eigentümlichkeit von keinem zum Vorschein kömmt.*

(... it would be desirable if for once there came an end to the boundless misunderstanding with which art, and espe-cially poetry, is being underrated by those who practice it and by those who want to enjoy it. So much has already been said concerning the influence exerted by the arts on human culture, but in the end it has always seemed as if no one took the question seriously. And that was only natural, for people did not think of what art, and espe-cially poetry, is by its nature. The public took note only of its modest exterior, which is of course inseparable from its essence, but which makes up for nothing to a lesser degree than for its total character. They took it for play because it appears in the modest form of play. And thus, it stands to reason, there could result from it no other effect than one of play, that is, amusement, practically the exact opposite of what it achieves when it is present in its true essence. For then, man immedi-ately gains composure in its presence, poetry gives him

peace, not the empty but the living peace wherein all energies
are active, and are not recognized as such only on account
of their inner harmony. It makes men close and brings them
together--not as play, where men are united only through the
fact that each forgets himself, and living individuality
appears in no one.)

More than such explicit statements on the nature and function of poetry, however, in which there is present, as in the
critical manifestos of English romanticism, the sense that a
new dispensation is at hand which will correct old errors, the
very warp and woof of Hölderlin's poetry itself implies the
supremely important role of the poet as visionary, as mediator.
In the poems too the statements are often entirely explicit,
and sometimes they voice discouragement, as in stanza 7 of the
elegy "Brod und Wein" (2:94):

> *Indessen dünket mir öfters*
> *Besser zu schlafen, wie so ohne Genossen zu sein,*
> *So zu harren, und was zu tun indes und zu sagen,*
> *Weiss ich nicht, und wozu Dichter in dürftiger Zeit.*

> (But meanwhile too often I think it's
> Better to sleep than to be friendless as we are, alone,
> Always waiting, and what to do or to say in the meantime
> I don't know, and who wants poets at all in lean years?)

But the stanza concludes:

> *Aber sie sind, sagst du, wie des Weingotts heilige Priester,*
> *Welche von Lande zu Land zogen in heiliger Nacht.*

> (But they are, you say, like those holy ones, priests of the
> wine-god
> Who in holy Night roamed from one place to the next.)

And abidingly Hölderlin has, as the English romantic poets had,
the sense that distinguishes them most crucially from the Vic-
torian poets who followed them, namely that the poet had come

into his inheritance, that he had a saving mission and the
power to fulfill it. These things are said clearly in "Wie
wenn am Feiertage" (2:119):

> *Und wie im Aug ein Feuer dem Manne glänzt,*
> *Wenn hohes er entwarf, so ist*
> *Von neuem an den Zeichen, den Taten der Welt jetzt*
> *Ein Feuer angezündet in Seelen der Dichter.*

> (And as a fire gleams in the eye of that man
> Who has conceived a lofty design,
> Once more by the tokens, the deeds of the world now
> A fire has been lit in the souls of the poets.)

Those who tended the fields for us, disguised as laborers,

>   *sie sind erkannt,*
> *Die Allebendigen, die Kräfte der Götter.*

>   (they now are known,
> The all-alive, all-animating powers of the gods.)

If you ask who they are--

>   *im Liede wehet ihr Geist*
> *Wenn es der Sonne des Tags und warmer Erd*
> *Entwächst, und Wettern, die in der Luft, und andern,*
> *Die vorbereiteter in Tiefen der Zeit,*
> *Und deutungsvoller, und vernehmlicher uns*
> *Hinwandeln zwischen Himmel und Erd und unter den*
>   *Völkern.*
> *Des gemeinsamen Geistes Gedanken sind,*
> *Still endend, in der Seele des Dichters,*

> *Dass schnellbetroffen sie, Unendlichem*
> *Bekannt seit langer Zeit, von Erinnerung*
> *Erbebt, und ihr, von heilgem Strahl entzündet,*
> *Die Frucht in Liebe geboren, der Götter und*
>   *Menschen Werk,*
> *Der Gesang, damit er beiden zeuge, glückt.*

                          (In song their spirit wafts
When from the sun of day and from warm soil
It grows, and storms that are in the air, and others
That, more prepared in the depths of time,
More full of meaning and more audible to us,
Drift on between Heaven and Earth and amid the peoples.
The thoughts of the communal spirit they are,
And quietly come to rest in the poet's soul,

So that quickly struck and long familiar
To infinite powers, it shakes
With recollection and kindled by
The holy ray, that fruit conceived in love, the work
      of gods and men,
To bear witness to both, the song succeeds.)

And the passage ends in the simile of Semele and the birth of
Bacchus, who appears again in "Dichterberuf"--as eloquent a
declaration of the poet's place in the world of men and before
God as it is possible to imagine; nor ever emptily magniloquent
because, as always in Hölderlin, the dark side of the picture
is fully recognized, the abuse or misuse of the poet described
with perfect simplicity and directness.

Some modern critics, Sir Herbert Read chief among them,
have made the concept of organic form the central one in the
romantic theory of poetry. "So he *is;* so he *writes,*" says
Coleridge, and Sir Herbert places the statement at the head
of the opening chapter of *The True Voice of Feeling.* This
whole question, like so many others, is no doubt adumbrated
somewhere or other in Hölderlin's essay "Über die Verfahrungsweise des poetischen Geistes," but it is also implied in some
strictures about translation that occur in a letter to Neuffer.
Hölderlin begins by agreeing with Neuffer on what translation
basically is (6:125; No. 83):

Du hast recht, das Übersetzen ist eine heilsame Gymnastik
für die Sprache. Sie wird hübsch geschmeidig, wenn sie sich
so nach fremder Schönheit und Grösse, oft auch nach fremden
Launen bequemen muss. Aber, so sehr ich Dich bewundere, dass

Du mit solcher Beharrlichkeit das Mittel zu Deinem Zwecke
vorbereiten kannst, so werd ich Dir doch einen Fehdebrief
schicken, wenn Du nach Vollendung beider Arbeiten, die Du
jetzt unter den Händen hast, eine neue der Art anfängst.
Die Sprache ist Organ unseres Kopfs, unseres Herzens, Zei-
chen unserer Phantasien, unserer Ideen; uns muss sie gehor-
chen. Hat sie nun zu lange in fremdem Dienste gelebt, so,
denk ich, ist fast zu fürchten, dass sie nie mehr ganz der
freie, reine, durch gar nichts, als durch das Innre, so und
nicht anders gestaltete Ausdruck unseres Geistes werde.

(You are right, translation is a healthful exercise for
language. It becomes pleasantly supple whenever it must so
accommodate itself to alien beauty and greatness, often
also to alien moods. But, much as I admire you for being
able to prepare the means to your ends with such persistence, I will send you a written challenge to a duel if,
after completion of the two projects you have on your hands
now, you start a new one of a similar nature. Language is
the organ of our minds, of our hearts, the emblem of our
imaginings, of our ideas; it is *us* it must obey. Once it
has lived in foreign servitude for too long, it is, I
think, almost to be feared that it will never again entirely become the free and pure expression of our minds,
shaped by nothing if not by inner necessity, to be thus
and none other.)

This is not so categorical as Shelley's statement in the *Defence*
about the sheer impossibility of translating poetry, and it is
even qualified in a later letter to Neuffer (6:169; No. 99):

Ich begreife jetzt, wie Du so gerne übersetzen magst.
Schiller hat mich veranlasst, Ovids Phaëthon in Stanzen
für seinen Almanach zu übersetzen, und ich bin noch von
keiner Arbeit mit solcher Heiterkeit weggegangen als bei
dieser. Man ist nicht so in Leidenschaft wie bei einem
eigenen Produkte, und doch beschäftigt die Musik der
Versifikation den Menschen ganz, der andern Reize, die
so eine Arbeit hat, nicht zu gedenken.

(I understand now how it is you enjoy translating so much.
Schiller has asked me to translate Ovid's *Phaëthon* into
ottava rima for his *Almanac*, and I have never yet stood up
from any work with such good cheer as from this. One is
not in such a state of agitation as with a production of
one's own, and yet the music of versification absorbs one

completely, not to speak of other charms that work of this
kind holds out.)

But even here the truth is not denied that the poet's ultimate
nature and individuality of being are involved only in the full
creative process: a truth or doctrine that is inextricably
involved in all romantic or postromantic preconceptions about
the artist and his creative function.

Although I do not believe it can be said, without great
care and exact qualification, that Hölderlin retreated into
madness as a means of escaping from the failure of his hopes
for his time,[12] it does seem justifiable to find in his work,
and even in his life, yet another example of a pattern that is
constantly repeated in European romanticism. The world's great
age was to begin anew, but it sooner or later became apparent
that it was not going to do so, and the individual romantic
poet, who had confidently believed that his idealistic vision
could be transmitted to the world around him and made effective
in transforming the lives of men, withdrew into one form or
another of alienation or defeat.[13] Hölderlin's letters often
voice a belief, but by no means a blindly confident or merely
emotional one, that the world can be improved and is about to
be improved, not by magic but by reason, good sense, truth,
and fortitude: not a very romantic-sounding array of instru-
ments, but not so different, either, from the strictly human
powers that Shelley evoked in *Prometheus Unbound* as being capable of banishing evil from the world. It is probably in
Hölderlin's only novel *Hyperion* that the typical romantic
pattern of disillusioned idealism is most clearly presented.
Hyperion is pulled between his instinctive hopes and aspirations, which he himself finds natural in a young man who sets
out in the world to find his ideal, and his eventual recognition of the *Unheilbarkeit des Jahrhunderts* (incurability of
the century). Diotima explains to him that he is looking

not only for the lost Adamas or Alabanda, but for a world
(1:119):

Du wolltest keine Menschen, glaube mir, du wolltest
eine Welt. Den Verlust von allen goldenen Jahrhunder-
ten, so wie du sie, zusammengedrängt in Einen glückli-
chen Moment, empfandest, den Geist von allen Geistern
bessrer Zeit, die Kraft von allen Kräften der Heroen,
die sollte dir ein Einzelner, ein Mensch ersetzen!--
Siehest du nun, wie arm, wie reich du bist? warum du
so stolz sein musst und auch so niedergeschlagen? warum
so schröcklich Freude und Leid dir wechselt?[14]

(You wanted no individuals, believe me, you wanted a
world. The loss of all the golden centuries, as you
felt them, compressed into *one* happy moment; the spirit
of all the intellects of a better time; the   strength
of all the energies of the heroes--all this one solitary
individual, one person was to replace for you. Do you
see now how poor, how rich you are? Why you must be so
proud and yet so downcast? Why joy and sorrow alternate
for you so dreadfully?)

At the end, and amply prepared for by much that has gone
before, we have Hyperion's diatribe against the Germans--
not his last word, by any means, but at least a momentary
completion of the curve by which, in countless instances,
romantic idealism is finally replaced by despair when it
is confronted with inescapable and unregenerate actuality.

For the English romantic, idealistic hopes for the
future of mankind were sometimes translated into political
activity, or at least into an eagerness to serve liberty.
Here too there may be noted a parallel with Hölderlin,
albeit a slight and tragic one. It is at least as significant as most of the observations that are based on records
from the years of Hölderlin's madness to note the faint and
transitory parallel with Byron's career that is suggested
by Hölderlin's fragmentary last letter to his brother (6:469;
No. 312). This letter, to be dated from 1822 or 1823, and
the only one that stands out, by reason of its grasp of

reality, from the letters of polite, habitual compliment to his mother, is the record, according to Beck's note (6:1123-24), of a brief period when news of the Greek insurrection had roused Hölderlin sufficiently to give hopes of a possible improvement in his condition: but the hopes were unfounded.

II

In noting the presence in Hölderlin's thought of such affinities as have been touched on here, I do not mean to deny the importance, in "placing" him in relation to his time and to the history of literature generally, of giving careful attention to his awareness of his forebears in the ranks of German classicism, or to the extent to which he shares some of their principles, too. Surely the crucial point here was made by Stephen Spender in a brief essay which appeared in *Horizon*, in the midst of all the excited claims being made for Hölderlin in 1943-44, when he insisted that Hölderlin must not be seen merely as a flashy eccentric to set up in opposition to Goethe, but as participating fully in Goethe's heritage and as having the same kind of weight and permanent value.[15] Yet this view, which is clearly the right one, is not essentially at variance with the suggestion here offered, that a reader familiar with English romanticism will be helped, in the process of developing a familiarity with Hölderlin, by recognizing the presence in his life and thought of principles that are intricately involved in the romantic movement. When we come to make direct comparisons on the level of actual poetic practice, however, the situation becomes more complicated. Here--at least at first sight --we notice more difference than similarity, but since no two of the English romantic poets write the same kind of poetry, either, this is not surprising. The usefulness of the comparison lies, again, in showing us exactly what kind of poet Hölderlin is, even in terms of his differences from certain

poets who are better known to us and who do share some central
conceptions of the poet's task with him.

To be reading Keats at the same time that one is reading
Hölderlin can be an interesting experience for what it tells
us about both writers, but it is also apt to be a troubling
one, since at first Keats comes off so badly from the comparison. In Keats's poetry, from beginning to end, direct descriptive imagery is given very full and free development, and Keats
has traditionally been praised for the vividness with which he
renders the whole range of sense impressions. Such rendering
is justified, too, in his philosophy of the gradations of human
experience and the necessity for grounding attainment of the
ideal in a proper assimilation of the actual, on the human,
earthly level. But coming back to the fresh, charming, sometimes naïve images of Keats's early discursive poems, after the
much more highly abstracted, rarefied imagery of Hölderlin, is
to find Keats, at least for a moment, somehow gross; to find
his specific images too fully fleshed out, too autonomous.
Nor is the problem automatically resolved when we move forward
in Keats's development to the great odes, as is shown by Ronald
Peacock's comparison of a passage from the ode "To Autumn"
with a passage--and eventually with a single line--from
Hölderlin's "Stutgard."

In this comparison, Peacock does not match his sensitivity
to Hölderlin with an equal sensitivity to what may be seen as
the ultimate value of Keats's ode:

Keats shows the season and its fulness in their appearance,
as something visible, communicating, it is true, a sense of
the force in nature that drives to ripeness, but discovering
it in a wealth of images. He gives, too, a *fanciful* picture
of a personified autumn. ... The poet's fancy chases the
sights of autumn and his verses show much artistic skill
--perhaps a little too much--and are in their way delightful.
Hölderlin, in strong contrast, makes the simplest of utterances:

"Gross ist das Werden umher."

The process itself, not its effects, arrests him; and his
simple utterance is more impressive than all Keats's fancy
because there is mystery in it, the mystery of natural
life; from the gravity and wonder of this comes the thrill
of the words.[16]

The comparison continues, always to the effect that Keats is
operating on a level merely of voluptuous melancholy, whereas
in Hölderlin's poetry "is a religious sense of forces tran-
scending man, and consequent upon this, a demand that man
acknowledge them. It is the religious consciousness of a
highly developed and civilized mind reverencing the divine
power of life itself."[17]

   No one will quarrel with the claims made here for Hölderlin. Even on the basis of the respective impressions of mind,
personality, and training that we receive from the letters of
the two poets, Keats seems boyish, amateurish, self-taught,
though we might not all be willing to exchange the vitality
and exuberance of his self-education for the uniform gray
light and the discipline of Hölderlin's seminaries. But one
comes to understand the full scope of the ode "To Autumn" not
by seeing it as an assemblage of individual fancies, more or
less mechanically joined to form a poem, but by seeing it as
a whole, which communicates, ultimately, on a level where
mysteries are sensed which are more than the sum of Keats's
allegedly fanciful observations, and expressive of a reverence
that emerges not from the lines or the stanzas taken one by
one but as an aura which hovers over the whole poem. Nevertheless, the comparison between Hölderlin and Keats as regards
their approach to image can be helpful for our understanding
of the essential quality of each poet, provided we do not use
one of them merely as an instrument to diminish the other.
The clarity and selectivity of Hölderlin's images is something
we do not habitually find in Keats, but to be aware of his
clarity and selectivity as one kind of standard is to be
doubly appreciative when we find Keats driving toward a deeper

kind of expressiveness, where very simple statements, almost unanalyzable, have very great depth:

> Aye, on the shores of darkness there is light,
> And precipices show untrodden green;
> There is a budding morrow in midnight,
> There is a triple sight in blindness keen.

As for the "preoccupation with the life-giving forces themselves," of which Peacock speaks as determining Hölderlin's superiority in handling the world of nature in his poetry, the English-speaking reader might have quite another writer in mind as his standard here: the writer who has Paul Morel say, explaining how he has managed to draw a spray of leaves in such a convincing way:

> ... it's because there is scarcely any shadow in it; it's more shimmery, as if I'd painted the shimmering protoplasm in the leaves and everywhere, and not the stiffness of the shape. That seems dead to me. Only the shimmeriness is the real living. The shape is a dead crust. The shimmer is inside really.

--the writer who brought into his books with truly incomparable vividness all the phenomena of the universe, from Orion and his dog, or a tangle of pale crocuses bending in a sharp spring wind, to the glistening movement of the paramecium under the microscope.

Hölderlin's use of image is entirely individual, and not at all easy to describe. We acquire at least a partial insight into what to expect from it if we have appreciated certain uses of image that we encounter in the letters and in *Hyperion*. Hölderlin is able to make a moving simile or an extended metaphor out of the simplest, most generic materials, comparable, if to anything in English poetry, to Wordsworth's use of extended image-motifs in *The Prelude* or *The Excursion:* but even Wordsworth is inclined to be much more specific.

In *Hyperion*, for example, Hyperion asks what life would be without hope *(1:37-38)*:

Ein Funke, der aus der Kohle springt und verlischt, und wie man bei trüber Jahrszeit einen Windstoss hört, der einen Augenblick saust und dann verhallt, so wär es mit uns?
*   Auch die Schwalbe sucht ein freundlicher Land im Winter, es läuft das Wild umher in der Hitze des Tags und seine Augen suchen den Quell. Wer sagt dem Kinde, dass die Mutter ihre Brust ihm nicht versage? Und siehe! es sucht sie doch.*

(A spark that jumps from the embers and is extinguished, and as in the dismal season one hears a gust of wind that howls one moment and abates the next, is that how it is supposed to be with us?
    Even the swallow looks for a friendlier land in wintertime, the wild animal runs about in the heat of day, and his eyes look for the spring. Whoever tells a child that his mother will not deny him her breast? And see! he looks for it all the same.)

The materials of the image, of the comparison, are so simple, so familiar, that they would certainly be hackneyed, inert in less skilful hands, but in Hölderlin these materials are combined, by style and by truth of feeling, into an eloquent and beautiful statement. Often, in the letters, an extended comparison will be grounded in such an unassuming set of circumstances that we instinctively think of it as modern (6:211; No. 122):

... ich bin ... wie ein alter Blumenstock, der schon einmal mit Grund und Scherben auf die Strasse gestürzt ist, und seine Sprösslinge verloren und seine Wurzel verletzt hat, und nun mit Mühe wieder in frischen Boden gesetzt und kaum durch ausgesuchte Pflege vom Verdorren gerettet, aber doch hie und da noch immer welk und krüpplig ist und bleibt.

... I am ... like an old plant that has fallen on the road, soil, pot, and all, that has lost its shoots and injured its roots, and now, with much effort, has been carefully set in fresh earth and, through extreme care, has just barely been saved from drying up, but is still withered and stunted here and there and will so remain.)

Whether or not Hölderlin is to be called a "modern" writer,
the fact remains that the modern reader meets in his poetry
conditions and qualities that are familiar to him in the poetry
of his own time. As twentieth-century readers of poetry, born
under the sign of Arthur Symons's query as to whether it is
possible "at the present day, to be quite simple, with the old,
objective simplicity in either thought or expression," we are
quite at home when faced with a body of closely-wrought poems,
expressive of a highly idiosyncratic vision, poems which are
apt to retain a degree of opacity even after long acquaintance,
but whose validity is never in doubt. The language of the
poems will not yield up all its meaning to non-German readers,
since the expressiveness of words in poetry depends on a long-
term awareness of their expressiveness in life-discourse.
Further, the plasticity and mobility that result from German's
being more highly inflected than English, less bound to a
normal order for the elements of a sentence, can be a cause
for unfamiliarity, for difficulty: Hölderlin's habit of placing *mir* as the last word in a run-on line can produce moments
of vertigo as we try to follow the development of his thought
through a poem whose meaning does not reach a point of rest
until the end. Some features of his form and style are immediately familiar to us, perhaps because so many of Rilke's
typical approaches have been brilliantly naturalized in English
by W. H. Auden. Such features--so notably present in "Menons
Klagen um Diotima" and "Brod und Wein"--are the sense of moving
very directly into the argument of the poem, with the poet
assuming an easy allusiveness which has the effect of establishing an immediacy that we instinctively think of as "modern."
In one sense, Hölderlin is, in the loftiness of his thought,
anything but a poet who encourages an easy familiarity, but
in another sense there are the candor and the unassumingness

of manner that draw us quickly and easily into his spell.
These qualities are present in the questions he poses, for
instance, at the beginning of "An die Deutschen," or his
willingness to make concessions that go against his argument,
his frankness in admitting difficulty or contrary argument:
these features contribute to an intimacy of rapport between
poet and reader that, again, we are apt to think of as modern.
Maybe we would also like to claim as modern Hölderlin's extreme
simplicity of statement, the stark directness of intuition,
when the words fit their meaning so closely as to leave the
translator no room to maneuver in solving his problems, as in
"Patmos" (2:165):

> *Nah ist*
> *Und schwer zu fassen der Gott.*
> *Wo aber Gefahr ist, wächst*
> *Das Rettende auch.*

> (Up close,
> That hard to hold fast, is God.
> But it is also in danger
> That rescue grows live.)

or in the second version of *Der Tod des Empedokles* (4:104):

> *Ich fühle nur des Tages Neige, Freund!*
> *Und dunkel will es werden mir und kalt!*

> (I feel the day declining now, my friend,
> And all is growing dark for me, and cold.)

In such simplicity the balances of weight become so delicate
that they are wholly destroyed by any alteration of the kind
that translation makes inevitable.

Such qualities may or may not be modern, and no doubt
they are not exclusively so, but there is one sense in which
Hölderlin is indubitably to be described as a modern poet,

and it is the only sense in which this sometimes dubious compliment has any real meaning. Any writer is modern who has
not yet given up his full meaning, whose work we still ponder
both to see exactly what it meant for its own time and exactly
what it may mean, in its full range of consequence, for our
time and our questions. The very fact that since the thirties
and forties Hölderlin has been accepted as a partisan by so
many schools of thought is a sign that our century has not yet
taken his measure. This, however, is something that any half-
way sensitive reader discovers for himself as, moving gradually
into Hölderlin's poetry, he discovers and learns to respect
its integrity, its depth, and its resistance to any process
of artificial assimilation or facile understanding.

Hölderlin and the Modern Sensibility

by Stephen Tonsor

T. S. Eliot remarks in his essay on "Seneca in Elizabethan
Translation" that "Few things that can happen to a nation
are more important than the invention of a new form of verse."
That poetry is always relevant to the larger concerns of
society is a truism which has been remarked on from the time
of Plato to Bob Dylan. Jacques Barzun observed that it is
impossible to understand German romantic political theory
unless one set it to music. But whatever the power of music
as an aid to cultural understanding, I believe it is easily
demonstrable that we moderns cannot know ourselves unless and
until we have read the poets. Poetry is always relevant.

But in what sense is poetry relevant? Poets, it seems
to me, fall, not easily but with some pushing and shoving,
into two categories. The greatest poets are those who speak
of the permanent things, those whose rhetoric crystalizes and
defines the perennial human condition and delineates those
things which from generation to generation and across the

First published in *Modern Age* 15 (1971): 143-47.

54

gulf of differing and estranged cultures are perceived by all
mankind to need utterance. Then body and soul together are
touched and the poet speaks for all mankind what we, had we
been able to formulate our incoherent thoughts, would have
said. The poet is mankind's better and more articulate self.

However, most of the poetry of the past two centuries has
not been a poetry of universal human relevance. It is the poetry
of a particular age, of a particular moment in time. However
great *The Waste Land* is as poetry, however deeply it spoke to
my generation, its preoccupations and its symbols are not such
as will carry it to a wide audience a century hence. Romanticism, which was so preoccupied with time and the historistic
quality of human experience, created a poetry which more than
any other is bound to a moment or an era. The relevance of
the poetry of the Romantics lies in its ability to crystalize
a moment, to identify the yearning and the aspirations of an
era, to encapsulate the metaphysical anxieties and the quest
for a subjective but intense realm of personal experience.
The universal is replaced by the infinite and the Greeks,
made over in the image of an alienated and irrational generation, demonstrated how even the certainties of classical humanism were forced to bow before the style of a new generation.
Hölderlin was among the first and was perhaps the greatest
to perceive the poet's mission as personal and time-contingent
utterance rather than universal statement. In the 1840's
when asked for a poem he replied, "As Your Holiness commands.
Shall it be about the spring, or Greece, or the spirit of the
age?" But, in fact, Hölderlin wrote about little other than
the "Spirit of the age"; the spirit of the age as it was embodied in his own experience. We of course rarely share
Hölderlin's experience but we share his intellectual world
and that fact makes him our contemporary.

Here I do not wish to imply that the elements of contemporaneity in Hölderlin were those elements which are commonly

listed in descriptions of pre-romanticism and romanticism. To
be sure, Hölderlin had, as had Herder, come to equate the conceptions of *Kind*, *Naturmensch*, *Volk*, and *Urpoesie*. Indeed
Hölderlin's poems return to these themes and equivalences time
and time again. Every thought and attitude in contemporary
society is colored by what A. O. Lovejoy described as the metaphysical pathos which clusters around these conceptions.

Nor is the organismic conception of nature the great bridge
between the poetry of Hölderlin and the sensibility of the
present. Certainly Hölderlin merges the cosmic process, the
environment, and the individual into one differentiated but
unitary consciousness. His successors have hardly equaled
the keenness of his perceptions in this respect and not even
the symbolists were capable of making language a more evocative
instrument for the purpose of getting behind the phenomena of
nature to its intrinsic spirit. The spiritualization of nature
is, after all, one of the commonplaces of the romantic mood.

The emphasis upon the singularity of place in the life of
the individual and the race, implicit even in the Swabian
vocabulary of Hölderlin, is not ultimately the element which
binds him to our own time as a contemporary. Ethnicity, local-
ism, the landscape of a particular place and a poetic vocabulary
which echoes a provincial vocabulary are to be found in varying
degrees among all the romantics. Local color is the easy pass-
port into the sentimentalized landscape of the romantic poet
and painter.

Those who have sought to account for the strong romantic
emphasis in the thematic materials and symbolic universe which
Hölderlin employs have emphasized the impact of Pietism and
particularly the Pietism of the Swabian school. No doubt
Köstlin, Bengel, Oetinger, and Hahn were enormously influential
and did much to tie Hölderlin to the world of the romantics and
pre-romantics. Still the Pietistic element in his poetry, if
anything, estranges us rather than makes us contemporaries.

Much the same thing must be said of the world of German idealistic philosophy which impinged so dramatically on the personality of Hölderlin in the form of his youthful friendship with Hegel and Schelling. They were able, taken together with the influence of Schiller and Goethe, to carry Hölderlin into the world of romanticism but all of them would have been unable to make Hölderlin our contemporary. However closely related to the modern sensibility those conceptions are they are not of the essence and they are, finally, not what Hölderlin is all about. None of them will give us the key to Hölderlin's tormented and tragic world and none of them will provide us with an explanation of Hölderlin's insight into our own frightening predicament.

Alienation has become a cant word, but then intellectual history is littered with cant words such as nature, grace, justification, rationality, and order. And no other word will serve to indicate the precise point of connection between ourselves and Hölderlin. Time and again Hölderlin says, "let us have done with man as he is; let us have done with things as they are and put on a new and more perfect humanity; live in a new and more perfect world." Hölderlin's Greece is not to be confused with the Greece of antiquity. It is Utopia; a historicist utopia, to be sure, rather than a utopia of the future but it is utopia, nonetheless. It is a symbol of estrangement and alienation overcome, of harmony restored, of ecstasy regained. It is, to employ the much-used phrase of Eric Voegelin, an immatization of the eschaton and that it is identified with the unattainable past makes the poet's yearning all the more poignant and the poet's pessimism and frustration all the deeper. Schiller and Goethe were correct in their skepticism of Hölderlin's classicism. Hölderlin's gods have as little to do with the Greeks as Nietzsche's Zarathustra has to do with Iranian religion.

But alienation from what? Not surely alienation from

God, that fall from grace and estrangement which is the consequence of sin. Hölderlin's estrangement is not from human
nature as it was or as it is but rather an estrangement from
human nature as it might be. That is the key to the philosophies of radical and revolutionary transformation which have
been such an important element in the contemporary world. It
is in terms of this alienation that we can understand the element of *Streben* which was so essential a feature of romantic
poetry and art and so intrinsic an element in the modern
sensibility. It is alienation, too, which makes understandable
the romantic preoccupation with the infinite, the romantic
flight from closed systems and limited universes. The romantic
painters, particularly Caspar David Friedrich, symbolized that
unknown and mysterious infinitude by a figure at a window or
peering out into some other vastness which cannot be glimpsed
by the beholder of the picture.

Infinitude, however, is always associated by Hölderlin
and by ourselves with the infinite deeps and vastnesses of the
personality and the consciousness. The description of the
landscape tends to abstractness and is usually, with the exception of the poet, unpeopled. The poet's vision is interior
even though he symbolizes his search by depicting an exterior
reality. Moreover, there is always a beyond, an ever receding
horizon, an unattainable distance. Nor can it be said that
Hölderlin's imagery is sensuous. It is intellectual rather
than sensate. There is a constant calling for intensity, a
frenzied movement toward the ecstatic but these elevated states
involve a mystical estrangement from the here and now.

The syntactical peculiarities of Hölderlin's poetry are
not aesthetic accidents or affectations. Hölderlin was a
self-conscious artist and his innovations point the way to
the new structure of art and poetry. The artist in the modern
period has attempted to break the power of the observer and
the reader to objectify experience. The movement in modern

poetry has been one from observation to participation and the
purpose of Hölderlin's syntactical experiments is involvement
and immediacy. Hölderlin's poetry abolishes the spectator,
the neutral observer. Indeed, the poet not only engulfs and
subjectifies the landscape but he absorbs the other completely
so that the reader becomes an aspect of the poet's projected
selfhood. To this end Hölderlin does not describe or depict,
he incites. Hölderlin's syntax leads the reader not only
inside the poem and the meaning of the poem but inside the
poet. The affinities between Hölderlin and Hopkins or Joyce
in this respect are all too clear.

Modernity is an art without boundaries; subject and object
are one; poet and reader are united, environment and organism
merge and, most importantly, creator and creature are indis-
tinguishable. The great revolutionaries in romantic poetry
and philosophy tended to begin their careers in theology.
They were, from Hölderlin and Hegel to Nietzsche and Joyce,
spoiled priests and stickit ministers. That distinction between the divine and the mortal which was so completely a part
of the Greek consciousness was expunged by the poets and philosophers of romanticism. Perhaps that is the single most important characteristic of modernity. It was the effort of the
romantic poet and philosopher to elevate man to the stature of
the deity.

I do not wish at this point to detail Hölderlin's theology, if indeed one can call it a theology. Romano Guardini
in his *Hölderlin, Weltbild und Frömmigkeit* has explored that
subject in detail, though I believe Guardini's work insuffi-
ciently critical and colored by the same romantic subjectivism
and lack of distance which characterize Hölderlin's poetry.
It is clear, however, that Hölderlin believed himself to be
living at a decisive moment in history. It is a moment of
longing and anxiety. The catastrophe which will usher in the
new age is at hand and Hölderlin casts himself in the role of

the apocalyptic prophet. As Guardini makes clear, this attitude of expectation and the certainty that a new age was at
hand is shared by Hölderlin and Nietzsche. It has been shared
by moderns generally. Eschatological anxiety is the mark of
the present era. What Guardini did not realize was that even
in Hölderlin's day both Christian and Gnostic eschatologies
were current and popular and that the turn of the century, the
revolution and the collapse of the empire, all led men to anticipate a decisive break in the cycle of the ages. That break
implied not only a new cycle of history but a transformed and
renewed humanity. Hölderlinian, Hegelian, Marxist, and Nietz-
schean anticipations all insisted upon an end to alienation.

Even more contemporary, however, was the conception held
by Hölderlin that the way to wholeness was not through ethical
transformation but rather through aesthetic experience. Men
became like gods through the exercise of their creative poten-
tialities.

> Then welcome, O silence of the world of shades!
> Contented I shall be, even if my lyre
> does not accompany me on that downward journey;
> *Once* I lived as the gods live, and that suffices.

The creative act, even in politics, is modeled on the work of
art, and aesthetics replaces metaphysics and theology throughout the whole of our era. Until Nietzsche, the reason why
this should be the case was unclear. It was Nietzsche who
perceived that in a world in which order has been dissolved in
anarchic chaos only the arbitrary order of art or of violence
is possible. (Our own generation has come to see that in a
world without order the order of art and the order of violence
are equivalents.)

That development in the human spirit still lay in the
future, however. For Hölderlin the act by which the human
raised itself to the stature of divinity was the creative

gesture. Religion and morality are swallowed up in aesthetics
and men transcend their creaturely and human limitations by
turning their lives into a work of art. It is, I believe,
mistaken to conceive of Hölderlin's gods as numinous forces or
religious entities as does Guardini. They are, in fact, the
transcendent spirit of art; they are what man might become were
he able to purge himself of the dross of the mundane. Art had,
in fact, become the great religious surrogate of Western society and remained such until it was replaced by violence.

But note that the creative act, that life as art, is not
the consequence of rational analysis. Rather it is a state of
consciousness in which the spirit or the soul projects on the
world of existential reality the forms which it has discovered
at the deepest level of its experience. It is for this reason
that the Dionysian and the unconscious have played such an
inordinately large role in contemporary culture. Here, as in
other areas, Hölderlin was a prophetic voice. Here, as in so
many other areas, Hölderlin anticipated Nietzsche by fifty years.

But consciousness is not method, is not analysis, and it
is for this reason that both Hölderlin and Nietzsche verge so
often on sentimentality. It is for this reason that poets,
musicians, painters,and philosophers who belong to the romantic
school but who do not share the consummate artistry of Hölderlin and Nietzsche lapse so often into sentimentality and bathos.
Die Wiederkunft des Dionysos, that creative aesthetic state
out of which men and their culture were to regenerate and to
recreate themselves, too often bore the stigmata of madness
or the triviality of silliness and sentimentality. In all of
these respects Hölderlin traveled the road of our culture
ahead of us.

But Hölderlin and Nietzsche found Dionysos and Christ in
an antithetical relationship. For both, the new age was to be
an age under the sign of Dionysos. Still Christ would not
die. Christianity is one of those historical experiences

which absolutely transforms history. Willy-nilly all those
who came after that historical experience are in some sense
Christian. Certainly a return to a pre-Christian state is
impossible. One can graft Aristotle on to Christianity; it
is quite impossible to graft Christianity on to Aristotle.
Hölderlin and after him Nietzsche, discovered that history
is a one-way street, that time's arrow moves unidirection-
ally. When Pan died at the beginning of the Christian era
his morbidity was quite complete and no amount of resurrec-
tionism by intellectuals living in what they believe is a
post-Christian era is capable of reviving him. Is it possible that both Hölderlin and Nietzsche broke themselves
on this stumbling block?

However unsuccessful Hölderlin and Nietzsche were in
reviving Dionysos they both anticipate and pave the way for
a mood which had its equivalent in the ancient world. When
E. R. Dodds concluded his study of *The Greeks and the Irrational* he said:

in writing these chapters, and especially this last one,
I have had our own situation constantly in mind. We too
have witnessed the slow disintegration of an inherited
conglomerate, starting among the educated class but now
affecting the masses almost everywhere, yet still very
far from complete. We too have experienced a great age
of rationalism, marked by scientific advances beyond
anything that earlier times had thought possible, and
confronting mankind with the prospect of a society more
open than any it has ever known. And in the last forty
years we have also experienced something else--the
unmistakable recoil from that prospect. It would appear
that, in the words used recently by André Malraux,
"Western civilization has begun to doubt its own
credentials."
What is the meaning of this recoil, this doubt? Is it
the hesitation before the jump, or the beginning of a
panic flight? I do not know. On such a matter a simple
professor of Greek is in no position to offer an opinion.
But he can do one thing. He can remind his readers that
once before a civilized people rode to this jump--rode
to it and refused it. And he can beg them to examine

all the circumstances of that refusal.

Was it the horse that refused or the rider? That is really the crucial question. Personally I believe it was the horse --in other words, those irrational elements in human nature.

Nothing I might add could speak more clearly of the contemporaneity of Hölderlin or link him more completely to the world of his beloved Greeks.

"Stifter einer weiteren Ahnenreihe"?

Hölderlin's Influence on German
Poets of the Twentieth Century

by Ingo Seidler

To say of an eighteenth-century poet that he is in some way
an early modern is one thing; to say that he has influenced
modern poets is another. While I have long upheld the first
proposition, I could not defend the second with anything like
the finality of Stefan George who--in the quote that is part
of my title--calls Hölderlin the "founder of a continuing
line of ancestors."[1] But before giving my own, rather qualified, account of the question of Hölderlin's "influence,"
I should like to state briefly in what sense Hölderlin's
poetry appears to me to be "modern." Neither Hölderlin's use
of, and faith in, mythology nor his particular brand of *Natur-
lyrik* strikes me as modern, or even as capable of being integrated into very modern developments. Also, the basic mold
of Hölderlin's language is clearly eighteenth-century, and
thus by definition not viable in our age. But out of those
very eighteenth-century historic and linguistic presuppositions Hölderlin has, especially in his late poetry, developed

a daringly free use of imagery that is without parallel in
classical, romantic, or realist poetry, and that does have
striking affinities with much later, symbolist and imagist,
expressionist and surrealist, techniques. Theodor Adorno,
in a polemical but perceptive article on Hölderlin's late
poetry, has already pointed to the paradox that some of the
most daring imagist devices of the late Hölderlin that have
earned him the title of an "early modern" may, in fact, be
traced back to Pindar.[2] Nonetheless, they do strike the
contemporary reader as contemporary devices. What seems to
us contemporary, or at least modern, is the independence of
Hölderlin's images from any rephrasable "message"; the images
are, as Gottfried Benn would say, pure expression. Modern,
too, is their independence of any traceable individual emotion
or single experience; Hölderlin's images are, in Rilke's
sense, objective. Modern is their unconcern with accepted
manners of evocation, their impatience with logical coherence,
their refusal to grow organically out of a psychologically
testable world view. Modern, in short, is Hölderlin's entire
shift from offering symbols to what Walther Killy calls *"ein
sinnlich schönes, an sich nicht verständliches Bild, dessen
Bedeutung erst aus dem Zusammenhang erschlossen werden muss"*
(a sensuously beautiful, in itself not comprehensible image,
whose significance can be ascertained from the context only).[3]

Still, can it be said that Hölderlin thereby became the
"founder of a continuing line of ancestors"? How much easier
it would be to make such a confident claim for other great
innovators, for example, the other two Germans of that amazing
crop of 1770, Beethoven and Hegel. Why, then, does one--why
do I--hesitate with Hölderlin? Are philosophy and music perhaps more easily traceable in terms of influences and "ances-
tral lines"? Or is it simply the fact that Beethoven and Hegel
exerted their influence both during their lifetimes and after,
without ever a break? Hölderlin's story was indeed different.

He belongs more with such untimely geniuses as Carlo Gesualdo
(music of the seventeenth century) or Georg Büchner (drama of
the nineteenth): artists who at first were not--and probably
could not be--integrated into the historical development.
Their very modernity stands, paradoxically, in the way of their
exerting influence--at least during their lives and long after.
If we are nowadays at all aware of such artists' existence,
and of their stature, it is because of a kind of artistic
"second coming." Such second comings, or rediscoveries, can
usually be dated with some exactness. In Hölderlin's case the
date is 1914, when his late hymns were first made available to
a wide, and wide-eyed, audience. This is not to say, as it
sometimes *is* said, that Hölderlin was completely unknown until
Norbert von Hellingrath brought out his edition of Hölderlin's
works. Nietzsche, for example, gave a perceptive account of
the poet's work and rank as early as 1861 (when Nietzsche,
incidentally, was seventeen years old);[4] Hofmannsthal read
him in a little Polish village (where he was stationed with
the Austrian army) in the 1890s;[5] Max Reger set Hölderlin to
music as early as 1903, and so the list could go on. But the
late, and that means the most modern, part of Hölderlin's
oeuvre *was* virtually unknown for more than a hundred years,
and when it was rediscovered it came into times so radically
changed in spirit, in presuppositions, in sensibility, and in
problems, that no small number of misunderstandings arose in
trying to cope with it. I shall, at least in part, have to
deal with such misunderstandings, particularly since I intend
to narrow down the scope of my rather panoramic subject by
inserting the words "actual," "direct," and "demonstrable"
before the word "influence" in my title.

We should then begin by asking ourselves, What are the
criteria that will allow us to speak of such actual, direct,
and demonstrable influence, and how can such influence be
distinguished from mere affinity, chance parallelism, and

accidental similarity? Without trying to be exhaustive, I
should like to suggest that the following conditions would
have to be met: (1) firsthand knowledge of Hölderlin's work,
(2) specific stylistic and/or thematic correspondences of some
degree of complexity and uncommonness, and (3) a body of control texts by the same author, but written before or after
the period of actual influence. Personal testimony, a fourth
possible criterion, although always interesting and often
helpful, I would consider neither necessary (see the example
of Trakl) nor, strictly speaking, sufficient (see the example
of Weinheber) to make a case for "actual influence." With
these three basic criteria in mind I should like to look at
four groups, or generations, of German poets: the symbolists,
the expressionists, the "Third Reich" poets, and the poets
writing since the end of World War II. For each of these
groups I shall try both to sketch a general account and to
focus on at least one representative in some depth.

I

Stefan George and his *Kreis* deserve to be treated first. If
we pass up such writers as Nietzsche and Spitteler as belonging
strictly to the nineteenth century, George would be the oldest
poet to be seriously considered here. Hellingrath, whose edition started the modern Hölderlin renaissance, also had close
ties to the *Kreis*, and some of the most eloquent advocates of
Hölderlin's importance during the first two decades of our
century (Gundolf, Kommerell, Wolters, Boehringer) were members
of George's inner circle. A great deal has been written about
George and Hölderlin, but it is important to distinguish the
contributions from within the *Kreis* and those of outsiders.
For the testimony of the *Kreis* invariably echoes George's own
dictum: Hölderlin is to be accepted into mankind's hall of
fame--along with Aeschylus, Pindar, Plato, Dante, as well as

(sometimes) Novalis, Napoleon (!), and Nietzsche--as one of
the eternal leaders. Hölderlin becomes the prophet of a "true
Hellas," but also of a secret Germany, a "cornerstone of the
German future," a "voice calling out for the new God," and,
more to the point, a "rejuvenator of both language and soul."[6]
At the same time he is *"ein hehrer ahn"* (a sublime ancestor)
of the *Kreis* itself. It is this latter function that seems in
the end the most important to George's disciples, as ample
testimony shows--in poetry (Robert Boehringer):

> *Er wäre unser einer säh er heute*
> *Da sich erfüllt die zeit der Dioskuren*
> *Erblühend Hellas jugend ...*[7]

> (He would be one of us if he today
> Now that the time of the Dioskouroi is fulfilled
> Saw the youth of Hellas blossom ...)

and in prose (Friedrich Gundolf):

> ... *nur George hat heute den lebendigen Willen und die*
> *menschliche Wesenheit die zuletzt in Goethe und Napoleon*
> *noch einmal Fleisch geworden, die in Hölderlin und Nietz-*
> *sche zuletzt als körperlose Flamme gen Himmel schlug und*
> *verglühte.*[8]

> (Today only George has the living will and human spirit
> that lately became flesh once more in Goethe and Napoleon,
> that in Hölderlin and Nietzsche most recently leaped to
> the sky and died out as incorporeal flame.)

This forcible annexation and distorting hero worship on the
part of the *Georgekreis* has assumed extraordinary proportions.
Even as late as 1950, Edgar Salin (in a lecture to the Hölderlin-Gesellschaft), after admitting that Hölderlin would perhaps
not have been just another member of the *Georgekreis* after all,
that he, in fact, "transcends George and his circle," in the
end relapses into the old cliché that makes Hölderlin the mere

prophet, but George the *bringer* of the German fulfillment--
again reducing the former to a John-the-Baptist figure charged
with announcing the future coming of the Master himself.[9]
Without question, George and his circle were instrumental in
spreading Hölderlin's fame--at least after 1914. (In the original edition of their anthology *Das Jahrhundert Goethes* [1902],
Brentano and even Platen were alloted more space than Hölderlin!) But it is also obvious that their image of Hölderlin
was perversely subordinated to the self-image of the *Kreis*,
and is thus misleading.[10] For in the end it must be admitted
that--despite George's prose homage of 1919 and his poems about
Hölderlin and *Hyperion*,[11] despite shared affinities with a
Pindaresque, hymnic tradition and a superficially similar
prophetic stance, despite a seemingly parallel concern with
the future fate of Germany--the willful artifice of George's
language, rhythm, imagery, and general poetic tone, its impe-
rial rigidity and mannered polish, have very little in common
with Hölderlin's verse. And where Hölderlin's uniqueness has
been seen in his combining *"Grossartigkeit der Begriffe und
Einfachheit des Ausdrucks"* (grandeur of conception and simplicity of expression),[12] in reading the poetry in George's periodical *Blätter für die Kunst* one is too often struck by its
combining paucity of conception and pomposity of expression.

In the absence of a paper on Hölderlin and politics in
this Symposium, a brief excursion on the subject of Hölderlin's so-called nationalism seems called for. Some important
distinctions are to be made here. One question to ask is,
of course, what an author makes of his nationalism; the other,
even more important question (as *we* ought to know, in 1970),
is what nationalism--what the nation--is making of itself at
a given historic point. In Hölderlin's time, politically
speaking, a "German nation" did not yet exist. What did exist
were various principalities that were being threatened by what
was very much a nation, the (then most belligerent) *grande*

nation. To identify with a *possible* German nation and entertain hopes for its future may not be particularly attractive
even at this point (and Goethe's example shows that such feelings were not inescapable); still, it does not by any means
seem morally objectionable. But by 1870 Germany *was* a nation,
and Nietzsche was one of the first to understand and warn that
nationalist identifications had now turned into something quite
different. By the time of World War I both George and Rilke
might have noticed that nationalism at this point was, at best,
in questionable taste. Rilke can be said to have seen this
after some initial confusion (treated more fully later); George
hardly did. By the time of World War II, identifying with the
German nation had passed from being in questionable taste to
being potentially criminal. This Weinheber should have known
and did not, but Hölderlin himself is hardly to be taken to
task for such later developments.

II

The most fully explored relationship to be discussed here is
that between Hölderlin and Rilke--and for good reason. Friedrich Beissner's article of 1936, Werner Günther's of 1951, and
Herbert Singer's book of 1957 are only the best among a host
of others on the subject.[13] All are aware of the fact that
Rilke (through the kind offices of Hellingrath himself) came
to know Hölderlin at a time of severe personal and artistic
crisis and that he was, as his letters attest, overwhelmed
by the encounter. The outbreak of World War I and Hölderlin's
sudden impact conspired to make Rilke produce five hymnic war
poems ("Fünf Gesänge, August 1914," which Rilke, incidentally,
wrote right into his new copy of Hölderlin's late poems).[14]
No doubt at least the beginning of this cycle has about it
something of that national enthusiasm and spirit of self-
sacrifice which, according to Thomas Mann, swept the entire

German nation in the summer of 1914, and which *are* related to
the spirit of Hölderlin's national and battle poems. The god
of war, *"Endlich ein Gott"* (a god at long last [R 2:87]), is
seen as a powerful, transpersonal, and uniting force: *"Heil
mir, dass ich Ergriffene sehe"* (Hail to me, that I should see
enrapt ones [ibid.]), and a national community (of which Rilke
had long despaired) suddenly seemed within reach (R 2:89):

> *... Und wir? Glühen in Eines zusammen,*
> *in ein neues Geschöpf, das er tödlich belebt.*
> *So auch* bin *ich nicht mehr; aus dem gemeinsamen Herzen*
> *schlägt das meine den Schlag, und der gemeinsame Mund*
> *bricht den meinigen auf.*

> (... And we? Fuse into One,
> into a new creature he animates with death.
> So too I no longer *am;* out of a heart held in common
> my heart paces its beat, and the one common mouth
> moves me to open my own.)

But this collective enthusiasm for the collective was not
to last. Already in the later poems of the cycle it is not
war, nor enthusiasm, but pain that is addressed. Also, Rilke
soon refused to show the poems, and in several letters (from
August 1914 to October 1915) "took them back" as no more than
a temporary aberration (RB 2:15):

> *In den ersten Augusttagen ergriff mich die Erscheinung des
> Krieges, des Kriegs-Gottes ..., jetzt ist mir längst der
> Krieg unsichtbar geworden, ein Geist der Heimsuchung, nicht
> mehr ein Gott, sondern eines Gottes Entfesselung über den
> Völkern.*

> (In the first August days the epiphany of war, of the war
> god, held me enrapt ..., now the war has long since become
> invisible for me, the spirit of a curse, no longer a god,
> but rather the unleashing of a god over the nations.)

And Rilke celebrates having found again *"mein altes, mein bis-*

heriges Herz (das ich nicht aufgeben kann)" (my old heart, the
heart I had until now, which I cannot give up [RB 2:7]).[15]
The fact remains that, right down to details of vocabulary,
syntax, and diction these poems reflect at least *one* aspect
of Hölderlin. But it seems a totally different person that
inspires Rilke's poem to Hölderlin (September 1914), an
"incomparable conjuror" whose every image was nurtured by an
entire life, and whose vast landscapes of the soul transcended
all personal, cozy, warm, and domestic poetry (R 2:94):

> *Was, da ein solcher, Ewiger, war, misstraun wir
> immer dem Irdischen noch?*

> (What--now that there has been such an eternal one,
>   do we still
> distrust what is earthly?)

Beissner, Günther, and Singer all assume a decisive influence
of Hölderlin on Rilke's *Duino Elegies*, and they demonstrate it
by echoes of themes (the heroic, the role of the poet, the
role of nature), by the use of symbols (star, storm, river),
and by stylistic devices (inverted attributes, repetitions,
absolute comparatives, neologisms, turning verbs into neuter
nouns). Although one would have to agree that some of these
features strongly suggest Hölderlin, it should also be noted
that many of them predate Rilke's acquaintance with the older
poet (some, like the frequent nominalizations, having been
trademarks of Rilke's style for years), and furthermore that
at least some of them seem to come from Klopstock rather than
from Hölderlin.[16] But stronger claims than any of these can,
in my opinion, be made for the *Sonnets to Orpheus*. It is here
that Rilke has found his late sparse and objective style, here
that (in the virtual canonization of Orpheus) mythic poetry
becomes once more a reality, here that Rilke consciously transcends, and explicitly rejects, all merely personal expression:

"In Wahrheit singen, ist ein andrer Hauch" (to sing in truth is
another breath [R 1:732]), namely, *"Gesang ist Dasein"* (song is
existence [ibid.]), a celebration of *all* existence, including
its most tragic aspects. And it is in these poems that, in a
manner truly akin to Hölderlin, the poet is seen as a mouthpiece
of transpersonal forces. Rilke, therefore, seems to be the one
poet whose contact with Hölderlin bore rich fruit--it enabled
him to initiate and sustain the third and most significant stage
of his development, that of the *Elegies* and *Sonnets*. And I also
think that a valid claim could be made for a parallel between
Rilke's last, more modest and idyllic poems and the deceptively
simple rhymed poems of Hölderlin's final years. Certainly what
Eugen Gottlob Winkler said of Hölderlin holds equally for Rilke:
*"Nicht träge Genügsamkeit, sondern ein unabschätzbares Mass an
Verzicht ist der Untergrund dieser Idyllik"* (Not inert compla-
cency but rather an inestimable measure of restraint is the basis
of this idyllic stance).[17]

As far as Hugo von Hofmannsthal is concerned, one's claims
would have to be much more modest, even though, in the fourth
of his five Vienna letters for the American periodical *The Dial*
(the five letters date from 1922-24), Hofmannsthal, after much
small talk about Viennese affairs, suddenly makes an extrav-
agant statement about Hölderlin as a symbolic leader of a new
kind of religiosity.[18] There are traces of Hölderlin in some
of Hofmannsthal's Ariel-like poetry, and perhaps no other poet
after Hölderlin has achieved Hofmannsthal's delicate balance
of Greek and Christian allegiances. But it can hardly be claimed
that this combination ever became a productive mythic, or even
metaphorical, reality in Hofmannsthal's poetic output.

III

Much work will still have do be done before anything final can
be said about the question of Hölderlin's actual influence on
expressionist poets.   Sweeping claims are still being countered
by angry disavowals.   Pinthus and Edschmid, Sternheim and Benn,
Lohner and Uhlig claim Hölderlin's ancestry for expressionism;
and the following poets have all been said, at one time or
another, to be part of a "Hölderlin tradition": Wilhelm Klemm,
Franz Werfel, Albert Ehrenstein, Georg Heym, Georg Trakl, and
Oskar Loerke.   Walter Muschg is convinced that Hölderlin's
prose, more than his poetry, helped shape the early, lyrical
prose of Alfred Döblin and Hans Henny Jahnn.[19]   Lip service to
Hölderlin's genius abounds: even Johannes R. Becher and Carl
Sternheim joined the then fashionable chorus.   On the other
hand, there are many scholarly studies on expressionism that
do not mention Hölderlin even once.[20]   And it is my conviction
that, apart from Georg Trakl (but this question I can leave to
Professor Fiedler), systematic study will probably yield better
results with some of the forerunners of expressionism than with
the expressionists proper.   Questions of achievement and final
rank aside, both Alfred Mombert and--particularly--Theodor
Däubler continue a mythic-visionary tradition that is unthink-
able without Hölderlin.   And Däubler also shares Hölderlin's
concern with reconciling Greek and Christian cultural elements,
as well as attempting some of his magic evocations of specific
geographical locations.   Still, these are no more than suppo-
sitions at a time when systematic analyses on these poets and
their relation to Hölderlin are lacking.   In the meantime, I
feel much more comfortable with a statement such as the following by Gottfried Benn, who, in his unsuccessful attempt
at "selling" expressionism to the Nazis in 1933, claimed not
specific influence but all of Hölderlin's late work as an
early instance of "expressionism":

... Nietzsche[s], ... *und ebenso* Hölderlins *bruchstückartige Lyrik sind rein expressionistisch: Beladung des Worts, weniger Worte, mit einer ungeheuren Ansammlung schöpferischer Spannung, eigentlich mehr* ein Ergreifen von Worten aus Spannung, *und diese gänzlich mystisch ergriffenen Worte leben dann weiter mit einer real unerklärbaren Macht von Suggestion.*[21]

(... *Nietzsche's,* ... and likewise *Hölderlin's* fragmentary lyric is purely expressionistic: a charging of the word, of few words, with an enormous accumulation of creative tension, actually more *a plucking of words out of tension,* and these wholly mystically enrapt words then live on with a genuinely inexplicable might of suggestiveness.)

IV

This is neither the time nor the place to solve the knotty problem of Hölderlin and National Socialism. Certainly a vigorous attempt was made (comparable to, but even more irresponsible than, that by the *Georgekreis)* at "naturalizing" and integrating Hölderlin into the system. The patriotic hopes of some of his hymns were perverted into nationalistic allegations. Always, of course, at the expense of Heine, Hölderlin was stylized (as Weinheber put it, and without a shade of self-irony) into "the last official poet of the Germans, to whom I had to adhere as my ancestor."[22] The same note is struck in Hermann Pongs's article of 1944 about Hölderlin's influence on German poetry since the turn of the century. Pongs's recipe is simple. His own idea of Hölderlin is that of the nation's heroic singer of self-sacrifice, purity, and (a highly militaristic kind of) "honor"; Pongs looks for, and finds, or fails to find, such "true essence" in the modern poets he discusses. The poets are praised when Pongs finds such echoes, and censured when he does not: both George and Rilke pass with their most warlike and nationalistic utterances but not with the rest of their work; Weinheber (whom Pongs calls "the most significant poet of the younger generation") and the old *Blut und Boden* novelist Emil Strauss predictably "pass" with flying colors. Even more crudely, Werner Bartscher's book *Hölderlin und die deutsche Nation* (Berlin: Triltsch, 1942) lists as Hölderlin's legitimate heirs more than twenty Nazi writers, from Hanns Johst to Will Vesper, from Rudolf G. Binding to Baldur von Schirach--in short, the entire *Reichsschrifttumskammer*--pointing out that the Hitler Youth, too, had made it their business to popularize the poet.[23]

Such claims need hardly be discussed. What should be mentioned, however, is another, largely apolitical, group of poets who thought they were following Hölderlin as their model by writing in Greek stanzas. Among them were such respectable, though conservative and slightly academic, poets as Rudolf Alexander Schröder, Friedrich Georg Jünger, Rudolf Borchardt, and Georg Britting. But I should like to concentrate on the most celebrated, and the most questionable, of these, Josef Weinheber, who for years was considered Hölderlin's twentieth-century reincarnation. To be sure Josef Nadler, Weinheber's biographer, denies that Hölderlin had "influenced" his poet; rather, he says, Hölderlin comes into play only when Weinheber's stature, his *geistige Figur*, is to be discussed.[24] In other words, according to Nadler, they are not father and son, but true brothers in spirit. Still, Weinheber himself, in 1940, formulated the following credo:

Wir ehren und verehren in Hölderlin den grössten Sprach-genius unseres Volkes. Und wie anders könnten wir rühm-licher seiner gedenken, als dass wir seiner Sprache, als des lebendig gebliebenen Ausdrucks seiner Seinsgewalt, nachfolgten?[25]

(We honor and revere in Hölderlin the greatest linguistic genius of our people. And how else could we commemorate him more honorably than by imitating his language as the perennially living expression of his power of being?)

Despite its shaky style, this passage is quoted often enough. What is not generally quoted is its very continuation:

> *Die Dichter, als Trunkene, leben in einer Welt der Trunkenheit, die eine andere als die gegebene und für sie die eigentlich nüchterne ist. Das, was sie zu sagen haben, ist irrationaler Natur. Durch sie hindurch geht das Wesentliche, das Göttliche, und spricht sich durch ihren Mund aus. Wie sie das Unsagbare, das Wesentliche, in eine dem Sterblichen fassbare Form bringen, das ist ihre Sache. Es bleibt ihnen ja auch zeitlebens Problem, und sie gehen an diesem Problem so oder so zugrunde. Der Dithyrambiker Hölderlin musste wahnsinnig werden, weil ihm der Reim versagt war.*

(The poets, as the drunken ones, live in a world of drunkenness, a world different from the one given, but a world that, for them, is the actually sober one. What they have to say is of an irrational nature. What is essential and divine goes through them, and finds expression through their mouths. How poets couch the inexpressible, the essential, in a form comprehensible to mortals, is their business. This indeed remains a problem for them all their lives and, in one way or another, this problem becomes their undoing. The dithyrambic poet Hölderlin had to go insane because rhyme was denied him.)

The dithyrambic poet Weinheber, to whom rhyme was not denied, did not have to become insane. Instead, he filled several volumes with Greek stanzas and in noble modesty explained, on another occasion:

> *Ich beuge mich unter das Gesetz der Form. Ich nehme es auch willig auf mich, die geprägten Formen weiter zu pflegen, weil ich mich ausserstande fühle, bessere aus mir heraus zu erfinden.*[26]

(I bow before the law of form. I also take it upon me willingly to go on cultivating the received forms, since I feel myself incapable of inventing better ones of my own accord.)

Thus speaks the true epigone, and proceeds to prove his point in volumes of formally correct, pseudoheroic, and chauvinistic poems. (In fairness it should be said that Weinheber also tried his hand, and much more successfully, at simpler, folksier poems, some of them even in Viennese dialect. But it is also true that even Josef Nadler, the editor of Weinheber's works, was moved to exclude some of the poet's most notorious hymns to the Führer, about the Anschluss, etc., from the complete edition.)

Among Weinheber's classical verse there are three poems to Hölderlin (one in each of the major Greek stanzas) and a set of ten variations on Hölderlin's ode "An die Parzen." This memorable tour de force, according to Nadler a work "both bold and perfect," would have to be read and interpreted in detail to be believed. The manner in which Hölderlin's terse poem becomes infected; develops boils; gets soggy, bloated, dismembered; and in the end turns totally absurd, is an impressive refutation of all epigone poetry; it can also serve as a demonstration piece for the difference between language as creation and language as an imitative spasm. Although I cannot at this point present the entire set of variations, I should like at least to substantiate my argument by contrasting Hölderlin's poem with one (and neither the worst nor the most tasteless) of Weinheber's "variations." To help recall the original, one of Hölderlin's best-known poems, here is the text (1:241):

> *Nur Einen Sommer gönnt, ihr Gewaltigen!*
> *Und einen Herbst zu reifem Gesange mir,*
> *Dass williger mein Herz, vom süssen*
> *Spiele gesättiget, dann mir sterbe.*

> *Die Seele, der im Leben ihr göttlich Recht*
> *Nicht ward, sie ruht auch drunten im Orkus nicht;*
> *Doch ist mir einst das Heilge, das am*
> *Herzen mir liegt, das Gedicht, gelungen,*

Willkommen dann, o Stille der Schattenwelt!
Zufrieden bin ich, wenn auch mein Saitenspiel
Mich nicht hinab geleitet; Einmal
Lebt ich, wie Götter, und mehr bedarfs nicht.

(One summer only grant me, you powerful Fates,
And one more autumn only for mellow song,
So that more willingly, replete with
Music's late sweetness, my heart may die then.

The soul in life denied its god-given right
Down there in Orcus also will find no peace;
But when what's holy, dear to me, the
Poem's accomplished, my art perfected,

Then welcome silence, welcome cold world of shades!
I'll be content, though here I must leave my lyre
And songless travel down; for *once* I
Lived like the gods, and no more is needed.)

In his ninth variation, Weinheber proposes to fashion a new
poem, in hymnic style, out of the *Wort-Urmasse* of the original
(W 2:41):

Geleitet vom Herzen nur,
gönnt sie mir doch, die Orkusstille!
Liegt nicht am süssen Frieden drunten
der Seele Welt mir gesättiget?

Mein das Kommen der Schatten,
Spiele williger Götter, mein!

Im Gesange, gewaltigen,
zu einen
mich Leben und Gedicht,
nicht bedarfs, dass das Herz
einen Sommer will wie einst.

Einmal,
wenn ich sterbe und Herbst ward,
Dann ist mir Reifem mehr gelungen:
Dann lebt auch ihr
zu mir hinab, auch ihr!

Ruht, o im Saiten-
spiel nicht das heilge Recht?
Bin ich nicht göttlich?

(Accompanied only by my heart,
grant it to me nevertheless, the stillness
        of Orcus!
Does not the soul's world lie down there,
for me, satiating me with its peace?

Mine is the coming of shades,
the play of willing gods, mine!

In song, powerful
to one,
me life and poem,
it is not needed that the heart
want a summer, as once.

Once,
when I die and have become autumn,
then I, who am mature, have succeeded at more:
Then you too live
downward to me, you too!

Does not holy right
rest, O in the song of the lyre?
Am I not divine?)

In one of his published speeches Weinheber bemoans the fact
that Hölderlin, as he sees it, has fallen among thieves (W 4:48):

Denn auch das Übel, dass Hölderlin zur Mode zu werden droht,
ist schon bemerkbar. Und es gehört wohl mit zu seinem bit-
teren Schicksal, dass er, in einem solchen Sinn zeitgemäss
werdend, heute bereits eine beängstigende Gefolgschaft von
affengelehrigen Schülern und Kopisten nach sich zieht, die
sich seines Tonfalls versichert, von seinem Wesen aber
keine Ahnung hat.

(For even *that* evil: that Hölderlin is threatening to become
the fashion, is already noticeable. And it is most likely
part of his bitter fate that he, growing timely in such a

sense, already today draws in his wake a fearsome coterie
of students and imitators possessed of an apelike docility
who, having mastered his music, yet have not the faintest
notion of his innermost essence.)

History does not record for whom this stern censure was intended, but it is hard to imagine anyone to whom it might have
better applied than to Josef Weinheber.

V

Peter Demetz, in his recent volume on postwar German literature, says of the *Gruppe 47* that "in literary matters they
were deeply suspicious of complex grammar, flights of poetry,
and Hölderlin."[27] Put in this apodictic form, it will be hard
to defend the statement, and Demetz himself later names one
important exception, Johannes Bobrowski, whose poetic tradition he rightly sees as extending back to Trakl, Hölderlin,
and Klopstock. A strong reaction against more than just the
Nazi abuses of Hölderlin does, however, characterize the
postwar era. After Günter Eich, in his 1948 poem "Latrine,"
rhymed *Hölderlin* with *Urin,* there was for fourteen years not
a single German poem among the many that continued to be written
in homage to Hölderlin.[28] Another sign of the relative disen-
chantment with Hölderlin was the many parodies and travesties
that were beginning to appear in new volumes of poetry. The
founder of *this* "continuing line of ancestors" seems to have
been Bertolt Brecht, who in other ways was deeply impressed
with Hölderlin in general and his bold *Antigone* translation
in particular, but who, already in *Die heilige Johanna der
Schlachthöfe* (1930), applied the famous central image of
"Hyperions Schicksalslied" to the stock market:

> *Den Preisen nämlich*
> *War es gegeben von Notierung zu Notierung zu fallen*

Wie Wasser von Klippe zu Klippe geworfen
Tief ins Unendliche hinab. Bei dreissig erst hielten sie.[29]

                                   (For to the prices
It was given to fall from quotation to quotation
Hurled like water from ledge to ledge
Deep down into the infinite. Only at thirty did they stop.)

In like manner, Hans Magnus Enzensberger displaces a famous line from "Patmos" into a poem that features a kind of pep rally of the general staff:

                          ... bekanntlich
wächst, wo gefahr ist, das rettende auch[30]

                      (... as is well known
there grows where there is danger the saving power
      also)

With a more modest effort of the imagination Enzensberger satirizes yet another old war horse, the opening stanza of Hölderlin's "Gesang des Deutschen" (2:3):

O heilig Herz der Völker, o Vaterland!
Allduldend, gleich der schweigenden Mutter Erd,
Und allverkannt, wenn schon aus deiner
Tiefe die Fremden ihr Bestes haben!

(O sacred heart of peoples, O Fatherland!
 All-Patient One, akin to silent Mother Earth,
 And all-downrated, be it that from your
  Bowels the foreigners have their bounty!)

a chauvinistic absurdity that *deserves* to be ridiculed, and one that I confess I find even more objectionable than the equally infamous closing lines of Hölderlin's "Der Tod fürs Vaterland" (1:299):

> *Dir ist,*
> *Liebes! nicht Einer zu viel gefallen.*

> (For you,
> Dear One! not *one* too many has fallen.)

also addressed, of course, to the Fatherland. With Enzensberger, the stanza reads:

> *deutschland, mein land, unhéilig herz der völker,*
> *ziemlich verrufen, von fall zu fall,*
> *unter allen gewöhnlichen leuten.*[31]

> (Germany, my country, unholy heart of peoples,
> rather notorious, as the case may be,
> among all ordinary folk.)

And Peter Rühmkorf, in *his* parodistic variation of Hölderlin's "Gesang des Deutschen," gives, with stanzas like the following, a devastating picture of the *Wirtschaftswunder* and its questionable side effects:

> *Noch schwillst du an von unterdrücktem Krieg,*
> *sinnest ein neu Gebild, das von dir zeuge,*
> *das, einzig wie du selbst, das aus*
> *Stroh geschaffen, goldene Körner treibt.*[32]

> (You still swell from a suppressed war,
> design a new machine that may stand you witness,
> one that, unique like you yourself, constructed
> of straw, will bring forth gold kernels.)

And Rühmkorf ends his poem on his variation of the one line from Greek antiquity that during World War II every German high school student knew by heart: *"Wanderer, kommst du nach Sparta, so verkündige dorten, du habest uns hier liegen gesehen, wie das Gesetz es befahl"* (Wanderer, should you get to Sparta, make it known there that you saw us lying here,

as the law directed). In the final stanza of Rühmkorf's "Variation" the wording becomes:

> *Auf Kippe und Gedeih, dass nie und keiner*
> *die Kreise jemals störe, Wanderer, komm du nach*
> *Deutschland, sage du habest uns hier*
> *unterliegen sehen, wie es der Vorteil empfahl.*

> (For better or for worse, so that none ever
> disturb the circles, wanderer, come now to
> Germany, say you have seen us defeated
> here, as vested interests have recommended it.)

The common denominator of these parodies lies, of course, in
their turning Hölderlin's words--and the words from classical
antiquity that inspired him--against his alleged apolitical
high-mindedness by applying them to down-to-earth situations
and social problems. But it should also be pointed out that,
far from going against "all that is holy in Hölderlin," such
critical verse might, in fact, be seen as continuing a different strand of Hölderlin's *own* work--I am thinking of his bitter
indictment of the Germans in *Hyperion*, or again, of the following lines from the hexameter poem "Der Archipelagus" (2:110):

> *Aber weh! es wandelt in Nacht, es wohnt, wie im Orkus,*
> *Ohne Göttliches unser Geschlecht. Ans eigene Treiben*
> *Sind sie geschmiedet allein, und sich in der tosenden*
> *   Werkstatt*
> *Höret jeglicher nur und viel arbeiten die Wilden*
> *Mit gewaltigem Arm, rastlos, doch immer und immer*
> *Unfruchtbar, wie die Furien, bleibt die Mühe der Armen.*

> (Ah, but our kind walks in darkness, it dwells as in Orcus,
> Severed from all that's divine. To his own industry only
> Each man is forged, and can hear only himself in the
>   workshop's
> Deafening noise; and much the savages toil there, for ever
> Moving their powerful arms, they labour, yet always and
>   always
> Vain, like the Furies, unfruitful the wretches' exertions
>   remain there.)

But there is also another, and more direct, line of influence continuing as an observable trickle among contemporary German poets. The two outstanding examples of this trend seem to me to be Johannes Bobrowski and Paul Celan. Bobrowski was probably the only contemporary poet who continued writing in Greek stanzas without thereby becoming derivative or academic: his language had the strength and suppleness to assimilate these forms without compromise. And his elegiac poems in free verse betray, by their very density and intensity, an acknowledged debt to Hölderlin. So does his imaginative use of landscapes, rivers, and cities, as well as his sensitivity to the shaped world around him and to atmospheric changes, his uneasy concern with his national identity, even his pious yet unorthodox religiosity. At the same time, Bobrowski's very acute social conscience does not seem to have any roots in Hölderlin. This vulnerable conscience Bobrowski seems to have in common with the other great contemporary in a hymnic and esoteric tradition, Paul Celan. To be sure, here the influence, though no less direct, is more qualified. It has, in fact, been argued that Celan, with poetic means that clearly stem from Hölderlin (although Celan should not be called an epigone, either), is turning against some of Hölderlin's most exalted hopes and cherished expectations. Götz Wienold has interpreted Celan's poem "Tenebrae" as a *Widerruf* (revocation) of Hölderlin. Lines out of "Patmos" (2:165):

> *Nah ist*
> *Und schwer zu fassen der Gott.*

> (Up close,
> That hard to hold fast, is God.)

are doubly inverted, and the confidence of the poet in God's symbolic *presence* in time of distress is thereby turned into a profound attack, based on His actual *absence* at a time of the most terrible distress--during the systematic murder of the European Jews.[33]   Another poem of Celan's, "Tübingen, Jänner," seems to reinforce that very gesture of revocation. Of the Hölderlin-like patriarch figure in the poem it is said that, were he to come into *our* time, all he could do would be to babble, and babble, and babble. True, here it is the age that is being indicted, in the name of the metaphorically resurrected poet. But Celan's third, and final, gesture of rejection came when he--of all contemporary poets the most akin to Hölderlin--took his own life in the spring of 1970 by throwing himself into the river Seine.

My own hopes for a vigorous continuation of hymnic, mythic, and generally exalted poetry are not very great. And I certainly cannot take seriously Professor Bertaux, who recently tried to demonstrate Hölderlin's relevance by linking his concept of nature to pollution control.[34]   But the very question of Hölderlin's relevance strikes me as strangely irrelevant: there is greatness that can do without the popular crutches of relevance. Indeed, it is such exemplary greatness that helps us understand the very relativity and transitory character of all "relevance." I, for one, am content to see Hölderlin as one of the miracles within the history of poetry. But all miracles have one thing in common: there are no repeats.

Hölderlin and Trakl's Poetry of 1914

by Theodore Fiedler

Trakl's interest in Hölderlin, a matter whose significance has all too readily been exaggerated by some and dismissed out of hand by others, can be traced throughout his oeuvre. As early as 1906, for example, in a rather hapless prose poem entitled "Barrabas. Eine Phantasie," Trakl employed the striking title of Hölderlin's hymn "Der Einzige" to identify the figure of Christ crucified. Yet it is not until late 1912 that Trakl's interest in his predecessor, apparently focused for the first time on the odes, elegies, and hymns of Hölderlin's maturity that were available to him, contributes to some sustained changes in his poetry.[1] Chief among these changes, as evident in the poems "Helian" and "Abendlied," is the emergence of a historical perspective that reflects the secularized historical fiction--a past millennium, present decadence, the new millennium--informing Hölderlin's mature poetry. Even then more than a year passes before Trakl's concern with this fundamental thematic component of his predecessor's poetry merges with a dramatic interest in aspects of Hölderlin's mature style, to effect a crucial development that results in the so-called hymnic poetry of mid-1914.

The first signs that Trakl's interest in Hölderlin's major
poetry was reviving after a year of dormancy occur not, as might
be expected, in a verse poem but in the poet's prose masterpiece
"Traum und Umnachtung," written during the first weeks of 1914.
One such sign is Trakl's isolated use of a kind of hyperbatic
syntax that is characteristic of Hölderlin's mature poetry.
I refer to the clause: *"Stille sah er und lang in die Sternen-
augen der Kröte"* (Quietly he looked and long into the starry
eyes of the toad [T 1:147]), in the poem's first section. A
more significant manifestation of Trakl's reviving interest in
Hölderlin in his unprecedented use of the word *Geschlecht* "race,
generation" in a pejorative manner in various sections of the
poem. Such usage recalls not only Hölderlin's odes "Der
Frieden" and "Dichterberuf," where contemporary humanity is
referred to respectively as a *gärendes* and a *schlaues Geschlecht*
(a seething and a sly race) but also "Der Archipelagus," in
which the poet laments:

*Aber weh! es wandelt in Nacht, es wohnt, wie im Orkus,
Ohne Göttliches unser Geschlecht.*[2]

(Ah, but our kind walks in darkness, it dwells as in Orcus,
Severed from all that's divine.)

Trakl, to be sure, narrows down the scope of the word *Geschlecht*
primarily to the protagonist's family in "Traum und Umnachtung"
but its frame of reference extends by implication at least to
Western man. Yet, unlike Hölderlin, who continually asserted
the regeneration of decadent humanity in the near future along
lines known from past eras, Trakl does not hesitate, at least
in the context of "Traum und Umnachtung," to send contemporary
humanity to its inescapable doom: in the final words of the
poem, *"die Nacht das verfluchte Geschlecht verschlang"* (night
swallowed up the accursed race [T 1:150]).[3]

Undoubtedly the most important manifestation of Hölderlin's mediation in "Traum und Umnachtung" is Trakl's frequent use of the conjunction *aber*. Not that Trakl had completely ignored such conjunctions as *aber*, *doch*, *denn*, and even *auch* ("but," "yet," "for," "also"; the last-named also appears once in the poem), which are an essential feature of Hölderlin's argumentative rhetoric, both in his mature poetry and in *Hyperion*. In fact, in mid-1912 after an almost principled avoidance of such conjunctions for three years, he used *aber* in "Träumerei am Abend," a poem that echoes "Brod und Wein" extensively.[4] For the next year and one-half Trakl employed *aber* and *doch* sparingly but conspicuously to indicate radical but usually obscurely motivated shifts in perspective and mood. Only in "Traum und Umnachtung," however, does the use of *aber* become widespread, occurring fully ten times. Its main function, analogous to its dialectical usage in Hölderlin's poetry (compare, for example, the use of *aber* in line 7 of the opening stanza of "Brod und Wein"), is to effect and emphasize the poem's rapid transitions from idyllic to demonic states and back again. Consider, for instance, the imposing opening of the third section of "Traum und Umnachtung" (T 1:149):

O des verfluchten Geschlechts. Wenn in befleckten Zimmern jegliches Schicksal vollendet ist, tritt mit modernden Schritten der Tod in das Haus. O, dass draussen Frühling wäre und im blühenden Baum ein lieblicher Vogel sänge. Aber *gräulich verdorrt das spärliche Grün an den Fenstern der Nächtlichen und es sinnen die blutenden Herzen noch Böses.*

(Oh, for the accursed race. When in soiled rooms each and every fate is fulfilled, then with moldering steps death walks into the house. Oh, would that it were spring outside, and that in the blossoming tree there sang a lovely bird. *But* the sparse green withers grey at the windows of the nocturnal ones, and the bleeding hearts still meditate evil.)

Here the poem moves almost breathlessly from the demonic opening apostrophe to the subjunctively stated idyll and back again,
at least momentarily, to the demonic via the conjunction *aber*.
Similarly, *aber* introduces a sudden reversal of imagery and
mood, a shift from the malign to the benign. As in the passage
immediately preceding, and hereafter throughout the essay,
roman type in the German quotations--corresponding to italics
in the English translations--indicates verbal parallels with
Hölderlin. The following passage opens the fourth and final
section of "Traum und Umnachtung" (T 1:150):

> *Tief ist der Schlummer in dunklen Giften, erfüllt von*
> *Sternen und dem weissen Antlitz der Mutter, dem steiner-*
> *nen. Bitter ist der Tod, die Kost der Schuldbeladenen;*
> *in dem braunen Geäst des Stamms zerfielen grinsend die*
> *irdenen Gesichter.* Aber *leise sang jener im grünen Schat-*
> *ten des Hollunders, da er aus bösen Träumen erwachte;*
> *süsser Gespiele nahte ihm ein rosiger Engel, dass er,*
> *ein sanftes Wild, zur Nacht hinschlummerte; und er sah*
> *das Sternenantlitz der Reinheit.*

> (Deep is sleep in dark poisons, filled up with stars
> and the white face of the mother, the one of stone. Bitter
> is death, the food of those burdened by guilt; in the
> trunk's brown branches, the earthen faces decomposed,
> grinning. *But* softly that one sang in the green shade of
> the elder bush, as we awoke from evil dreams; with sweet
> playing a rose-colored angel approached him so that he,
> a shy wild animal, slept into the night; and he saw the
> sidereal countenance of purity.)

Some two months later Trakl continued his close imitation
of Hölderlin's use of conjunctions in two poems that mark an
important juncture in Trakl's relationship to his predecessor's
poetry. Indeed, "Gesang des Abgeschiedenen" and "Abendland,"
both originating in the second half of March 1914, point in
opposite directions as far as Trakl's poetry of 1914 is concerned. Unlike "Abendland," the first of whose several versions already anticipates the long strophes and short dithy-

rambic lines of the "hymnic" poetry of mid-1914, "Gesang des
Abgeschiedenen" is one of the last poems Trakl wrote in the
predominantly long-line, free verse style that has its roots
in the "Helian" complex of late 1912/early 1913. This fact
tends to undercut the possibility that the poem, whose rhythm
is partially determined by a largely dactylic stress pattern,
represents a deliberate imitation of Hölderlin's elegiac hexameter, though it does not rule out that possibility entirely.
Not surprisingly, the lines that most clearly recall Hölderlin's hexameter, lines 12 and 15 of "Gesang des Abgeschiedenen" (T 1:144):

Liebend auch *umfängt das Schweigen im Zimmer die Schatten der
    Alten,*
Denn *strahlender immer erwacht aus schwarzen Minuten des
    Wahnsinns ...*

(*Lovingly* too the silence in the room surrounds the shadows
    of the old,
For ever more radiant there awakens from the dark minutes
    of insanity ...)

also contain the conjunctions *denn,* which occurs once more in
the poem, and *auch.* Hölderlin, like Trakl after him, usually
positioned such conjunctions at the start of a line, as in the
first and final lines of this passage from the initial stanza
of the elegy "Heimkunft" (H 1:182):

Denn *es wächst unendlicher dort das Jahr und die heilgen
    Stunden, die Tage, sie sind kühner geordnet, gemischt.
Dennoch merket die Zeit der Gewittervogel und zwischen
    Bergen, hoch in der Luft weilt er und rufet den Tag.
Jetzt* auch *wachet und schaut in der Tiefe drinnen das
    Dörflein ...*

(*For* more endlessly there the year expands, and the holy
    Hours and the days in there more boldly are ordered and
        mixed.

Yet the bird of thunder marks and observes the time, and
  High in the air, between peaks, hangs and calls out a
      new day.
Now, deep inside, the small village *also* awakens ...)

It is noteworthy that Trakl's use of the conjunctions *denn*
and *auch*, indicative of causality and continuity, gives rise,
in "Gesang des Abgeschiedenen," to an illusion of narrative
coherence that is decidedly absent from almost all of his
poetry written after mid-1909, especially those poems originating after mid-1912. The sharp play of opposites—of benign
and malign forces represented in seemingly autonomous imagistic
scenes—that normally determines the structure of Trakl's mature
poems is discarded in favor of an overarching harmony more
appropriate to the almost hymnic celebration of the protagonist's ultimate entry into the blue realm of *Abgeschiedenheit*.
Not that conflicts are absent from the poem. But we become
aware of them only as they are being absorbed into the metaphysical blue realm that pervades the poem and constitutes
Trakl's otherworldly analogue to Hölderlin's future millennium.
Clearly the conjunctions must play a crucial role in this process of subordination and subsumption. Thus the conjunction
denn serves to reinforce the benign qualities of the symbolic
Abendmahl immediately preceding the emergence of a serious
conflict in this passage from the middle of "Gesang des
Abgeschiedenen"(T 1:144):

Schon dämmert die Stirne dem sinnenden Menschen.

Und es leuchtet ein Lämpchen, das Gute, in seinem Herzen
Und der Frieden des Mahls; denn *geheiligt ist Brot und Wein*
Von Gottes Händen, und es schaut aus nächtigen Augen
Stille dich der Bruder an, dass er ruhe von dorniger
      Wanderschaft.
O das Wohnen in der beseelten Bläue der Nacht.

(Already the brow of the thinking man darkens,

And there shines a small lamp, the good one, in his heart
And the peace of the supper; *for* bread and wine are
Consecrated by God's hands, and quietly, out of
      night-filled eyes
Your brother looks at you, so that he might rest from his
      thorny wanderings.
Oh, to live in the spirit-filled blue of night.)

The hymnic apostrophe to the beneficent blue realm that rounds
out this passage of course also helps to contain the emerging
conflict by implicitly satisfying the brother's intuitively
discerned desire to be at peace. Indeed, through use of the
conjunction *auch* at the beginning of the next stanza Trakl
extends the conciliatory powers of this blue realm to a historical plane which, in the words *Geschlecht* and *Enkel*, recalls
at least the rhetoric of Hölderlin's historical fiction if not
its substance (ibid.):

Liebend auch *umfängt das Schweigen im Zimmer die Schatten*
      der Alten,
Die purpurnen Martern, Klage eines grossen Geschlechts,
Das fromm nun hingeht im einsamen Enkel.[5]

(Lovingly *too* the silence in the room surrounds the shadows
      of the old,
The purple martyrs, lament of a great *race,*
That, piously, fades away in the lone *grandchild.)*

Trakl's use of such rhetoric does not end here, however. In
the poem's concluding stanzas, essentially an elaboration of
the all-embracing blue realm of *Abgeschiedenheit* and the benign fate of the poem's variously identified protagonist in
it, Trakl goes on to characterize his fictive blue realm at
least in part in terms of the Hölderlinian concepts of *Mass*
and *Gesetz,* virtues that are requisite for human progress and
the new millennium.[6] In the words of the closing lines of

Trakl's poem (ibid.):

Denn strahlender immer erwacht aus schwarzen Minuten des
       Wahnsinns
Der Duldende an versteinerter Schwelle
Und es umfängt ihn gewaltig die kühle Bläue und die leuchtende
       Neige des Herbstes,

Das stille Haus und die Sagen des Waldes,
Mass *und* **Gesetz** *und die mondenen Pfade der Abgeschiedenen.*

(For everymore radiantly there awakens out of black minutes
       of insanity
The patient one at the petrified threshold
And powerfully the cool blue and the radiant decline of
       autumn surround him,

The still house and the legends of the forest,
Proportion and *law* and the moonlit paths of the departed.)

     It is fair to say, I think, that Trakl's use of Hölder-
lin's mature poetry helped him to achieve in "Gesang des Abgeschiedenen" a relatively unique and, in some ways, final
expression of his predominantly elegiac mode of 1913 and
early 1914. By the same token, it would be intriguing to
discuss the first of two published versions of the much more
complicated poem "Abendland," which contains even more extensive signs of Hölderlin's mediation, as a kind of twentieth-
century analogue to the hymn "Patmos," for example. Yet my
chief interest in "Abendland" in the present context is the
poem not so much as an end in itself as in its capacity as
process, not so much in several self-sufficient works as steps
in the evolution of a new kind of poetry. Thus I propose to
read the various stages of "Abendland" as a series of experiments partially on Hölderlinian forms that culminate, in
however circuitous a fashion, in Trakl's darkly apocalyptic
mode of mid-1914. Before proceeding, however, I would like

to describe briefly the poem's somewhat complicated genesis.
In retrospect the poem's first stage consists of two distinct
poems, one already bearing the title "Abendland," the other
—which takes up such central motifs from "Gesang des Abgeschiedenen" as the eucharistic meal, the suffering brother,
the benign otherworldly blue night, and religious patience—
bearing the title "Wanderschaft." These poems were then integrated virtually unchanged as parts 1 and 3 into a much longer
five-part poem also called "Abendland" that was published in
the journal *Der Brenner* (this latter text is hereafter referred
to as the *Brenner* version). In addition to the poem's first
stage the new critical edition of Trakl's works has also
brought to light a third version of the poem, which reduced
the five-part *Brenner* version from 138 lines to a three-part
poem consisting of only 48 lines. This version differs from
the final authorized one published in Trakl's second and last
book of poetry *Sebastian im Traum* only with regard to its third
section, although, as we shall see, this difference is rather
remarkable especially in point of Hölderlin's mediation.[8]

At the outset it should be noted that Trakl's adaptations
of his predecessor's poetry in "Abendland" do not fall into a
consistent pattern and only a few carry over into the poetry
of mid-1914. Take, for instance, Trakl's rather mechanical,
primarily visual adaptation of the long strophic forms and
terse lines of Hölderlin's hymns which constitute two of the
three essential characteristics of his later poetry. Both
the long-stanza and the short-verse form suddenly emerge full-
blown in the first stage of "Abendland," whose longest stanza
totals fifteen lines. Yet in the *Brenner* version this same
stanza is broken up, without any really noticeable difference, into two shorter stanzas. It is not until the third
version of the poem, apparently written in an attempt to
substitute another kind of monumentality for the one that had
been lost in a deletion of ninety lines, that Trakl reinstates

the long-stanza form. Another case in point is Trakl's use of
Hölderlin-derived conjunctions in the poem. Though clearly not
as crucial to "Abendland," where they effect no more than short
spurts of causality and continuity, as they were to "Gesang des
Abgeschiedenen," *denn* and *auch* occur conspicuously in the first
and second stages of the former. One conjunction also appears
in the third version and even *aber* appears once in the *Brenner*
version. Yet no occurrence of either conjunction is attested
in the poem's final text nor beyond that in the poetry of
mid-1914.

    The various stages of "Abendland" also reveal a variety
of syntactical innovations modeled on the hyperbatic syntax of
Hölderlin's mature poetry which, with one exception that I shall
discuss shortly, play either a minor role or no role at all in
the poetry of mid-1914. Nonetheless, as part of a process of
experimentation they are clearly crucial to the evolution of
Trakl's new voice. One of the more obvious examples of such
syntactical innovation is Trakl's sudden use of appositions,
both nominal and adjectival, as in the following example from
the *Brenner* version, part 3, which also recalls a morphological
aspect of Hölderlin's so-called "austere" style (T 1:406):

> *Gelehnt an den Hügel der Bruder*
> *Und Fremdling,*
> *Der* menschenverlassene ...

> (Reclining on the hill the brother
> And stranger,
> The *man-forsaken one ...)*

Other kinds of Hölderlin-inspired hyperbata in the *Brenner*
version of "Abendland" are fewer in number but nonetheless
illustrate the extent of Trakl's experimentation with his
predecessor's style. Hölderlin's mediation is audible, for
example, in the inverted word order of these lines from part 2

of the *Brenner* version (T 1:404):

> Und es fallen der Blüten
> Viele über den Felsenpfad.

> (And of *blossoms* there fall
> *Many* over the cliff path.)

These two lines recur in the final version of the poem (T
1:409-10) and may well have a direct source in these lines
from the opening stanza of Hölderlin's ode "Mein Eigentum"
(H 1:150):

> ... wenn schon der holden Blüten
> Manche der Erde zum Danke fielen.

> (... even if, of the lovely *blossoms*
> *Many* fell to earth, for thanks.)

A somewhat more dramatic instance of hyperbatic syntax reminiscent of Hölderlin is provided by the following passage from
part 5 of the *Brenner* version (T 1:407):

> Gross sind die Städte aufgebaut
> Und steinern in der Ebene; ....

> (*Great* are the cities, built high
> And of *stone* on the plain; ....)

The asymmetrical distribution of the attributes *gross* and *stein-
ern* immediately brings to mind the gnomic opening of the authorized version of "Patmos" (2:165):

> Nah ist
> Und schwer zu fassen der Gott.

(Up *close*,
That *hard* to hold fast, is God.)

While Trakl was unfamiliar with this opening, similar sentence
structure occurs elsewhere in Hölderlin's mature poetry, as,
for example, in lines 92-93 of the hymn "Die Wanderung"
(H 1:204-5):

Unfreundlich *ist und* schwer *zu gewinnen*
Die Verschlossene ...

(*Unfriendly* and *hard* to win over
Is the recluse ...)

One final example of such syntactical asymmetry from part 3 of
the *Brenner* version (T 1:406):

Vieles ist ein Wachendes
In der sternigen Nacht
Und schön die Bläue, ...

(*Much is awake*
In the starry night,
And beautiful, the great blue, ...)

is the more remarkable for the fact that Trakl seems to have
attempted, in the phrase *"Vieles ist ein Wachendes,"* something
of the enigmatic power of the well-known gnome from Hölderlin's
hymn "Der Rhein"--*"Ein Rätsel ist Reinentsprungenes"* (A mystery
are those of pure origin [H 1:206]). It is doubtful whether
Trakl clearly perceived Hölderlin's formulation of such gnomic
truths in his hymnic poetry as a distinctive feature of the
poet's high office. But it is almost certain, given the final
version of "Abendland" and the poetry that follows it, that he
fully appreciated the authoritative stance which they and
related prophetic utterances in Hölderlin's mature poetry

imply.[9]

The passage just quoted is not the only instance where Trakl models the diction and imagery of "Abendland" after his predecessor's poetry. *"Schwerttragender Engel"* (Sword-carrying angel), for example, a line from the first stanza of the *Brenner* version of part 2 (T 1:404), surely echoes Hölderlin's nominal epithet for Christ in "Patmos"--*"der Gewittertragende"* (the thunder-bearing one [H 1:218]). Another passage from "Patmos," the one depicting Pentecost (H 1:219):

> *Darum auch sandt' er ihnen*
> *Den Geist, und freilich bebte*
> *Das Haus und die* Wetter Gottes rollten
> Ferndonnernd über
> *Die* ahnenden Häupter, *da schwersinnend*
> *Versammelt waren die Todeshelden,* ...

> (That's why he sent them the
> Ghost, and of course, the house
> Shook and *God's thunderclouds rolled*
> *Far-rumbling over*
> Their *dawning minds,* as, heavy of heart,
> Heroes in death, they were gathered, ...)

may well have passed through Trakl's mind as he wrote the final stanza of the *Brenner* version, part 2 (T 1:405):

> *Anders* ahnt *die* Stirne *Vollkommenes,*
> *Die kühle, kindliche,*
> *Wenn* über grünendem Hügel
> Frühlingsgewitter ertönt.

> (But the *mind,* the sober, the childlike,
> *Has foreknowledge* of perfection differently
> When *over the greening hill*
> *The spring thunderstorm resounds.)*

It is noteworthy that Trakl's adaptation of Hölderlin's poetry tapers off sharply in his final revision of the *Brenner*

version of "Abendland" (in the revision whose result is the
shortened "3. *Fassung*" [T 1:409-10]), especially if we take
into account his suppression of many of the imitative innovations present in the *Brenner* version. In fact, Trakl adds
only two features to the third version of the poem that recall
Hölderlin. The more important of these is the compound epithet *fern verstrahlend* modeled on a kind of participial compound that is fairly widespread in Hölderlin's elegies and
hymns. The Pentecostal passage from "Patmos" just quoted
contains an instance of such a compound in *ferndonnernd*.

Yet, as though in counterpoint to Hölderlin's generally
declining influence on the third version of "Abendland," the
poem's final draft contains the most dramatic instance of
Hölderlin's mediation in all of "Abendland." It is a curios-
ity of literary history that the source of this mediation,
the poem "Lebensalter," is not one of Hölderlin's great odes,
elegies, or hymns. Along with "Hälfte des Lebens," certainly
a superior work of art and the one poem most frequently cited
as indicative of its author's modern sensibility, Hölderlin
had salvaged "Lebensalter" from the ruins of his hymnic enter-
prise. Moreover, like "Hälfte des Lebens" it is easily one
of Hölderlin's most pessimistic poems, though it differs from
the latter thematically insofar as its rejection of the poet's
usual assumptions about history is more or less explicit. For
in "Lebensalter" the triadically structured historical fiction
that informs Hölderlin's major poetry gives way to a dualistic
one that leaves the poet stranded in the present without recourse to past or future utopias. From a secluded vantage
point, the poet registers the incomprehensible but nonetheless
irrevocable passing of a past civilization momentarily evoked
in the poem's three opening apostrophes (H 1:226):

> *Ihr Städte des Euphrats!*
> *Ihr Gassen am Palmyra!*
> *Ihr Säulenwälder in der Ebne der Wüste, ...*

(You cities of Euphrates!
You streets at Palmyra!
You forests of pillars in the desert plain, ...)

Given Trakl's fundamentally pessimistic nature, it is hardly surprising that the poem struck a responsive chord. Specifically, he adapted its three opening apostrophes, yet another
type of Hölderlin's hyperbatic syntax, to fuse images and imagistic scenes from the respective conclusions of the second and
third versions of "Abendland" and transform them, as it were,
into an apocalyptic vision of the Occident, indeed of the cosmos itself. As late as the third version of "Abendland," the
concluding section of the poem had still dealt primarily with
the fate of the individual, the outsider, the *Fremdling*. Moreover, if we briefly turn to the final lines of that version
(T 1:410):

> *O Liebe, es rührt*
> *Ein blauer Dornenbusch*
> *Die kalte Schläfe,*
> *Mit fallenden Sternen*
> *Schneeige Nacht.*

> (O love, a blue
> Bush of thorns touches
> The cool temple
> With falling stars,
> Snowy night.)

we can discern the outlines of an enigmatic but nonetheless
positive, religiously motivated resolution. But the hopeful
tone, dependent on the quiet apostrophe *"O Liebe,"* which
permits a positive reading of the inexplicably falling stars
here, as well as the appositionally functioning "snowy night"
with its benign qualities, are both decidedly absent from the
conclusion of the fourth and last version of "Abendland" (T
1:139-40), where Trakl's three anguished and resounding, but

carefully positioned apostrophes help to create the visionary
terror that encompasses the outsider, civilization, nature,
and the cosmos without exception (T 1:140):

> Ihr grossen Städte
> Steinern aufgebaut
> In der Ebene!
> So sprachlos folgt
> Der Heimatlose
> Mit dunkler Stirne dem Wind,
> Kahlen Bäumen am Hügel.
> Ihr weithin dämmernden Ströme!
> Gewaltig ängstet
> Schaurige Abendröte
> Im Sturmgewölk.
> Ihr sterbenden Völker!
> Bleiche Woge
> Zerschellend am Strande der Nacht,
> Fallende Sterne.

> (You great cities
> Built of stone
> On the plain!
> So speechlessly
> Does the homeless one
> With dark brow follow the wind,
> Bare trees on the hilltop.
> You streams glimmering far-off!
> Powerfully, rain-promising
> Red dusk bodes fear
> In a roll of stormclouds.
> You dying peoples!
> Pale wave
> Shattering on the night beach,
> Falling stars.)

One cannot help feeling at times that the most appropriate
voice in which to recite this conclusion of the final version
of "Abendland" and the related poetry of mid-1914 is a piercing
scream. For what Trakl employs, and employs effectively, to
integrate the three adapted structural elements that mark
these poems--the monumental stanza; the terse dithyrambic
line, which exposes each word to special emphasis; the bold,

expansive apostrophes—is a certain shrillness of tone without
parallel in the German lyric tradition. Such a tone of course
is largely a reflection of the profound personal and cultural
pessimism that finds expression in these poems and still informs the final war poems "Klage" and "Grodek" that Trakl wrote
in the last months preceding his death in November 1914. Yet
one should not underestimate the role that Hölderlin's poetry,
especially the poem "Lebensalter," played in the evolution of
Trakl's new-found public voice and the emergence of correlative
concerns.

It is hardly surprising, then, that Trakl should attempt,
in the poem "Der Abend," one of the more subdued examples of
his new apocalyptic mode, what seems to be an oblique but
nonetheless deliberately conceived analogue to Hölderlin's
poem "Lebensalter." As does his predecessor in "Lebensalter,"
Trakl addresses the poem's two apostrophes not to contemporary
humanity, although his words are also clearly meant for its
ears, but to vestiges of a past order of things and to the
moon which serves the poet as a vehicle for the resurrection
of this order. Indeed, Trakl takes up almost half of the
one-stanza, seventeen-line poem to locate these spectral
remnants of more viable pasts, and thus the potential agents
of historical change in the present, in a fairly rugged natural
terrain safely outside the decadent center of civilization.
In terms of the poem's thematic concerns it is important to
note that the generic figures that constitute these vestiges,
the dead heroes and embracing lovers, play a crucial role in
joining Hölderlin's past and future worlds. In the poem's
middle section the regenerative forces inherent in these embod-
iments of past glory are represented in the form of a blue
light mysteriously radiating toward a modern urban wasteland,
the city, where present decadence, embodied in the *"verwesend
Geschlecht,"* is perpetuating itself and thus preparing an
ominous future for its innocent progeny. The rhetoric of

Hölderlin's historical fiction is in part again recalled in
these words of "Der Abend" (T 1:159):

> *So bläulich erstrahlt es*
> *Gegen die Stadt hin,*
> *Wo kalt und böse*
> *Ein verwesend* Geschlecht *wohnt,*
> *Der weissen* Enkel
> *Dunkle Zukunft bereitet.*

> (Thus, bluish, it radiates away
> In the direction of the city,
> Where, cold and evil,
> There dwells a decaying *race* of men,
> One preparing
> For white *grandchildren*
> A dark future.)

The implicit upshot of this oblique interplay of opposing
epochs is the absolute decline of vanished pasts as a viable
force in reshaping the here and now. At least I, for one,
find little comfort or hope for change manifest in Trakl's
sudden apostrophic transference of his now grieving vestiges
of past glory to the pristine refuge of a remote mountain lake,
as expressed in these concluding lines (ibid.):

> *Ihr mondverschlungnen Schatten*
> *Aufseufzend im leeren Kristall*
> *Des Bergsees.*

> (You shades swallowed up by moonlight
> Heaving a sigh in the empty crystal
> Of the mountain lake.)

Indeed, Hölderlin's own final statement in "Lebensalter"
(H 1:226):

> *... fremd*
> *Erscheinen und gestorben mir*
> *Der Seligen Geister.*

                                    (... strange
                    To me, remote and dead seem
                    The souls of the blessed.)

seems a good deal less wrenching by comparison.

What has emerged in the preceding discussion is, I hope,
a clear sense of the selective nature of Trakl's interest in
Hölderlin. Unlike a poet such as Josef Weinheber, who wrote
chauvinistic odes in the Hölderlinian manner, Trakl made no
attempt to assimilate all of Hölderlin to his purposes. Instead, he contented himself with experimental adaptations of
Hölderlin's elevated style which were readily discarded once
they had served their initial purpose lest they become uninte-
grated mannerisms. This is not to say, of course, that his
experimentation lacked a larger aim. Especially in the case
of "Abendland" Trakl seems to have been groping with the aid
of Hölderlin's poetry toward a more monumental and expansive
mode of expression that would better accommodate the increasing urgency of personal and public concerns. Nor should Trakl's
experimentation imply an absence of felt existential affinities, however reductive his perception of Hölderlin may have
been. Indeed the reductive nature of this perception, in so
far as it can be reconstructed from the only evidence at our
disposal, namely Trakl's poetry, should throw some light on
the theme of this conference. Above all I would guess that
Trakl saw in his predecessor a paradigm of the poet apart,
the poet as outsider, which, as M. H. Abrams has observed in
his recent essay "Coleridge, Baudelaire and Modernist Poetics,"
is one of the fundamental assumptions of literary modernism.[10]
And though Hölderlin shared with a generation of European
romantics a fundamentally different view of the poet and his
function, most of his life and some aspects of his oeuvre,
when read out of context, corroborate Trakl's assessment.

Hölderlin and the Twentieth Century:
Is Elevated Style in Poetry Possible Today?

by Aleksis Rannit

I

The personal remarks that I should like to make are those of
a verse maker and a critic of both literature and the fine
arts, but first of all those of a subjective reader. The
Hölderlinian panorama has been constantly widening in a geographical sense, and I myself, coming originally from Estonia,
a country situated between East and West, cannot see Hölderlin
--our awareness of him and commitment to him--as a purely Western phenomenon. Rather, he is a reality that today belongs to
the whole of Europe. The radiance of the German poet reached
Northern and Eastern Europe long ago; he has been studied,
misinterpreted, admired, and translated not only by Russians,
but by other East European critics and poets as well. At the
end of my essay I shall note a few names that may suggest the
present existence of a Hölderlinian atmosphere and of a diction
similar to his--far beyond the bounds of Stuttgart and Tübingen,
Weimar and Jena.

II

Let us first turn to Hölderlin's familiar *Seelenlandschaft*, and try to add a few descriptive words to it. As is well known, Hölderlin's passion for Greece was the expression of his own empirical estrangement from contemporary life, and his view of the harmonious relationship of nature, men, and gods among the Greeks represented his ideal of existence. In the elegy "Brod und Wein" we find an expression of this faith tormented by the poet's affirmation that the Greece he knew cannot be revived (2:93):

Aber Freund! wir kommen zu spät. Zwar leben die Götter,
   Aber über dem Haupt, droben in anderer Welt.

(But, my friend, we have come too late. Though the gods are
      living,
   Over our heads they live, up in a different world.)

There is, therefore, an elegiac strain in Hölderlin's work, to which the late elegy "Menons Klagen um Diotima" and the fragmentary tragedy *Der Tod des Empedokles* offer clear testimony. And yet one must, strangely enough, not take Hölderlin's sadness or estrangement too literally, since it seems clear enough that, secretly, he also wanted sadness and seclusion. In "Die Heimat," one of the moving odes from around the year 1800, celebrating a harmonious coexistence of nature and of society in the poet's mind, Hölderlin ends by saying (2:19):

Denn sie, die uns das himmlische Feuer leihn,
   Die Götter schenken heiliges Leid uns auch,
      Drum bleibe dies. Ein Sohn der Erde
         Schein ich; zu lieben gemacht, zu leiden.

(For they who lend us heavenly light and fire,
   The gods, with holy sorrow endow us too.
      So be it, then. A son of Earth I
         Seem; and was fashioned to love, to suffer.)

Throughout his life, appeals to many people in his letters
notwithstanding, there were important moments when he thoroughly
enjoyed his aloneness. Along with this there is also a sense
in which Greek antiquity is not lost for him. In his poetic
vision Hölderlin succeeded in transplanting the Greeks to a
German soil and their gods to a German sky; he thus domesti-
cated them and made them very much alive in his own immediate
surroundings. One important consequence of this dual experience, in the letter as in the life, seems to be that, however
dark Hölderlin's spiritual landscape became, especially after
his separation from Diotima, within his individual pantheistic
Naturphilosophie he was never isolated from the larger and
unified world of nature. In his poetry, the poet either stands
in this larger landscape, as he puts it in his last completed
hymn "Mnemosyne" (2:197):

> *Prophetisch, träumend auf*
> *Den Hügeln des Himmels* ....

> (Prophetic, ...
> ..., dreaming on
> The mounds of heaven ....)

or, as he says considerably earlier, in "An die Natur" (1:191):

> ... *von Blüten übergossen,*
> *Still und trunken* ...

> (... inundated with blossoms,
> Quiet and drunken ...).

    More important still, when in his youth Hölderlin begins
to look with pleasure at the actual details of nature, his
symbolizing habit of mind lends the act of observation an
unusual intensity. He looks at flowers, fruits, and trees,

not only as objects in themselves, but as prototypes of the divine as well. It is in this, I would say "medieval," minne-singer-like, attitude of Hölderlin's that we find the peculiar freshness indwelling in his individualistic naturalism. Natu-ral ideas and objects are perceived by him in the abstract. They are less satisfying or even pleasing in themselves than symbolic of ideal, elevating, and protective qualities in the life of man. A perception of this order makes possible Höld-erlin's discovery of nature as a *garden*. In the Frankfurt epode "An Diotima" the poet sings (1:210):

Komm und siehe die Freude um uns; in kühlenden Lüften
      Fliegen die Zweige des Hains,
Wie die Locken im Tanz; und wie auf tönender Leier
      Ein erfreulicher Geist,
Spielt mit Regen und Sonnenschein auf der Erde der Himmel;
      Wie in liebendem Streit
Über dem Saitenspiel ein tausendfältig Gewimmel
      Flüchtiger Töne sich regt,
Wandelt Schatten und Licht in süssmelodischem Wechsel
      Über die Berge dahin.

(Come, take a look at the joy all around us; in cooling breezes
      Fly, wave the twigs of the grove,
As do your locks in the dance; and as on a lyre resounding a
      Mind who brings comfort and joy,
So does the sky now play on earth with rain and with sunlight;
      As in some amiable strife
Over the concert of strings there stirs a thousandfold
      Crowd of fleeting tones,
Shadow and light now wander in sweetly melodious changes
      Over the hills and away.)

In a sense, "discovery" is the wrong word here. The enchanted garden, be it Eden or the Garden of the Hesperides, has been one of humanity's most consoling myths; its reappearance in Hölderlin's poetry and in that of the romantic school consti-tutes but partial evidence, however important, of the reawak-ening imaginative faculty of poets and artists.

At the beginning, Hölderlin's garden is the enclosed grove,

where Diotima and his other friends can sit and move on the grounds. Sometimes this garden—as, for example, in the ode "Mein Eigentum"—is small. But it is noble and very sensitively colored, as are landscape elements in the paintings of Martin Schongauer on the one hand, or, nearer our own time, in the compositions of Edward Burne-Jones on the other. To be sure, Hölderlin does not seek, as did Vergil, the myth of ideal rusticity, nor did he ever try to reproduce a factual landscape (rendered convincingly, for instance, by such an "empiricist" as Hubert van Eyck). Rather, in most instances visible in the poetry, Hölderlin's garden is a far larger enclosure, sung in hymns to nature-in-general, and it includes ideas of a cosmic landscape. However intimate or universal, classical or romanticized, Hölderlin's vision becomes, his garden is always Eden-like. It is a Paradise not yet forfeited, and never completely lost.

Hölderlin had, from the outset, an immense penchant for the poetization of nature. One may suspect that he was eager to give the intellect opportunities for fresh conquest in poetry. He would do this by giving the disorder of natural scenery a logical form, the *open* form of the *romantic* artist. Hölderlin conceived the basis of landscape poetry (and the foundations of his other poetry as well) to lie in a peculiar nonstatic balance of the horizontal and vertical elements in his structural design. Among the *horizontal* elements of verse structure I hazard to place those lines of text that are complete in themselves and separated from adjacent lines by punctuation; among the *vertical* elements are to be classed occurrences of enjambement, the running over of a given line to the following line or even stanza. With the aid of Dionysius of Halicarnassus and the principle of *harmonía austêrá*, which Hölderlin's critics translate as *"harte Fügung"* (rough-hewn construction), Hölderlin may well have taken seriously an architectural metaphor in poetry that we tend to take for granted and even to gloss over.

He may have recognized that the spacing of prosodic horizontals
and verticals and their rhythmic organization could exert the
effect of a rhythmic diagonal analogous to the architrave or
similar bracing devices in architecture. Still, it seems, he
very seldom if ever subscribed to a principle now recognized
as important in Roman rather than in Greek architecture, the
golden section. In this his structural insights differ greatly
from the landscape structure of a Nicolas Poussin and from late
classical architecture, or from their near-ideal correlate in
Augustan poetry, Vergil. Hölderlin's is not the closed form
of his teachers Alkaios and Asklepiades or of his admirers
George and Weinheber.

The dramatic unity of form Hölderlin achieves is rather
similar to that attained by John Constable or by Vincent van
Gogh, to oriental asymmetrical harmony, or to the refined
shifting and dislocation of the compositional axis in Gothic
art. Throughout Hölderlin's work there runs a restless flowing line, curling and uncurling in agitated intonational and
phonetic accents, as this happens, again on another frequency,
for example, in the convoluted draperies of German Gothic.
The vibrant luminism of this movement charges the statuesque
body of form, and, combined with psychical tension, creates,
as early as Hölderlin's middle and early final periods, a
free style, sometimes even the freest form possible. One
recalls the Tintoretto-like downpour of the famous lines in
stanza 5 of the hymn "Der Rhein" (2:144):

> *Denn wo die Ufer zuerst*
> *An die Seit ihm schleichen, die krummen,*
> *Und durstig umwindend ihn,*
> *Den Unbedachten, zu ziehn*
> *Und wohl zu behüten begehren*
> *Im eigenen Zahne, lachend*
> *Zerreisst er die Schlangen und stürzt*
> *Mit der Beut und wenn in der Eil*
> *Ein Grösserer ihn nicht zähmt,*
> *Ihn wachsen lässt, wie der Blitz, muss er*

Die Erde spalten, und wie Bezauberte fliehn
Die Wälder ihm nach und zusammensinkend die Berge.

(For where the banks at first
Slink to his side, the crooked,
And greedily entwining him,
Desire to educate
And carefully tend the feckless
Within their teeth, he laughs,
Tears up the serpents and rushes
Off with his prey, and if in haste
A greater one does not tame him,
But lets him grow, like lightning he
Must rend the earth and like things enchanted
The forests join his flight and, collapsing,
        the mountains.)

We recall it all the more, since the very sinuosity of this
utterance is underscored by a corresponding passage in "Der
Rhein," in strategic *dis*location placed in stanza 10 (of fifteen stanzas; placement in stanza 11 opposite 5 would create
symmetry). In the latter passage the life of the demigod,
Rousseau, reflects the life of the river; the man of genius
speaks as the river speaks (2:146):

Wem aber, wie, Rousseau, dir,
Unüberwindlich die Seele,
Die starkausdauernde, ward,
Und sicherer Sinn
Und süsse Gabe zu hören,
Zu reden so, dass er aus heiliger Fülle
Wie der Weingott, törig göttlich
Und gesetzlos sie, die Sprache der Reinesten, gibt
Verständig den Guten, aber mit Recht
Die Achtungslosen mit Blindheit schlägt,
Die entweihenden Knechte, wie nenn ich den Fremden?

(But he whose soul, like yours,
Rousseau, ever strong and patient,
Became invincible,
Endowed with steadfast purpose
And a sweet gift of hearing,
Of speaking, so that from holy profusion
Like the wine-god foolishly, divinely

And lawlessly he gives it away,
The language of the purest, comprehensible to
    the good,
But rightly strikes with blindness the irreverent,
The profaning rabble, what shall I call that stranger?)

These two great hymnic passages suggest two pillars of an asymmetrical structure that has surrendered its classical stasis to the displaced stress of a dynamic musical freedom.

Although both the contour and the overall profile of the wording in "Der Rhein" are intense and sharp, Hölderlin's style in general is neither linear nor sculptural, but rather *painterly*. It is syllabic lighting and coloring in their great sweep that produce the vitality of the verses. Endowing the form with chromatic qualities and pictorial subtleties never entails mere virtuosity or imitation. On the contrary, in central works such as "Brod und Wein," "Germanien," "Patmos," the verse achieves unique heights in the free ecstatic expression of both the dynamic visions and rhythms of Hölderlin. Original imagery and language, for all their occasional near-incomprehensibility, are strangely compelling in their emotive power and sense of urgency.

Notwithstanding the tragic coloring of his desire to merge with the Absolute, Hölderlin has really made the universe his own garden of wholeness. And, whatever his indebtedness to the rhythmic genius of an Asklepiades or a Pindar, Hölderlin treats established metrical schemes in a thoroughly original manner. He thus becomes an innovator in so-called free poetic structure. Having arrived at this double security, the philosophical and the stylistic, Hölderlin could employ with full sonority his originally cultivated *Naturstimme*. The unity of thinker and singer, as well as his unity in rapture with all created things, was undoubtedly an ideal condition for producing the kind of rhapsodic, decentralized, yet convincingly elevated style of which Hölderlin is the unique master.

III

Artistic completion is generally the result of a combination
of biopsychical talent and erudition. Erudition, the structural development of inner form, can be described, but it is
probably impossible to measure the color and temperature of
the living word, of the voice of the word, itself. One may
hear Hölderlin's voice as being that of a tenor who later
became a baritone, and then even a *basso profondo*. Starting
as a lyric tenor, he changed voice into *tenore robusto* with
the vigor necessary for the expression of a strong passion.
Finally, at times as *basso profondo*, low-ranging but beautifully warm, he was capable of manifesting great solemnity.
Solemnity as such, whether of spacious volume or of rhetoric,
is not easily appreciated today by formalist critics. Thus
now, after the expressionist and neo-expressionist periods
have had their day, Hölderlin may suddenly seem old-fashioned.
We are still living with poetry too much as chamber music, as
private conversation, with a poetry that may be characterized
by the Hölderlinian adjective *gesang-los*.

Needless to say, elevated rhetorical style will never
disappear from the literary scene, but will, rather, always
coexist with intimate poetry, much as realism, for example,
will never cease to exist, but will constantly be present as
somehow parallel to abstract art. A number of significant
European poets of this century have, directly or indirectly,
felt the great breath of Hölderlin's diction. Some of them,
like Vjačeslav Ivanov, Marina Cvetaeva, Stefan George, Rainer
Maria Rilke, Georg Trakl, Gottfried Benn, Hermann Hesse, Josef
Weinheber, Pierre Emmanuel, and Johannes Bobrowski, have con-
fessed their affinity to Hölderlin. The relationship with
Hölderlin of others like Eino Leino, Uku Masing, Marie Under,
Władysław Broniewski, or František Halas, needs still to be
investigated. Finally, there are some modern variations on a
Hölderlinian kind of poetry-as-energy-discharge: I am thinking

of poets like Dylan Thomas, George Barker, and Charles Olson.

I have mentioned the Russian poet Vjačeslav Ivanov (1866-1949) first, because his Dionysian impulse, combined with exalted phraseology and spirituality, is analogous to that of Hölderlin. Ivanov is still a great unknown in European letters, despite the fact that Ernst Robert Curtius considered his book *The Exchange of Letters between Two Corners* "the most important pronouncement on humanism since Nietzsche." Ivanov wrote a number of poems to Diotima, in his case Lydia Zinov'eva-Annibal, his passionate love and deceased wife who, like Susette Gontard, died early. Professor Emery E. George has translated an elegy from Ivanov's book of poems *Cor ardens* (Moscow: Skorpion, 1911) which, for the sake of graphic design and musicality, is presented here first in the original Russian, followed by a transliteration and the English translation:

Знаешь и ты, Диотима, кому твой певец эти мирты
   ивой увенчан свивал: розы вплетались твои

в смуглую зелень желаний и в гибкое золото плена.
   Розой святила ты жизнь; в розах к бессмертным ушла.

(Znaeš' i ty, Diotima, komu tvoj pevec eti mirty
   ivoj uvenčan svival; rozy vpletalis' tvoi

v smugluju zelen' želanij i v gibkoe zoloto plena.
   Rozoj svjatila ty žizn'; v rozax k bessmertnym ušla.)

(You, Diotima, know, too, for whom in my song I have woven
   myrtle the willow now crowns. Roses were bound in your dark

 green of desire, the ductile metal of prisoning passion--
   hallowing life in a rose; rose-tombed, you rose to the gods.)

A careful and provocative comparative study of two great figures like Hölderlin and Ivanov is a much-needed undertaking. Both poets believed firmly in the existence of a higher reality of which the objects of this world are but a reflection. Each searched for his place within Greek and Christian religions and philosophies, the Platonic ideal being preserved in the poems of Ivanov with much greater force even than in Hölderlin's work. This circumstance may of course be interpreted as a tribute to both poets, as well as to the deep-running affinity between them. O. Deschartes, the friend and lifelong scholar-companion of Vjačeslav Ivanov, wrote to me from Rome on November 24, 1970:

> Vjačeslav Ivanov loved Hölderlin's poetry and valued it highly. This is of course natural: the classical form of Hölderlin's art and his authentic, immediate experience of Dionysos (even where the Hellenic god is not mentioned by name) have moved Vjačeslav Ivanov deeply.
>
> During a visit by Herbert Steiner to Pavia in 1932 (where Vjačeslav Ivanov was living and teaching at the time), I remember that between Steiner and Ivanov there developed a conversation about Hölderlin. Ivanov spoke inspiringly of Dionysos and Herakleitos in relation to Christianity, a link which Hölderlin was first to discover. Steiner became enthusiastic about it and asked Ivanov to write an article for *Corona* (a highly-regarded German-language journal to which Ivanov was one of the contributors). Ivanov gave his promise, but had no time to do it.

Another Russian poet of considerable distinction in the twentieth century, Marina Cvetaeva (1892-1941), to whom Rilke dedicated a long elegy, was an ardent admirer of Hölderlin. Professor Marc Slonim of Geneva, a personal friend of Cvetaeva, recalls, in a recent article of reminiscences in the *Novyj Žurnal* (No. 100, Winter, 1970), that Cvetaeva knew many of Hölderlin's poems by heart, and would occasionally recite them in the company of friends. There is in the collection of Professor George Cvetaeva's personal copy of *Remeslo* (Crafts-manship) (Berlin: Helikon, 1923), considered her best book of poems, with the following lines from the second draft of Höld-erlin's rhymed Frankfurt hymn "Diotima" inscribed on the title page in her own hand (1:219):

> *O Begeisterung, so finden*
> *Wir in dir ein selig Grab,*
> *Tief in deine Wogen schwinden,*
> *Still frohlockend, wir hinab,*
> *Bis der Hore Ruf wir hören*
> *Und, mit neuem Stolz erwacht,*
> *Wie die Sterne wieder kehren*
> *In des Lebens kurze Nacht.*

> (O enthusiasm, so we
> Find in you a blessèd grave;
> Quietly, in exultation,
> Deep we submerge in your waves.
> Till we hear the call of the Hour,
> And, awakened with new pride,
> We return, as do the stars,
> Into the brief night of life.)

In her own continuous *Begeisterung* (fervor) Cvetaeva loved
abrupt and incantatory rhythms as well as expansive gestures
that recall Hölderlin's odes. But unlike Hölderlin's poetic
gestures, hers are expressionist hammer blows of unbounded
passion and sudden, rough colloquialisms—yet embedded in an
archaic diction. Nevertheless, in the poetry of both Cvetaeva
and Hölderlin, there is an analogous streaming of words with
the help of a rhythmical swing in practically every verse line,
as well as of numerous instances of enjambement, adding up to
a linguistic correlate of what Hölderlin himself calls, in
"Elegie," *"schäumendes Blut"* (foaming blood [2:71]).

  Of the other great but largely unknown European poets
with the Hölderlinian touch, the Finn Eino Leino (1878-1926)
and the Estonian Marie Under (born 1883, lives in exile in
Sweden) come to mind. Both Leino and Under are possessors of
uninhibited lyrical spontaneity and of remarkable discipline
within the open form. Like Hölderlin, these poets have created
their own modes of expression instead of conforming to an
accepted pattern, and, like Hölderlin's best work, theirs is

of a unique imperative kind that springs from vividness of
imagery, rhythmic energy in phrasing, and directness of language. In addition, like Hölderlin, they have been possessed
by a patriotic vision of destiny.

A study entitled "Hölderlin and the Twentieth Century:
Is Elevated Style in Poetry Possible Today?" could include
many more names than I have mentioned. A panoramic review
of the whole contemporary culture of lofty and sublime expression might also include artists and musicians, as for example
the Italian sculptor Giacomo Manzù or the French composer
Olivier Messiaen. How much poorer we would be today without
the balance of their impelling rhetorical works. The innovators and visionaries of today have aesthetic and human conflicts similar to those Hölderlin had. In their case, but
especially in the case of Hölderlin, their spiritual father,
the message of elevated humanity comes through with extraordinary force, because the genius of the man dominates the
talent of the poet.

Sophokles the Elusive

by Gerald F. Else

Others abide our question. Thou art free.
We ask and ask: thou smilest and art still,
Out-topping knowledge.

So wrote Matthew Arnold of Shakespeare. He was acknowledging
a characteristic that we sense only in the very greatest poets:
a characteristic that outtops not only knowledge but that which
knowledge depends on: limitation, opposition, choice. Is
Shakespeare a partisan of Lear? Which does Homer prefer, whom
is he "for": Achilleus or Hektor, the Achaeans or the Trojans?
We feel the inappropriateness of these questions, as we would
feel their inappropriateness to nature or to God. The greatest
poets have that indeterminateness which Keats called "negative
capability": the capacity to go beyond distinctions and prefer-
ences, to *include*.

I

I will not try here to prove that Sophokles was one of the very
greatest poets. I myself think that he was, but the calculation
is impeded by the sparseness of the evidence. We feel, and

119

rightly, that the kind of greatness I am talking about requires
amplitude as well as quality for its demonstration. Inclusive-
ness has to be seen in a work of corresponding size, a poem as
long as the *Iliad*, the whole of the *Divine Comedy*, the middle
and late plays of Shakespeare taken all together; and of Sophokles we happen to have only 7 plays (out of 123) plus a few
hundred short fragments. The corpus is too slender to include
the whole, a whole.

Yet if we look closely at this slender corpus we find a
strange, a disquieting, state of affairs. The usual hallmark
of a limited--a "small"--poet is that we readily understand him.
We can "get around" him, define him, penetrate his meaning,
without difficulty. But that is just what we cannot do with
Sophokles. We may admire him, perceive--or sense--his artistry,
be swept along by his dramatic rhythms, but we do not understand
him. In every one of the seven plays, the deeper we penetrate
the more we become aware of impenetrable mysteries that lie
beyond us. Why do the three earliest plays, *Aias*, *Antigone*,
Trachiniai, each fall into two semi-independent halves? Is or
is not the *Oidipous Tyrannos* a play of fate? How can the mur-
ders of Aigisthos and Klytaimnestra, in *Elektra*, be presented
as if they added up to a cloudlessly happy ending? Why does
Sophokles allow things to go so badly awry, in the *Philoktetes*,
that he has to invoke a deus ex machina (Herakles) to set them
right again?

Some of these questions have to do with the form of the
plays, some with their content or meaning. But that distinction gives us little help or comfort, because for Sophokles,
in a very important sense, form *is* content--the medium is the
message--or in any case form and content are so close they
cannot be disentangled.

In the last century this cardinal fact was recognized in
a way, but a way so crude and unhelpful that no good came of it.
It was generally accepted that Sophokles was (1) a supreme

dramatic and literary artist, and (2) an outstandingly pious
person. But since the plays were not really read as plays, but
as specimens of Greek grammar and literary composition, and
since piety was understood to mean, in principle, no surprises,
a tendency grew up to enshrine Sophokles as the supremely
"classical" author, that is, the unrivaled embodiment of dramatic art and religious orthodoxy at one and the same time.
Aischylos was an austere religious teacher, rather like the
Hebrew prophets; Euripides was an agnostic and a rationalist
and therefore upsetting, but *interesting;* Sophokles, on the
other hand, was neither too prophetic nor too rationalistic,
but just right: beautiful, edifying, and--dull.

Tycho von Wilamowitz, son of the famous Junker scholar
Ulrich von Wilamowitz-Moellendorff, punctured the balloon.
In a book, *Die dramatische Technik des Sophokles* (Berlin:
Weidmann, 1917), published by his father (Tycho was killed in
World War I), he maintained--and cited considerable evidence
for his thesis--that Sophokles was neither a consummate dramatic
architect nor a conventional moralist, but a man of the theater
who would sacrifice anything for the immediate effect of a particular scene.

Tycho's brash attack has been outlived, but scholarship
has not returned to the naïve idealizing view of Sophokles.
I do not wish to give a review of Sophoklean scholarship here,
but merely to reaffirm that we have reached no consensus and
no answer to the persistent questions.

The mystery I spoke of a minute ago as being at the heart
of Sophoklean drama has to do, when all is said and done, with
the relationship between god and man. The difficulty impinges
differently--that is, is seen from a different angle of vision
--in each play. In *Aias,* for example (the earliest extant
Sophoklean drama), we are presented near the beginning and
near the end of the play with a view of Aias that will not
square with what we see of him in the rest of it. Athene,

at the end of the prologue, and Menelaos and Agamemnon, in the
last scene, agree that the hero is *kakos:* a rebellious, unruly,
subversive human being; but that is not the way we perceive him.
In the middle of the play *(Aias* 645-92) we are privileged to be
present at a crucial soliloquy by Aias himself, in which he
seems to entertain, indeed to welcome, the idea of yielding to
the Atreidai as one yields to a force of nature (670-73):

> As snow-packing storms give place to fruitful summer,
> and the dark circle of night stands to one side
> for white-steeded day to blaze her morning light.[1]

We are left to infer that Aias will yield, and as night and
winter do; and that is not in harmony with our idea of him
either.

Which is the true Aias: the dour, intransigent rebel, as
Athene and the Atreidai see him, or the wise yielder? Neither.
He is not a rebel for rebellion's sake; and he will not yield
merely because night and winter do. He will not yield; sooner
than do that, he will take his own life. He is consistent; he
is Aias, a man, a hero, a unique person. But his ultimate
relation to the underlying truths, whatever they are, remains
mysterious. We feel Aias's greatness; we hear his traditional
enemy, Odysseus, acknowledge it; at the end of the play no one
has successfully gainsaid it; but how do the gods stand towards
him? No final or explicit answer to that question ever comes
through to us.

Antigone is not much less mysterious. We catch the measure of her heroic spirit at the beginning of the play, by contrast (Sophokles loves contrasts) with her loving, unheroic
sister Ismene. Ismene will not join in the mad plan to defy
King Kreon's edict that Eteokles, who died defending his city,
shall be accorded full burial honors while his brother Polyneikes, the attacker, is cast out, "a prey to dogs and birds" *(Ant.*
194-206). No sooner has Kreon appeared, to justify the edict

and state his principles of government, than we hear how someone, mysteriously, has given symbolic burial to the corpse of
Polyneikes. Who? How? Our natural reaction is that *we* know
who did it. We heard Antigone just now, vowing to do just that.
Antigone is the "holy sinner"; she did it. But did she?

Kreon leaves after impressing his command on the guard:
the criminal must be apprehended, come what may; and immediately
thereafter the chorus sings its first regular song, the famous
ode to man, as Hölderlin translates it (5:219):

> *Ungeheuer ist viel. Doch nichts*
> *Ungeheuerer, als der Mensch.*

> (Many are the wonders. Yet none
> More wondrous than man.)

Man, who sails the wintry sea, plows the unwearying earth, sub-
dues the animals of air, sea, and mountain; has fashioned speech
and wind-swift thought and city-building ways, shelter and
medicine; only from death he will devise no escape (5:220):

> *Hochstädtisch kommt, unstädtisch*
> *Zu nichts er, mit dem das Unschöne*
> *Ist und die Frechheit.*
> *Nicht sei am Herde mit mir,*
> *Noch gleichgesinnet,*
> *Wer solches tut.*[2]

> (To a citadel he comes, cityless,
> To nothing, he, with whom unbeautiful
> Behavior rests and presumption.
> Let him not stay at one hearthside,
> Nor be of a mind with me,
> Whoever acts that way.)

And with this pious disclaimer still on its lips the chorus
turns its attention to an incredible sight: Antigone led in by
the guard, a prisoner. Antigone a criminal, a defier of the

king's laws, caught in open folly?

The scene thus begun develops rapidly into the famous confrontation in which Antigone not only admits her infraction of the king's edict but contrasts it with the unwritten, unshakable laws of God (5:223):

> *Nicht heut und gestern nur, die leben immer,*
> *Und niemand weiss, woher sie sind gekommen.*

(Not just today and yesterday: they live
Forever; and no one knows where they are from.)

This confrontation of the two laws, of "Zeus" and of the state, is the feature of the play which the discursive understanding finds easiest to grasp: it perceives the tension between Antigone and Kreon as a clash of ideas. This is the basis of Hegel's famous categorization of the play. In part 2 of the *Ästhetik* he says:

Alles in dieser Tragödie ist konsequent; das öffentliche
Gesetz des Staats und innere Familienliebe und Pflicht
gegen den Bruder stehen einander streitend gegenüber,
das Familieninteresse hat das Weib, Antigone, die Wohl-
fahrt des Gemeinwesens Kreon, der Mann, zum Pathos.
Polynikes, die eigene Vaterstadt bekämpfend, war vor
Thebens Toren gefallen, und Kreon, der Herrscher, durch
ein öffentlich verkündetes Gesetz droht jedem den Tod,
der jenem Feinde der Stadt die Ehre des Begräbnisses
zuteil werden liesse. Diesen Befehl aber, der nur das
öffentliche Wohl des Staats betrifft, lässt sich Antigone
nichts angehen, sie vollbringt als Schwester die heilige
Pflicht der Bestattung, nach der Pietät ihrer Liebe zum
Bruder. Dabei beruft sie sich auf das Gesetz der Götter;
die Götter aber, die sie verehrt, sind die unteren Götter
des Hades (Sophokles "Antigone", Vers 451, ...), die
inneren der Empfindung, der Liebe, des Blutes, nicht die
Tagesgötter des freien, selbstbewussten Volks- und
Staatslebens.[3]

(Everything in this tragedy is consistent; the public law of
the state and inner, familial love and duty toward a brother
confront each other in hostile opposition; the interests of
the family are taken passionately to heart by the woman,
Antigone; the welfare of the community by the man, Kreon.
Polyneikes, fighting against his own native city, had fallen
before the gates of Thebes, and Kreon the ruler, by way of a
law publicly decreed, threatens everyone with death who should
accord that enemy of the city the honor of burial. Antigone,
however, does not concern herself with this command, which
pertains solely to the public good of the state. As a sister
she fulfills the sacred duty of burial in accordance with her
dedicated love for her brother. In so doing, she invokes as
her authority the law of the gods; however, the gods whom she
reveres are the underworld gods of Hades [Soph. *Ant.* 451, ...],
the inner ones of feeling, of love, of blood ties, not the
gods of open day, those of the free and self-assured life
of a nation and state.)

Thus *Familieninteresse* and *Wohlfahrt des Gemeinwesens* stand
against each other, as Albin Lesky says in his technical *Referat*
on Greek tragedy, as *"zwei in sich gleichberechtigte Prinzipien"*
(two principles that, taken by themselves, are equally justified).[4] The strife between them, this clash of equal thesis
and antithesis, can only be solved--but it *can* be solved--in
and through the higher synthesis of the *Geist* (spirit).

Hegel's reading has dominated interpretation of the *Antigone* down to the present day, and not only in Germany. Yet one
feels in one's bones that it cannot be correct. Feeling cries
out that Antigone is right--must be right--and Kreon wrong.
And it is not merely sympathy for Antigone that points in that
direction. The chorus discreetly indicates disapproval of
Kreon's action; his own son Haimon pleads with his father to
recognize that he may be wrong; Teiresias tells him flatly that
he *is* wrong; and in the end Kreon is a broken man: both son and
wife self-destroyed, nothing is left for him to live for. As
the last lines of the play proclaim, the gods teach presumptuous
men, in old age, to be wise.

So there is a growing tendency nowadays to agree that in
the end Antigone is justified and Kreon refuted. But is it

really a case of justification and refutation? These rhetorical, intellectually bound terms do not do justice to the play
as a whole--any more than it does justice to the *Aias* to say
that after all Aias was a great though limited man and his
greatness must be recognized. Other things happen in the
Antigone besides a resolution of the clash of ideas between
family and state, things that are mysterious and troubling.
In the first part of the play we have not one but two burials
--symbolic burials--of the corpse of Polyneikes. How is this
doubling to be explained? Could the gods be at work here, as
the chorus suspects (278-79)? After the argument between Haimon
and his father, the chorus sings (781-800) of the invincible
power of love: a power to which Haimon never referred. We had
not realized that Eros was really involved here. That is followed immediately by a long antiphonal section between Antigone
and the chorus in which she is deeply troubled: she feels mocked
and isolated, abandoned by the gods; and *that* is followed immediately, in Kreon's presence, by her profoundly felt and profoundly moving address of greeting to her tomb (891-93):

> *o tymbos, o nympheion, o kataskaphês*
> *oikêsis aieiphrouros, hoi poreuomai*
> *pros tous emautês, ...*

as Hölderlin translates it (5:242):

> *O Grab! o Brautbett! unterirdische*
> *Behausung, immerwach! Da werd ich reisen*
> *Den Meinen zu, ...*

> (O grave! O bridal bed! subterranean
> Home, ever watchful! There I will travel
> To my own, ...)

a speech whose power is in some kind of mysterious relationship to Antigone's utter abandonment and powerlessness. Whence does she derive this strength?

II

Even when we turn to one great poet translating another--to Hölderlin's highly individualistic poetic *compte rendu* of Sophokles' text--we find that the latter-day artist does not necessarily offer us aid and comfort in the form of even implicit univocal answers to the riddles that disturb us in the original. Hölderlin's apprehension of Sophokles' meaning is not merely a reception of ideas, concepts; it consists much more of a direct openness to his *language:* its shapes and tensions, its implications, the concreteness yet ambiguity of its images. Taking the second stasimon (choral song) of the *Antigone* as an example, we can demonstrate Hölderlin's sensitivity by comparing his translation with a well-known English version, that by Dudley Fitts and Robert Fitzgerald.[5]

We must preface this brief study by saying that Hölderlin's translation has two built-in shortcomings: (1) his command of Greek was not perfect and he occasionally committed errors; (2) the Greek text he used contained some inferior readings, not in full tune with Sophokles' meaning.[6]

We have just witnessed the crucial scene in which Antigone, vis-à-vis Kreon, freely admits her deed (the symbolic burial of her brother) and is condemned to death. The chorus (representing us, in a sense) has suffered the emotional impact of that tense encounter, but sees it in a much larger context. The death of Antigone is the last episode in the long tragic history of Oidipous's house, embracing the deaths of Labdakos, Laios, Oidipous himself, his sons, and now his daughter, perhaps both daughters. Why has it all happened? The chorus does not know for sure; it can only feel, pray, and grope for an answer.

The ode *(Ant.* 582-626) consists of two pairs of strophe
and antistrophe: it ends with "spring of sorrow" in Fitts-
Fitzgerald (FF) and with *"ohne Wahnsinn"* (without madness)
in Hölderlin (H); the lines that follow immediately, beginning
"Hämon kommt hier" are not part of the ode.[7] The meter combines dactyls and iambs, but the prevailing rhythm is the
sterner and more energetic iambic.

H's translation is, with slight exceptions (caused mainly
by the two factors mentioned above), rigidly literal; the only
poetic adornment is from Sophokles' (S) own images. Thus the
first line of the ode runs, literally: "Happy (those) to whom
life (time) is untasting of evils." H keeps the initial plural
("solcher") and the durative force in *"nicht schmecket"* (is
untasting); FF give us "the man who has never tasted." But
FF's most important alteration is "God's vengeance" for "evils."
S does not identify the source of the "evils" until the next
line, and nowhere in the ode does he speak of vengeance. "God's
vengeance" generalizes and interprets; *"nicht schmecket das
Übel"* (literally, "does not taste the evil") conveys the naked
experience of evil (including the suggestion of its bitter
taste).

H's *"wenn sich reget"* is not as strong as it might be
(Greek *seisthêi* "is shaken"; cf. "seismic"), but H's *"einmal"*
(once) is exact and *"von Himmlischen"* (from the divine) (inde-
terminate plural) marvelously so: "God" and even "heaven" are
overdetermined to a modern ear. In other words, H's vagueness
exactly renders S's vagueness *(theothen* can mean "from [a] god,"
"from gods," or "from the divine," indifferently).

Now (stanza 1, line 3 of the ode) comes what might seem
an aberration, and a willful one, on H's part: *"Wahnsinn"* for
Greek *ata (atê)* "doom, curse, madness." That his choice is
deliberate is apparent from the ends of the third and fourth
stanzas: *"Wahnsinn kostet"* (costs madness) and *"ohne Wahnsinn"*
(without madness) render S's *"ektos atas"* each time. FF give

"curse" and "sorrow" in stanzas 3 and 4, respectively, "damna-
tion"in stanza 1, line 3, and they seem justified, for the handbooks tell us that *atê* means "madness" in Homer but "doom" or
"curse" in tragedy. But *ata* is the leitmotiv of this ode, an
ostinato refrain appearing at the beginning (end of the second
line, *ouden atas*, responding to *kakôn* at the end of the first;
so the content of the "evils" is *atê)* and at the ends of stanzas
3 and 4.

If we now note the end of stanza 2, we find in the same
place: *"logou t'anoia kai phrenôn Erinys,"* H's *"ungehaltnes
Wort und der Sinne Wüten"* (literally, "folly of speech and fury
in the mind"). H is right and FF and the handbooks are wrong.
The theme of the ode is not "doom" or a "curse" as such, but
very precisely *madness,* a madness that has recurred in each
generation of the house of Labdakos: in Laios (the chorus in
Aischylos' *Seven against Thebes* [750 and 756] says explicitly
that he was driven by folly and madness when he begot Oidipous);
in Oidipous himself, who begot his sons "with maddened mind"
(ibid., 781); in the sons (653, 686-87, 700); and now in Antigone, for the chorus, in the *Antigone,* sees her too as impelled
by madness: *"der Sinne Wüten"* (fury of her mind). And where
does the madness come from? Somehow, ultimately, from the
gods; but how and why, S does not say.

In the remaining lines of stanza 1 H has made a mistake
or two (there is no *"Hütte"* [hut] in the original) and been
misled at one point by a poor text. But the demoniacal force
of the storm (which is, of course, an image for the madness)
comes through magnificently, with a hammering of syncopated
iambics that is astonishingly close to the original. In the
following parallel quotation, the last three lines of stanza
1 of the ode in the texts of S and H, the English (here immediately following S) is not from FF, but is my literal rendition of S (marked 1r/S):

S   *kylíndei býssothén keláinán*
lr/S   it rólls úp fróm the dépths, the bláck sánd
H   *Von Gründ áus wälzt síe das dúnklé*

       thína kái dysánemói
       ón the shóre; and tórn by wínds
       Gestád úm, dás zersáusté,

       stonôi, bremoúsin ántiplêges áktái.
       with gróans they róar, the gále-confrónting héadlánds.
       Und vón Gestöhne ráuschen díe geschlágnen Úfer.

(As a last touch, the way in which *"Ufer"* [banks] echoes *"Übel"*
at the end of the first line of the ode corresponds exactly to
the way in which *"aktai"* [shores, headlands] responds to *"aiôn"*
line 1, and *atas*, line 2, in S!)

     The last two lines of FF's first stanza are respectable
verses:

       When the long darkness under sea roars up
       And bursts drumming death upon the windwhipped sand.

but not in any way equal to H as a rendering of S.

     Time and space are lacking to continue our comparisons.
One could point out how FF convert the chorus's earnest prayer
at the beginning of the third stanza (strophe 2) into a rhetorical question followed by a declarative statement, while H
preserves the prayer; the beauty and faithfulness of (ibid.):

       kátechéis Olýmpoú,
       mármaroéssan áiglán.

       Behältst dés Olýmpos
       Mármórnen Glanz dú, ...

```
        (You hold the marble
        Gleam of Olympus.)
```

the simplicity of (5:231):

> *bis dem, der an nichts denkt,*
> *Die Sohle brennet von heissem Feuer.*

```
        (until the unthinking man's
        Sole burns with hot fire.)
```

But perhaps enough has been said to suggest some of Hölderlin's qualities as translator of Greek poetry, in spite of his less than perfect command of the language and the inadequate text he had at his disposal.

In the face of aesthetic triumph against such odds, one thinks of the meaning of the act of translation as "making new" (to borrow Ezra Pound's strictly pertinent formulation); of translation not as imitation but as a mode of making, commenting, reexperiencing, apprehended as an essential unity of the creative intellect. No afterthoughts on Hölderlin's experience of the *Antigone* could more tellingly confirm it as a discovery of *language* than the poet's own "Anmerkungen zur Antigonae" (5:269):

> *Die tragische Darstellung beruhet, ... darauf, dass*
> *der unmittelbare Gott, ... in der Gestalt des Todes,*
> *gegenwärtig ist.*
> *Deswegen ... die dialogische Form, und der Chor im*
> *Gegensatze mit dieser, deswegen die gefährliche Form,*
> *in den Auftritten, die, nach griechischerer Art, not-*
> *wendig faktisch in dem Sinne ausgehet, dass das* Wort
> mittelbarer faktisch *wird, indem es den sinnlicheren*
> *Körper ergreift; ....* Das griechischtragische Wort
> *ist* tödlichfaktisch, *weil der Leib, den es ergreifet,*
> *wirklich tötet.*[8]

```
        (Tragic imitation is based, ... on the notion that
        the immediate god, ... is present in the figure of death.
```

Hence ... the dialogue form and the chorus to contrast
with it, hence the danger-filled plot in the scenes, which
in a more Greek manner has its outcome with necessary effectiveness in the sense that the *word* becomes *immediately
effective* in its act of seizing the more sensuous body;
.... The *Greek-tragic word is death-effective* because the
body it seizes really kills.)

Hölderlin's understanding of the poetic power of the drama is
involved precisely in the insight that language is *"der Güter
Gefährlichstes"* (the most dangerous of possessions [2:325]),
that words are first of all deeds; this is how latter-day minds
wondering about the mystery of Sophokles are to comprehend the
power of the Greek dramatist's way with words (5:270):

Und so ist wohl das tödlichfaktische, der wirkliche Mord
aus Worten, mehr als eigentümlich griechische und einer
vaterländischeren Kunstform subordinierte Kunstform zu
betrachten.

(And so, most likely, *that which is death-effective, the
real murder composed of words, is to be regarded more as
a peculiarly Greek art form, one subordinated to a more
native form in art.)*

Dramatic progression in the *Antigone*, as Hölderlin sees
it, is in the nature of a revolution of the spirit. It is a
total and uncompromising turnabout in the very core of man:
it is *"vaterländische Sache"* (native concern), in whose course
*"jedes, als von unendlicher Umkehr ergriffen, und erschüttert,
in unendlicher Form sich fühlt, in der es erschüttert ist"*
(each live being, as if seized and shaken by infinite revolution, feels itself in that infinite form in which it is shaken
[5:271]). For--and in the "Anmerkungen zur Antigonae"this is
perhaps the most lapidary insight of them all--*"vaterländische
Umkehr ist die Umkehr aller Vorstellungsarten und Formen.
Eine gänzliche Umkehr ... ist aber, ... dem Menschen, als
erkennendem Wesen unerlaubt* (native turnabout is a turnabout

in all conceptions and forms. A complete turnabout ... however, is not permitted to man as a cognitive being [ibid.]).

Antigone's mystique (or madness, if that it may be called) is precisely to effect such a total turnabout. And so the question, "Whence does Antigone derive her strength?" may help answer itself--in part. Have her gods planted in her an awareness of the power, the murderous power of language? Is this what Sophokles is trying to "tell us"? We do not know; I do not believe we will ever know--if indeed the purpose of aesthetic experience is to impart knowledge of this kind. What we may be sure of is that we are free to look--and listen-- to the end. The chorus meditates on Danaë, Lykourgos, and the daughters of Phineus--all targets of divine grace or jealousy or cruelty--and immediately Teiresias is at hand to speak of the will of the gods, against Kreon. The *Umkehr*, the turning point in the dramatic sense, has come. Antigone has reached her nadir, Kreon his zenith, and the true balance is about to be restored.

The fabric of the *Oidipous Tyrannos* is more tightly knit, the "logical" connections between one link in the chain and the next more carefully wrought, but a demonstration like that for the *Antigone* could be made here too. Everywhere, beneath the smooth surface of this most famous of all plots, are deep-running currents, unseen concurrences of power and weakness, attraction and repulsion, down to the final *Umkehr*. What is the relation of the gods to these hidden currents? Is the *Oidipous* a play of fate, engineered by the gods? Or is it Oidipous himself, as modern interpreters are fond of saying, who drives the action to its goal, pushes himself to the catastrophe?

III

It will remain difficult to understand Hölderlin's interpretation of *Antigone* and *Oidipous*, as a whole; I make no claim
to such total understanding. I do perceive that this interpretation is religious, that Hölderlin takes both plays seriously as religious documents and finds their meaning somehow
embodied in their very fabric rather than in concepts that are
verbalized or verbalizable by chorus or actors. All I am
prepared to say is that there is a deep residue of mystery
embedded in both the plays Hölderlin translated, and in every
other one of the Sophoklean seven--a residue which classical
scholarship, with its explicitly and overtly rational techniques, has not yet managed to explain. Therefore, just
possibly, Hölderlin's poetic, intuitional, religious approach
might deserve a respectful hearing even now, 170 years later.
Possibly Sophokles is smiling; in any case he is silent.

The Concept of Enlightenment
in Hölderlin's Poetry

by Wilfried Malsch

Anyone who has derived his view of Hölderlin mainly from the older schools of German literary criticism would presumably not expect to find a concept of the Enlightenment in his work. He might rather believe that Hölderlin's hymns are, as Friedrich Gundolf expressed it, *"das Ertönen anhaltender Weihe, beständigen Verkehrs mit den Göttern"* (the voice of perpetual consecration, of continuous contact with the gods.)

In the framework of the history of ideas Hölderlin certainly does not belong to the epoch of the Enlightenment with its rationality and its concept of a world of calculable regularity. Moreover, it is even controversial in recent research whether the poetry of Hölderlin belongs to that part of European romanticism that German critics are used to calling *deutsche Klassik,* or to the other part, the so-called *deutsche Romantik,* or, like the work of Jean Paul and Kleist, to neither of them, as having a unique quality of its own. From the point of view of our Symposium it seems easier to interpret Hölderlin as an early modern on the basis of his apparently unrelated singularity than on the basis of his historical position. This impression, however, is convincing only to the extent that we neglect his completed poems, preferring instead his

135

incomplete fragments and even the obscure sketches from his later years. Similarly, the obscurity of the completed later hymns seems "modern" to us only to the extent that we omit from consideration their structure of historical thought, which reorganizes the religious images of earlier ages.

I do not deny that, with little historical knowledge, we can be most attracted to the "modern sensibility" of Hölderlin's dark, gloomy, and puzzling image sequences and his paratactic sentences in solemn rhythms which, like poems by Mallarmé, seem to elevate us into a dream of freedom beyond any natural or historical possibility and removed from the restrictions of temporal existence. More recently, however, now that Baudelaire's concept of the modern lyric is already becoming a classical concept of modernity, and now that the school of Stefan George, together with Heidegger's prophecy, is losing ground, the holy mist is lifting from Hölderlin's more obscure poems and the critic can again take the liberty to try to enlighten the reader about their structure and images. But even if these are related to contemporary concepts and imagery, Hölderlin the poet cannot really be considered an early modern in the context of the history of poetry—even though he may have stimulated some poetic forms in the work of Rilke, Trakl, Celan, or others.

It is also noteworthy that the so-called *werkimmanente Interpretation* (interpretive comment on the poem itself) has, in fact, led toward more historical conclusions. Research on Hölderlin's theory of poetry has pointed out his systematic calculation of the laws underlying poetic creation. This observation could lend credence to the fashionable modern view of calculated creativity, but only if one failed to take into account that this understandable demand for a sense of order in our critical perceptions—canonized by Horace's *Ars Poetica* —has ruled the whole history of poetry. Our recognition, on the other hand, that Hölderlin understood the *kalkulables Gesetz* of poetry as being connected with the law of historical progress

and the perfectibility of mankind, places him clearly in his
own time. An excellent example of this approach to Hölderlin
is provided by the contributions of Lawrence Ryan, who started
by explaining Hölderlin through Hölderlin, but now places him
in the context of his time, particularly with reference to the
effects of the French Revolution in Germany.

The additional emphasis now placed on Hölderlin's relationship to his own times is partly to be attributed to another,
and by far the most radical attempt to "modernize" Hölderlin,
namely by seeing him as a Jacobin. Some critics read his novel,
his odes, and his elegies as coded revolutionary signals, or
as reflections directed to or drawn from conspirators in Jena
or Swabia. Actually, we do not have enough evidence of Hölderlin's involvement in revolutionary conspiracies to support
such speculations. We can be certain only that he was a
republican, but never a Jacobin in the sense established by
the *terreur* of the Montagnards. But we can indeed consider
Hölderlin's poems as revolutionary signals if we relate them
to his conception of the progress of mankind.

The progress and perfectibility of mankind are concepts
of the eighteenth-century Enlightenment that remained fundamental concepts throughout the age of Goethe, even though
German philosophers and poets of this age opposed and even
scoffed at the Enlightenment as unhistorical rationalism or
merely popular philosophy. But in another sense such concepts
retained a pervasive influence. For in Germany, probably owing
to Hamann and Herder, they were also understood in a way preformed by the Christian tradition, especially as manifested in
its heretical line of the *damnatas opiniones Judaicas*, which
--via Bengel and Oetinger--extended to Herder and Novalis as
well as to the Tübinger Stift and to Hölderlin.

The closest historical link between the eighteenth-centry
Enlightenment and Hölderlin's generation is perhaps Friedrich
Schlegel's review of Condorcet's last work *Des progrès de*

l'esprit humain, which foresees an increasing perfectibility
of mankind. But Schlegel had already adapted this view to the
more historical interpretation by Herder, as did Hölderlin and
others. Herder's interpretation transmitted to them not only
the view of modern historicism that every epoch has its own
kind of perfection and its own justification, but also the
vision of the wandering human genius that realizes itself in
uncountable ways under ever-changing historical conditions,
but is ever advancing toward its goal of perfection. Many of
Hölderlin's poems, as well as his novel *Hyperion*, enable us to
see this influence.

The concept of human genius signifies a potential that
has been given to man by nature, but one that has to be actu-
alized by historical means. However, the accomplishments,
neither of any age nor of any individual have hitherto exhaus-
ted the possibilities or fulfilled the promise of the perfectibility of human nature. But every accomplishment is at the
same time a testimony and a sign for the future destiny of
the whole of mankind.

Herder's concept contains a method for looking at history
that has seldom been used since Hegel, but was widespread in
the age of Goethe. This method was preformed by the Christian
typology of the Bible. According to this concept, for example,
the type of human being represented by Adam has found its more
distinct complementary type in Christ. Both types represent
the same basic strain of humanity, but the earlier does it in
a less, the later in a more distinct configuration. Analogously,
history is understood by medieval biblical typology as a progression toward the distinct revelation of human destiny. This
Christian idea of progress, which is prefigured in earlier ages
but has to be accomplished in the future, came to Herder from
Hamann. But Herder secularized the idea and used its typological method to interpret the universal historical view of the
Enlightenment. Herder did not oppose Christianity, but he did

eliminate the distinction between it and humanity, as did Lessing in his essay *Die Erziehung des Menschengeschlechts*. More clearly than Herder, Lessing pointed out that the books of divine revelation contain pictorial prefigurations of true reason, which were created to educate an immature mankind toward a mature understanding of the truth.

As a consequence of this, the German Enlightenment did not arrive at such a clear confrontation with Christianity as De Maistre saw in the struggle of revolutionaries and conservatives in France. Moreover, the French Revolution was often interpreted in Germany at that time as being figuratively related to the Reformation and to the millennial reappearance of Christ.

In Schelling's, Hölderlin's, and Hegel's collaborative document, the essay entitled "Das älteste Systemprogramm des deutschen Idealismus" (4:297-99), political and social freedom are prophesied in Christian terms and likened to the advent of the Spirit of Pentecost: *"Ein höherer Geist vom Himmel gesandt, muss diese neue Religion unter uns stiften, sie wird das letzte, grösste Werk der Menschheit sein"* (a higher spirit sent by heaven must found this new religion among us, it will be the last, greatest work of mankind [4:299]). This messianic expectation did not conflict with the adoration of classical antiquity, certainly not with Winckelmann's vision of Periclean democracy. On the contrary, Winckelmann's vision gave to the universal historical expectation its prefiguration within the early temporal and national limits of Greece. It was, in this form, the archetype for the universal concept of the future, as understood during the age of Goethe. It also prefigured the republican hope that was expressed in the seminary at Tübingen, as described by Christoph Theodor Schwab in his biography of Hölderlin (7:448):

*Da die Idee eines Freistaates in Frankreich ins Leben
getreten war, so glaubte sich eine Jugend, die in den
Alten zu Hause war, berechtigt, die Wiederkehr ihrer
aus der Vorzeit überkommenen Ideale von der Zukunft zu
hoffen.*

(Since in France the idea of a free state had sprung to
life, a young generation at home in the classics believed
itself justified in hoping for a future return of their
ideals inherited from ancient times.)

In Hölderlin's hexameter hymn "Der Archipelagus," ancient
Athens is seen as the prefiguration of the longed-for *Heimat*,
as the mother who shall give birth to the goal of history--
"Dass ... Ein Geist allen gemein sei" (that ... one spirit be
common to all [2:110]). This is the same expectation as that
clarified in the previously mentioned "Systemprogramm." Greek
and Christian conceptions are thematically integrated also in
the elegy "Brod und Wein." Here the expected birth of the
Spirit of Pentecost is recognized in the birth of the "common
spirit" among the people of Greece (2:92):

*Wo ist das schnelle? wo brichts, allgegenwärtigen Glücks voll,
    Donnernd aus heiterer Luft über die Augen herein?
Vater Aether! so riefs und flog von Zunge zu Zunge
    Tausendfach, es ertrug keiner das Leben allein; ....*

(Where is the swift? And full of joy omnipresent, where does it
    Flash upon dazzled eyes, thundering fall from clear skies?
Father Aether! one cried, and tongue after tongue took it
        up then,
    Thousands, no man could bear life so intense on his own; ....)

And this "common spirit" of ancient Athens prefigures the "new
religion," which is prophesied in terms of Christian conceptions. Basically, however, the concept of this new religion
is a messianic and idealistic modification of the Enlightenment
idea that beneath the world's diversities there is a common
body of faith, a natural religion universally present in the

human heart. This modification remains nevertheless true to
the principles of Kant's *Die Religion innerhalb der Grenzen
der blossen Vernunft*.

Using insights derived from Lessing's *Die Erziehung des
Menschengeschlechts*, the "Systemprogramm" tries to meet the
challenge of the historical situation that tells its authors
that on the one hand—as Kant had complained—religious diversities further wars and aid man's tyranny over man, and thereby prevent the advent of the common spirit; but that on the
other hand—as Lessing had seen—people need a religion that
is in agreement with their origin and degree of maturity.
The answer offered by the "Systemprogramm" is to enlighten
positive religions and mythologies, in order that people may
recognize them for what they really are, namely poetry. This
recognition would eliminate superstitious beliefs, and would
further embody the truths of reason in religious images acceptable both to the educated and to the uneducated (4:299):

*So müssen endlich Aufgeklärte und Unaufgeklärte sich die
Hand reichen, die Mythologie muss philosophisch werden,
um das Volk vernünftig, und die Philosophie muss mytholo-
gisch werden, um die Philosophen sinnlich zu machen. Dann
herrscht ewige Einheit unter uns. Nimmer der verachtende
Blick, nimmer das blinde Zittern des Volks vor seinen
Weisen und Priestern.*

(So finally the enlightened and the unenlightened must join
hands; mythology must become philosophical in order to make
the people think, and philosophy must turn mythological in
order to make the philosophers open to sensuous experience.
Then eternal unity will prevail among us. No more the con-
temptuous glance, no more the blind trembling of the people
before its wise men and priests.)

Hölderlin's poetry attempts to enlighten us about past
mythologies so that these can be recognized as poetic prefigurations of the anticipated future of mankind. As Hölderlin
writes in the "Thalia-Fragment" of *Hyperion* (3:180):

So verblühen die schönen jugendlichen Myrten der Vorwelt,
die Dichtungen Homers und seiner Zeiten, die Prophezeihun-
gen und Offenbarungen, aber der Keim, der in ihnen lag,
gehet als reife Frucht hervor im Herbste.

(Thus the beautiful youthful myrtles of ancient times
wither, the works of Homer and of his times, the prophecies and revelations; but the seed that lay in them goes
forth as ripe fruit in autumn.)

It is indeed true that Hölderlin preferred Greek religion
for this purpose. But this conception of a progression of
mankind from morning to evening, from spring to autumn, from
Orient to Occident, from Greece to Hesperia is, as we have
already seen, preformed by the Judeo-Christian tradition. And
beginning with the elegy "Brod und Wein" and continuing through
"Patmos," Hölderlin's poetry also attempts to enlighten us
about Christian mythology so that it can be understood not only
in its poetic configuration of the expected future, but also
in its difference from and in its typological identity with
Greek religion. In his later poems Hölderlin continues to
achieve his principal intention by pointing out that there
ought to be no domination of man over man, either on earth
or in the heavens of the mythologies. With the advent of the
Prince of Peace in the vision of the hymn "Friedensfeier,"
there is no longer any such domination, either in human imagination or in social reality: *"Da Herrschaft nirgend ist zu*
sehn bei Geistern und Menschen" (Since domination is to be
seen nowhere among spirits or men [3:534]). Now the natural
potential of mankind can be fulfilled. But this promise of
the Prince of Peace is not derived entirely from our own time:
"Von heute aber nicht, nicht unverkündet ist er" (Not being of
our day, he comes not unannounced [ibid.]). Indeed, any Sunday
the young Hölderlin could listen to Isaiah's prophecy that
there will come the *"Held, Ewigvater, Friedefürst"* (mighty God,
everlasting Father, Prince of Peace [Isa. 9:6]), born of a

mortal virgin.

The coming of the Prince of Peace will not occur, however, before he is understood in his origins as the spiritual god who wants to be realized on earth. Peace will not come before (3: 535):

> *Der Hohe, der Geist*
> *Der Welt sich zu Menschen geneigt hat.*

> (The high one, the Spirit
> Of the World has inclined unto men.)

The spirit's coming into real life is manifested in the mythological sons of God, born of virgins. Spiritual begetting and virgin birth are in Hölderlin's poetry also a symbol for the genesis of the poem, as expressed in "Wie wenn am Feiertage" (2:119):

> *von heilgem Strahl entzündet,*
> *Die Frucht in Liebe geboren, der Götter und*
> *Menschen Werk,*
> *Der Gesang, ...*

> (kindled by
> The holy ray, that fruit conceived in love, the work
> of gods and men,
> ..., the song ....)

In Hölderlin's understanding, poetry anticipates life in peace and harmony. Consequently, should history reach this goal, mankind would have realized the poetic anticipation. In the hymn "Friedensfeier" we hear (3:536):

> *Viel hat von Morgen an,*
> *Seit ein Gespräch wir sind und hören voneinander,*
> *Erfahren der Mensch; bald sind wir aber Gesang.*

> (Much, from morning on,
> Since we are a conversation, and hear from one
>   another,
> Man has learned; but soon we will be song.)

In order to recognize the Prince of Peace, man must have an understanding of the meaning of the spiritual God and of his tendency to become embodied in natural human life, as it is prefigured in the birth of the Son (3:535):

> *Und nun erkennen wir ihn,*
> *Nun, da wir kennen den Vater ....*

> (And now we recognize him,
> Now that we know the Father ....)

The Christian Son of God is, however, considered "Der Einzige." Yet the hymn "Friedensfeier" evokes the identical promise of the various prefigurations of the coming Prince of Peace by obscuring their mythological differences. Because of his being the latest within the typologically identical succession, the departed gods seem to prefer him as (3:536):

> *ihr Geliebtestes auch,*
> *An dem sie hängen, ...*

> (also their most beloved,
> To whom they are attached, ...)

But Christ is only another prefigurative promise, like the other types of the Son, and is not in himself the fulfilling advent of the Prince of Peace. It is precisely the obscure contours of the Son in "Friedensfeier" that make it even clearer that Christ is typologically related to Herakles and Dionysos. Apparently, the "shame" of the singer in the hymn "Der Einzige" is caused by the domination of the Christian religion over the poet's imaginative and moral development (2:163):

Es hindert aber eine Scham
Mich, dir zu vergleichen
Die weltlichen Männer.

(And yet a shame forbids me
To associate with you
The worldly men.)

But after having compared Christ with the other divine sons
and having recognized their typological identity beneath their
mythological diversity, the singer overcomes his shame and
rejoices (ibid.):

                         Herrlich grünet
Ein Kleeblatt.

                         (Splendidly there sprouts
A cloverleaf.)

The cloverleaf, symbolizing the three prefigurations of the
Prince of Peace, enlightens us about Isaiah's prophecy. The
poetic interpretation of this promise accomplished in Hölderlin's
hymn unites that promise with all the mythological promises of
a Golden Age, demanding the realization of these images in a
naturally fulfilled human life (3:536):

                    und eher legt
Sich schlafen unser Geschlecht nicht,
Bis ihr Verheissenen all,
All ihr Unsterblichen, uns
Von eurem Himmel zu sagen,
Da seid in unserem Hause.

                         (nor shall our race
Ever lie down to sleep until
All you who were promised,
All of you immortals,
Are here with us in our house
To tell us about your heaven.)

In conclusion, then, Hölderlin understands his later poems as enlightening interpretations of past mythologies. The method of this poetic interpretation is that of Herder's historical writings. It is preformed by the Judeo-Christian tradition, but adapted to the universal view of history developed during the Age of Enlightenment. The structure of this method can be described as looking into the past with the eyes of hope, in order to discover in the prophecies and promises of the past the future of mankind. Hölderlin's poetry employs this method with the intention of liberating mythological and religious images from superstitious beliefs and redirecting them through the inspiration of hope.

In his fragmentary essay "Über Religion" Hölderlin opposes his concept of poetic enlightenment to the concept of rational enlightenment that had prevailed in the eighteenth century. Rational enlightenment is based, as I have said, upon the concept of a world of calculable regularity: *"vom ... notwendigen Zusammenhang der unverbrüchlichen, allgültigen, unentbehrlichen Gesetze des Lebens"* (of ... the necessary context of the unbreakable, universally valid, and indispensable laws of life [4:276]). But this concept—as Hölderlin goes on to say—does not exhaust man's desires and dreams of happiness or the rules of love, friendship, and human relations, which are interrelated within a wider and more involved context than that of a merely mechanistic world. They are fused in what Hölderlin calls *"dieser höhere Zusammenhang"* (this higher context [4:275]), one that includes both the memory of a remote and vanishing past and hope for a future as yet out of reach. Hölderlin states that this higher context is the real sphere of human life, but that it cannot be entirely recognized by theoretical means. It can only be represented by means of imagery, as in religion. Therefore religion is understood as the repetition in the conscious mind of this higher context. But because religious and mythological images are *"dichterische Vorstellungen"* (poetic representations), religion per se is poetry. Hölderlin's later poetry is actuated by this idea: it challenges us to see former religions and mythologies as forms of poetry, in order to release us from the domination of images, but to give us, at the same time, through imagery, the free enjoyment of the higher context or sphere in which we live. Contrary to the usual concept of enlightenment, Hölderlin describes the free enjoyment of our higher context through poetic imagery: *"Und dies ist eben die höhere Aufklärung, die uns grösstenteils abgeht"* (And this is just that higher enlightenment that concerns us for the most part [4:277]).

"In What Sense Is Hölderlin an Early Modern?" Perhaps in the same sense, I should say, in which the second Isaiah is the first early modern, in that he enlightened the Jews with regard to the loss of Paradise and redirected their view from the past to the future. According to one of Novalis's "Blütenstaub" fragments, which Hölderlin very probably read, the Jews found in Babylonian captivity *"eine echt religiöse Tendenz, eine religiöse Hoffnung"* (a genuinely religious orientation, a religious hope [N 2:443]). The religion of hope was born in exile. The recognition of the exile of mankind was then, as now, a modern approach.

In the elegy "Brod und Wein" Hölderlin asks what has become of the ancient Oriental and Greek songs of the "children of God" in the Golden Age. The following distich answers this question by anticipating the fulfillment of Occidental history (2:95):

Was der Alten Gesang von Kindern Gottes geweissagt,
Siehe! wir sind es, wir; Frucht von Hesperien ists!

(What of the children of God was foretold in the songs of the ancients,
Look, we are it, ourselves; fruit of Hesperia it is!)

Seasonal and Psychic Time in the
Structuring of Hölderlin's *Hyperion*

by Lawrence O. Frye

The notion of seasonal time conjures up the old cliché that a person is a creature of his earth and that his moods and behavior are controlled by the annual seasons through which he lives. He blossoms in the spring, is in full bloom in the summer, is harvested in the ripeness of his fall, and dies in the winter. One year will do to represent the life of man; several cycles are credible but can be tiring. We all know that Hyperion is not such a man. The first letters of the narrating Hyperion tell us that while he can hear the *"Wonnegesang des Frühlings"* (joyous song of spring), he also sees and feels an opposing *"Totengarten"* (garden of the dead [1:9]) around himself.[1] Seasonal time also suggests that Hyperion's basic experiences of ebb and flow, of the *"in Ausflug und in Rückkehr zu sich selbst"* (in excursion and in return to oneself [1:65]) of life, are graphically modeled after the elliptical orbit of the planet around the sun; but such a motion of repeated orbiting would not seem to do justice to the thought in *Hyperion* that man emerged from an all-uniting center of life and will return, with and through his newfound spirit of consciousness,

148

to that center.[2]

Despite objections, I will retain the concepts of planetary orbits and seasonal sequences as an entrance into the
structure of the novel *Hyperion*. The reasons are twofold, and
simple. First, it is a stressed thematic concern that *"alles
altert und verjüngt sich wieder"* (everything grows old and
rejuvenates itself again *[1:27]*), but that man is *"ausgenommen
vom schönen Kreislauf der Natur"* (exempted from the beautiful
cycle of nature [ibid.]). The latter are simultaneously both
statement and question by the narrating Hyperion, after having
endured the double loss of Adamas and of his own past life.
Later, toward the end of volume 1, book 2, Diotima echoes the
experience: she has been forsaken by May and summer and fall.
Now, she continues: *"die Blüte des Mais und die Flamme des
Sommers und die Reife des Herbsts, die Klarheit des Tags und
der Ernst der Nacht, und Erd und Himmel ist mir in diesem
Einen vereint"* (the blossom of May and the flame of summer
and the ripeness of autumn, the clarity of day and the seriousness of night, and earth and heaven are united for me in
this one thing *[1:135]*). Two expressions for the course of a
human life are presented here. One may, as Diotima had, live
faithfully in tune with the rhythm of seasonal change; self-
regeneration flows with the regeneration of nature every spring.
For Hyperion, such regularity of life signifies the constancy
of life and self-renewal--in fact, the harmony of an eternal
spring. On the other hand, we see that man may leave this
repeating cycle, as Hyperion himself says earlier, in the self-
impelled striving to be all. What interests us, however, is
that in her description of her wayward path from nature's
course, Diotima still phrases the journey as a seasonal experience: Hyperion is the new sun of her life's orbit. In other
words, natural time and psychic--or inner--time, while they
might not be synchronous, can participate in analogous rhythms,
namely the rhythms of seasonal periods. The fascination and

complexity of the novel owe much to the superimposing of shifting inner time periods onto the earth's cycles in its movement
about the sun. The complexity is compounded in that each character has his own peculiar cyclical timing and, moreover, his
own variations in tempo. The seasonal clocks run sometimes
faster, sometimes slower in a period than seems quantitatively
warranted. The tendency of the novel, I believe, is to demonstrate at the ripe moment that all of the seasonal cycles, both
natural and psychic, can reestablish a harmonized synchronization.

The second reason for retaining the notion of orbiting
bodies and seasons is the basis for the above observations:
there must be a standard of earth time from which to gauge the
relationship of a character's inner experience of time to his
external world. Accordingly, there is scarcely a moment in
Hyperion's life for which we are not made aware of the season.
The elimination of dates for the letters is answered by an
awareness of the natural rhythms of the year.[3]

As I take a brief look at the seasonal framework for the
four parts of the novel I must concentrate here on the time
covered in the past, narrated life of Hyperion. The relationship of the narrator's time to that of his past is also
a crucial aspect of the topic, but can only receive cursory
attention in this presentation. The past of Hyperion begins
in the spring (in volume 1, book 1) and reaches at the end of
this book the transition period between winter and spring. A
scant two-year cycle passes with the encounters with Adamas
and Alabanda. That is, a narratively effective two years pass;
presumably more time is consumed by Hyperion's boyhood, but the
experienced time represents only those two years. Book 2 of
volume 1 opens, accordingly, in the spring once more and closes
about the end of summer. Thus the duration of the Diotima
experience presented in this book is reduced to two seasons.
Book 1 of volume 2 consequently opens in the fall and lasts

just short of one year by closing in roughly midsummer--precisely on July 4, 1770, the day before the Cheshme naval battle. The narrative of the last book then picks up with a brief retrospective view of the following summer day and lasts about the same three and one-half seasons as the preceding book, by ending in the spring in Germany.

This delineation is quite mechanical, although it serves as a necessary frame of reference. What can be observed from it is that, negatively, the four books are not divided simplistically into equal periods of time, although the last two books are comparable in this respect. What does emerge is the fairly clean opposition of the first two books to the last two in terms of their seasonal beginnings: whereas spring is the opening key twice in volume 1, the reverse time of year preludes in volume 2--clearly as fall in book 1 and, in book 2, as the briefest two-letter sojourn in summer before again lingering in the fall. I find it credible, for understanding Hölderlin's intentions in setting up this reversal in the seasonal structure, to conjecture that this is his variation on a Platonic notion concerning aging and rejuvenation.

Immediately before the trip to Athens near the end of volume 1, book 2, the narrating Hyperion enters with comments which anticipate the impending departure, in the past, of Hyperion from his cradle of love--and thus anticipate the main course of volume 2. He writes: *"Ich seh, ich sehe, wie das enden muss. Das Steuer ist in die Woge gefallen und das Schiff wird, wie an den Füssen ein Kind, ergriffen und an die Felsen geschleudert"* (I see, I see how it must end. The rudder has fallen into the waves and the ship is seized, like a child by the feet, and hurled against the cliffs [1:136]). Plato writes in his *Politikos:*

And now the Pilot of the ship of the Universe (for so we may speak of it) let go the handle of its rudder and retired to His conningtower in a place apart. Then destiny

and its own inborn urge took control of the world again
and reversed the revolution of it. Then the gods of the
provinces, who had ruled under the greatest god, knew at
once what was happening and relinquished the oversight
of their regions. A shudder passed through the world at
the reversing of its rotation, checked as it was between
the old control and the new impulse which had turned end
into beginning for it and beginning into end.[4]

The justification for bringing Plato into the discussion is
given by Hyperion himself when, in the first book, he and
Alabanda read Plato together, *"wo er so wunderbar erhaben
vom Altern und Verjüngen spricht"* (where he speaks in such a
wonderfully exalted way of aging and rejuvenation [1:46]).[5]
Plato distinguishes between the age of Kronos and the age of
Zeus. In the former, a timeless Golden Age prevails and man
is born in full maturity from Mother Earth, grows young, re-
enters the earth and continues the cycle; in the age of Zeus,
man is born of parents as child and grows old, then to die.

The aspect unique to the two growth forms is their respective planetary motion counterparts. In the Kronos age,
an external force--the "Pilot of the ship of the Universe"--
controls the revolution of the skies; in the age of Zeus, in
which we live under the experience of time, revolutionary
direction is reversed and the force of motion is given over
to the moving body itself. From the structural implications
of Plato's two-motion theory, we observe the semblance of a
Zeus period dominating Hyperion's life as the main tendency
of volume 2--until the late fall season sets in toward the
close of the last book of the novel. The signals for this
period accumulate, however, as early as the closing section
of volume 1, namely in late summer. The occasion, in fact,
for Hyperion's foreshadowing warning that "the rudder has fallen into the wave"--a comment from this late summer time--is
Diotima's lament that she has been forsaken by "May and summer
and fall." As Hyperion will graphically do, Diotima begins

her own seasonal course independent of, and to a large extent
in reverse to, the seasonal course of the earth. Her sun, as
she says, is no longer the natural sun of the earth but rather
Hyperion. But to complicate matters, her new inner cycle is
not the same as Hyperion's. The source of his new inner cycle
no longer lies outside himself but rather within. He finally
experiences what Adamas once said he would, and what Plato
makes a feature of in the age of Zeus: the god within him,
self-impelled momentum.

A compulsion for neatness does not reveal a clean Kronos
era in volume 1 as counterpart to the Zeus tendencies of volume 2. Enough signs are there to posit a basic Kronos inclination. One important aspect in this respect is the reiterated
feeling that Hyperion is directed through his life by forces
outside his control. But especially in his early, pre-Diotima
days, he often feels a counterforce which erodes any enduring
calm of equilibrium that would embrace one in a Golden Age of
Kronos. The very fact that the time is the eighteenth century
and not Greece in its glory necessitates some awareness of
distinctions in time. It is only in the spring with Diotima
that a Kronos-style forgetfulness engulfs Hyperion for any
duration with a sense of oneness of self and world. The point
is that each dominant tendency in the novel breeds variations
on itself, and coexists with the countertendencies of its opposite era. One can see the absurdity of seeking a pure dichotomy between the two volumes of the novel; for while each represents distinct tendencies and also carries the seeds of its
opposite in itself, the avowed aim of the novel is to represent
the ultimate reconciliation of opposites.

In applying the Kronos concept to the novel, the differing
aspects of time assume more unity if we recognize more than the
Platonic version of Kronos. Through the Platonic relationship
of opposition between Kronos and Zeus, we can describe the
reversal of motion that underlies the reversed structuring of

seasonal progression in the two halves of *Hyperion*. The Kronos
figure himself, however, is also a vessel of opposites. The
one tradition that Plato utilizes in the *Politikos* myth identifies Kronos as the ruler of the Golden Age, in which he is
the source of "a renewal of life," "an immortality" (270a), of
the age's "deathlessness and agelessness" (273e); in Hölderlin's
seasonal framework, spring is the period suited to experiencing
such renewal and timelessness of life. On the other hand, another Kronos tradition emerges in the novel: that imminent in
the figure of Melancholia.[6] The characteristic of melancholy
is disposed to flourish in the summer season; in fact, according to its nature, it links summer with winter. These latent
relationships assume correspondences in the larger structural
scheme. Both books of volume 1 open in the spring and close
first in winter and then in summer; in other words, opening and
closing seasons simply reflect on a structural level these two
main, opposing Kronos traditions.

The melancholic strain becomes most clearly apparent in
the summer period with Diotima in volume 1, book 2, namely at
the same time in which we detect the conditions of transition
into the Zeus period of volume 2. The mood of Hyperion is a
contrasting blend of bliss and melancholy, appropriately combining the extremes of the paradisiac effect of Diotima's
presence and the anticipation of depression in his ultimately
losing her: *"O es ist ein seltsames Gemische von Seligkeit
und Schwermut, wenn es so sich offenbart, dass wir auf immer
heraus sind aus dem gewöhnlichen Dasein"* (Oh, it is a peculiar
mixture of blessedness and melancholy when, as revelation would
have it, we must always be outside normal existence [1:123]).
The scene is the beginning of Hyperion's six-day separation
from Diotima and is experienced as a kind of eclipse, in which
the world intervenes between himself and her, blocking out her
life-giving light: *"und die Welt lag zwischen ihr und mir, wie
eine unendliche Leere"* (and between her and me the world lay

as an endless void [1:124]). Consequently his sense perception
is as if benumbed, the external world as if blocked out, and
he retreats to within himself, to an internal world of thought
and fantasies. In keeping with this internal retreat, his
external habitat is night. Physically, the heat of the summer
sun burns so intensely that one retreats to protective shade;
mentally, the lives of the people around Hyperion seem so
sterile and barren that the present is avoided for the self-
protective life of inner reverie. These features of the summer
season have been anticipated in the two preceding summers of
book 1, if never so extensively as now. The preceding summer
in Smyrna, in fact, is linked to the present Diotima summer in
that Hyperion's private fantasies were then envisioning the
Diotima to come (1:38):

_Mein Herz verschloss jetzt seine Schätze, aber nur, um sie
für eine bessere Zeit zu sparen, für das Einzige, Heilige,
Treue, das gewiss, in irgend einer Periode des Daseins,
meiner dürstender Seele begegnen sollte. ..._
  _Wie in schweigender Luft sich eine Lilie wiegt, so regte
sich in seinem Elemente, in den entzückenden Träumen von
ihr, mein Wesen._

(My heart now locked away its treasures, but only in order
to save them for a better time, for that one-and-only, holy,
true one, who in some period of existence would surely encounter my thirsting soul. ...
  As a lily rocks itself in the quiet air, so my being moved
in its element, in its enchanted dreams of her.)

Although the first summer of the novel, following Adamas's
departure, passes very briefly and without being specified as
a particular season, certain features of Hyperion's feelings
share in the summer syndrome: his turning away from the deso-
lateness of his own times and feeding on his own imagination's
ability to produce better worlds in which to live. In particular his mind dissolves the distinctions of historical time by
projecting itself into a mythic-heroic past (1:28):

*Wie Flammen, verloren sich in meinem Sinne die Taten aller
Zeiten in einander, und wie in Ein frohlockend Gewitter die
Riesenbilder, die Wolken des Himmels sich vereinen, so ver-
einten sich, so wurden Ein unendlicher Sieg in mir die
hundertfältigen Siege der Olympiaden.*

(As flames, the deeds of all time were lost in one another
in my senses, and as the giant images, the clouds of heaven
unite in one exultant thunderstorm, so did the hundredfold
victories of the Olympics unite and become one endless
victory within me.)

The tendency here to daydream one's self out of the present
into an amorphous, timeless, and idealized past, and the tendency in the Smyrna summer to envision a likewise glorified
future, are combined in the visions of the Diotima summer.
The mind lives in past and future only; both are extratemporal
forms of time which, in their escape from the laws of time and
space, create a paradise of existence that protects the mind
from the bleakness of present circumstances *(1:125)*:

*Da übte das Herz sein Recht, zu dichten, aus. Da sagt'
es mir, wie Hyperions Geist im Vorelysium mit seiner hol-
den Diotima gespielt, eh er herabgekommen zur Erde, in
göttlicher Kindheit bei dem Wohlgetöne des Quells, und
unter Zweigen, wie wir die Zweige der Erde sehn, wenn sie
verschönert aus dem güldenen Strome blinken.
    Und, wie die Vergangenheit, öffnete sich die Pforte
der Zukunft in mir.
    Da flogen wir, Diotima und ich, da wanderten wir, wie
Schwalben, von einem Frühling der Welt zum andern, durch
der Sonne weites Gebiet und drüber hinaus, zu den andern
Inseln des Himmels, an des Sirius goldne Küsten, in die
Geisterhalle des Arcturs--*

(There my heart exercised its right to create fictions.
There it told me of how, in a Proto-Elysium, Hyperion's
spirit played with his beloved Diotima before it came
down to earth, there in divine childhood near the euphony
of the fountain, and under branches, as we see branches
on earth when they glance back at us, intensified in
beauty, out of the golden stream.
    And as the past, the portals of the future opened in me.

There we flew, Diotima and I, there we wandered like
swallows, from one springtime of the world to the other,
through the far realm of the sun and out beyond it, to
the other islands of heaven, to the golden coasts of
Sirius, into the spirit hall of Arcturus.)

Such images of the lone dreamer in divine contemplation,
in extremes of emotion which blend or fluctuate between deep
sadness and ecstatic bliss, are characteristic of the melancholic aspects of the Kronos-Saturn man. Relevant to the
passage just quoted, in its depiction of the mind leaving the
temporal constrictions of this world for other worlds, is
Hölderlin's own formulation in his "Anmerkungen zur Antigonae"
on the countertendency under the influence of Zeus (5:268):

Im Ernste lieber: Vater der Zeit oder: Vater der Erde, weil
sein Charakter ist, der ewigen Tendenz entgegen, das Streben
aus dieser Welt in die andre *zu kehren* zu einem Streben aus
einer andern Welt in diese.

(In seriousness rather: Father of time, or: Father of Earth,
because it is his character, against the eternal tendency,
to turn *man's striving from out of this world into the next*
into *a striving out of the other world into this one.)*

Hyperion's visions are completed, however, in even more specific form as he projects his image of Diotima *(1:126):*

Ich lebt in Gedanken an sie. Wo bist du, dacht ich, wo
findet mein einsamer Geist dich, süsses Mädchen? Siehest
du vor dich hin und sinnest? Hast du die Arbeit auf die
Seite gelegt und stützest den Arm aufs Knie und auf das
Händchen das Haupt und gibst den lieblichen Gedanken dich
hin?

(I lived in thoughts of her. Where are you, I thought,
where will my lonely spirit find you, dear girl? Are you
gazing, lost in thought? Have you laid your work aside;
are you propping your arm on your knee and your head on
your little hand, and are you surrendering to sweet
thoughts?)

The description of Diotima's bearing and mood is that of the
traditional personification of melancholy.[7]
 The results of reentering the reality of summer after the
six-day separation assume two opposing tendencies. At first,
the nocturnal vision seems to be translated into both a psychic
and a natural reality of the present. The heavenly bliss of
experiencing a Golden Age type of perpetual regeneration, of
eternal youth, is felt by Hyperion when he sees Diotima again:
"Es ist hier eine Lücke in meinem Dasein. Ich starb, und wie
ich erwachte, lag ich am Herzen des himmlischen Mädchens. ...
als blickt' es eben jetzt zum ersten Male in die Welt" (There
is here a gap in my existence. I died, and when I awoke once
more, I lay at the heart of the heavenly girl. ... as if she
were glancing into the world just now for the first time [1:
128]). Hyperion, who has died a psychic death, is now reborn
and greeted as the alter ego of the sun. Moreover, in his
divine birth as star, he stands there as the incarnation of
spring--clearly as perpetual youth: *"Aber er ist ja da, er ist*
hervorgegangen, wie ein Stern; er hat die Hülse durchbrochen
und steht, wie ein Frühling, da" (But he is of course here,
he has gone forth like a star; he has broken through the pod
and stands there like a spring [1:129]). In turn the whole
earth around them is as a new earth, harmonized with the paradisiac youth of the couple: *"Alles in und um uns vereinigte*
sich zu goldenem Frieden. Es schien, als wäre die alte Welt
gestorben und eine neue begönne mit uns, so geistig und kräf-
tig und liebend und leicht war alles geworden" (Everything in
and around us united in a golden peace. It seemed as if the
old world had died and a new one had begun with us, so soulful
and energetic and loving and light had everything become [1:
132]). This is the temporary realization of the nonmelancholic
aspect of Kronos, fateless and timeless, uniting creatures in
free association through love. In the same letter, however,
the tyranny of temporality encroaches. *"Mir war, als hätt ein*

unbegreiflich plötzlich Schicksal unsrer Liebe den Tod geschwo-
ren, und alles Leben war hin, ausser mir und allem" (It seemed
to me as if an incomprehensibly sudden fate had sworn death to
our love, and all life was lost, outside me and everyone [1:
134]). Thereupon, Diotima also feels that she has been alienated from the seasons.

This experience of time and, specifically, of death to
their love can be viewed from two perspectives, compatible at
this point. On the one hand, the awareness of transience in
the nature of things, painful as it may be, is a corrective to
the flights of the imagination away from the laws of time.
Conscious submission to the demands and restrictions of our
present existence is, mythically, recognition of the reign of
Zeus, *"Vater der Zeit."* Here we are introduced to the main
tendency of volume 2 of the novel. On the other hand, the
awareness of the coming terminal point in time, of death, is
an aspect of the melancholic nature of Kronos; he is the god of
death, the dethroned ruler for whom an earthly existence has
come to an end.[8] Historical time will now dominate Hyperion's
life--first in his visit to Athens, and then on the battlefield
of contemporary Greece. Furthermore, the human experience of
historical time and natural, seasonal time will suffer a falling apart.

In looking back from this summer with Diotima to the pre-
Diotima periods in Hyperion's life, we first note similarities,
alluded to earlier, between summer and winter experiences. We
have seen how the Kronos figure embraces extreme opposites:
brooding sadness and ecstatic bliss, ageless youth and desolate
death. The opposite seasons of summer and winter, when the
earth is closest to and farthest from the sun, can also, in
their opposition, be united through certain qualities. Their
polarity is most obviously a natural one: the "flame" and vege-
tative luxuriance of summer versus the cold and barrenness of
winter. But, to follow a familiar theme of Hölderlin, as the

sun in its hyperintensity can kill, one sees the possibility of
coincidence--in death--of these two ends of nature. The subjective image of summer experienced as a winter is more explicit.
The Smyrna summer finds Hyperion, in his human isolation from
the unreceptive people around him, seeing his surroundings as
a winter landscape *(1:37)*:

*Ich war es endlich müde, mich wegzuwerfen, Trauben zu suchen
in der Wüste und Blumen über dem Eisfeld. ...
Auch die Schwalbe sucht ein freundlicher Land im Winter, es
läuft das Wild umher in der Hitze des Tags und seine Augen
suchen den Quell.*

(Finally I was tired of throwing myself away, of looking
for grapes in the desert and flowers over the ice field. ...
The swallow too looks for a friendlier land in wintertime,
and the wild animal runs about in the heat of day, and his
eyes look for the spring.)

We have seen how the mind, to preserve itself from the
intense extremes of the world outside, turns inward and denies
recognition to the finite world of one's conscious mind. Such
a mental act occurs in the one specific winter of volume 1--at
the end of book 1--when Hyperion despairs of his seemingly
annihilated world. Another comment from the "Anmerkungen zur
Antigonae" seems appropriate to his condition (5:267):

*Es ist ein grosser Behelf der geheimarbeitenden Seele,
dass sie auf dem höchsten Bewusstsein dem Bewusstsein aus-
weicht, und ehe sie wirklich der gegenwärtige Gott ergreift,
mit kühnem, oft sogar blasphemischem Worte diesem begegnet,
und so die heilige lebende Möglichkeit des Geistes erhält.*

(It is a great aid to the soul working in secret that at
the highest point of consciousness it avoids being conscious,
and before it is seized for good by the ever-present God, it
encounters the latter with bold, often even blasphemous
words, and thus preserves the holy, living possibilities
of the spirit.)

Likewise, when Hyperion broods on the mind reaching out into the infinite, he can affirm only the void: *"Und kühn frohlok-kend drängen auch unsere Geister aufwärts und durchbrachen die Schranke, und wie sie sich umsahn, wehe, da war es eine unend-liche Leere"* (And bravely rejoicing, our minds also pressed upwards and broke through the boundary, and as they looked around, alas, what was there was an infinite emptiness [1:79]). As in the later summer, the time passes in self-isolated dream-ing through which the imagination tries to create new universes in which to escape time and death: *"Es ist, als wolltest du noch eine Sonne schaffen, und neue Zöglinge für sie, ein Erden-rund und einen Mond erzeugen. So träumt ich hin"* (It is as if you wanted to create a second sun and new pupils for it, as if you wanted to beget an earth and a moon. That is what I dreamed [1:72]). The narrating Hyperion gives the basic formulation for the similarity between this winter experience and the sum-mer experiences: *"Ein Vergessen alles Daseins"* (A forgetting of all existence [1:72, 73]). The distinction made is that in the latter all is as if found; in the former all is as if lost in an inner night.

An important temporal relationship for volume 1 emerges from this brief comparison of the summer and winter seasons. The summer visions in the Diotima section represent psychic aberrations in time from the course of the natural cycle. The mind attempts to escape from the aging process of nature, as one season yields to the next, by winding the inner timepiece back and regenerating youth, wandering then "from one spring of the world to another" (1:125). This suspension of the flow of time in one constant illusion of spring works for a while out of season. As long as Diotima is Hyperion's only world, even the trip to Athens seems *"wie das Leben einer neugebornen Insel des Ozeans, worauf der erste Frühling beginnt"* (like life on a newborn island in the ocean, on which the first spring is beginning [1:137]). Although the ruins of Athens bring Hyperion to a rude reawakening to historical time, the perception is being made at the end of volume 1 that the mind is at least tentatively able, and even self-compelled, to create a rhythm of inner life that is no longer forthcoming from nature when needed. An inner generation of time which is out of tune with the natural cycle is, however, an exception to the basic tendencies of the first volume.

The experience of Hyperion at the end of his Alabanda episode is one other clear, brief, and futile attempt to escape awareness of his circumstances. He feels bitter disappointment from his break with Alabanda, and a decline in his prospects which is consonant with the natural decline of this late fall to early winter period. A Kronos type of experience is subsequently described: the forgetting of time and regression back to childhood. He returns to Tina, his birthplace; it is to be a return, not simply to a geographical place but to the beginnings of life, to his childhood in all its restrictive comfort: *"Nur in kindlicher einfältiger Beschränkung fand ich noch die reinen Melodien"* (Only in childlike simple confinement could I still find the pure melodies [1:64-65]). In fact, on the boat, when it is still in coastal waters, his mind and memory are turned off and he experiences a childlike slumber: *"Mit einer wunderbaren Ruhe, recht, wie ein Kind, das nichts vom nächsten Augenblicke weiss"* (With a wonderful tranquility, quite like a child who knows nothing of the next moment [1:65]). The rude awakening is not, however, to regenerated youth but to his inability to hold the fleeting moment.

How strong is the irony of these moments? Hyperion cries out against subjection to *"eine fremde Gewalt"* (an alien force [1:67]) which determines his time as it does the earth's; it deflects him into his inner grave as it deflects the earth into its winter period in its elliptical orbit around the sun. When, by contrast, he has tried to return to a world-forgetting childhood, he has awakened looking back, to be sure, but not at childhood but rather with eager memory toward his Alabanda world slipping away. Two poles of time, the slumber of the mind and memory, are both unsatisfied. Memory may be more personal, historical, egocentric: it feeds on the real associations with Adamas and Alabanda; it makes the mind more aware of itself as something distinct--especially in the distant aridity of winter. But it is not yet strong enough to look to the future of its possibilities and, in this winter, its past does not comfort: even the first hints of spring are smothered by unfulfilled memories of the past *(1:75-76)*. And so the summer-type fantasies of the mind are in intensified combat, to the point of mutual negation, with more self-conscious recollections of crippled hopes. Of three alternatives--inner grave, childhood, future--the first, a naïve sharing of his hibernation with nature, has been canceled out by being seen as unconsoling force. In decline, nature's seasonal cycle is not Hyperion's desired tempo. Rather than the winter letting him feel its necessity in the cycle of life, it seems to engender the opposing struggle to be free of the cycle--even while being so much a part of it that spring touches him on an unconscious level.[9]

The periods leading up to this winter are less laden with conflict and are generally more naïve in their portrayal of the synchronization of the natural seasons and the inner cycles of Hyperion. This is especially effective, since no real period of natural decline is described until the Alabanda encounter. The narrator dwells on the spring seasons, brief as they are. Spring and youth are not merely coincidental. Spring *is* youth. Spring is not merely one season of four, it is the sun of regeneration, and that sun symbolizes eternal, timeless youth: it is the *"ewig jugendliche Sonne"* (eternally youthful sun *[1:22]*). To the extent that none other than the ascending sun appears to exist, the feeling of a golden harmony with an ageless world seems natural. All is in effortless communion--child, sun,

stars, planets, plants--for a natural peace. There are signs
enough of time and death in the ruins and the people, but nature
manages to dominate with her illusion of the Golden Age. The
episodes contribute to the illusion: a reincarnation of spring
via a visit to the sun god of Delos with Adamas. And, structurally: Hölderlin puts two springs nearly back to back, with
only the brief summer-like season intervening to cover the
disappointment from Adamas's departure until the arrival in
Smyrna. When Adamas had departed, the hint of a symbolic death
was conveyed: the departure took place at the grave of Homer
(1:26). So that Hyperion might not seem to have his private,
symbolic deaths and births prematurely out of tune with nature's,
his inner regeneration is saved for spring near Smyrna, at
Homer's birthplace *(1:31-32)*.

The Alabanda episode, the first of three explicit fall
seasons in the novel, is peculiarly ambivalent for both the
representation of Hyperion and our conception of Alabanda.
Alabanda is a composite image of youth and the opposing period
of his appearance, the declining fall season. An association
complex which has been developing since the departure of Adamas
is now projected onto the image that Hyperion has of Alabanda.
The heroic era becomes a model for Hyperion to hold up to his
own age and, more importantly, a temporal and psychic refuge
from its inadequacies and from the impotence of his own contemporary role. Hyperion's birth-death association, first with
Homer's grave and then with the poet's birthplace, introduced
him indirectly into a heroic age of the past. The summer in
Tina, with its feature of psychic hibernation away from the
awareness of time progression, was filled with *"Riesenbilder"*
(images of giants) of a time when *"wie mutig, seelige Natur!
entsprang der Jüngling deiner Wiege! wie freut er sich in
seiner unversuchten Rüstung"* (how spirited, blessed nature!
the youth leaped from your cradle! How he rejoiced in his un-
tested armor! [*1:28*]). Even in the Smyrna spring the landscape

was infused with the dynamics of a heroic era: *"Zur Linken stürzt' und jauchzte, wie ein Riese, der Strom in die Wälder hinab"* (To the left, shouting with joy, the stream, like a giant, tumbled down into the woods [*1:33*]). What had existed in the mind and beyond the sharp contours of historical time as images of the heroic assumed the semblance of temporal reality in nature--as the regeneration of youth in spring. Now in the fall, at what is naturally the season opposed to regeneration, the youth experience assumes human form. The heroic is the element in common to both seasons in their opposition.

There is no rationale for a consistent application of the Kronos-Zeus dichotomy to all questions of temporal relationships in the novel, but here again I believe the Kronos figure is relevant and helpful to our understanding. The image cast of Alabanda is initially not merely heroic but titanic. The time sense is thereby made less specific, mythically closer to the beginnings of man, and part of the Kronos legend. (It is also here that the Platonic thoughts on aging and rejuvenating are introduced.) The first sight of Alabanda is as if of a titan: *"Wie ein junger Titan, schritt der herrliche Fremdling unter dem Zwergengeschlechte daher"* (Like a young titan, the splendid stranger walked along among the race of dwarfs [*1:40*]). Attributes of the titans such as wildness, disregard for authority or restrictions of any kind, self-centered power to break through finite limits--all appear in the descriptions of Alabanda. In an astronomical metaphor Hyperion takes pleasure, and not for the first time, *"diesem Geist auf seiner kühnen Irrbahn zuzusehn, wo er so regellos, so in ungebundner Fröhlichkeit, und doch meist so sicher seinen Weg verfolgte"* (in watching this spirit follow its bold wayward path, where he pursued his way so lawlessly, in such unbounded joy, and yet for the most part with such sureness of step *[1:51]*). A more Platonic aspect of the titan in the Kronos era is suggested by an interjection on the part of the narrator: *"Wo bist du?*

*Ich glaube fast, du bist ins unbekannte Land hinübergegangen,
zur Ruhe, bist wieder geworden, wie einst, da wir noch Kinder
waren"* (Where are you? I almost believe you have gone over to
the unknown land, to peace, that you have once again become as
you once were, when we were but children *[1:44])*. The suggestion is a reversal of growth of the titan, born in full youth
from nature's womb, backwards to childhood.[10]

Of particular interest to us is that the youth image implies the exclusion of the aging process from life and thus
counteracts any personal identification with nature's periodicity. This tendency is also evidenced in the treatment of
personal histories. We are told that Alabanda relates his past
to Hyperion but, unlike the later time with Alabanda in the
fall of volume 2, book 2, we hear only: *"Er erzählte mir nun
sein Schicksal; mir war dabei, als säh ich einen jungen Herku-
les mit der Megära im Kampfe"* (He now narrated to me his life;
it seemed to me in the telling as if I were seeing a young
Herakles in combat with Megaera *[1:52])*. The metaphor translates personal history into the heroic form. Our time sense
is being manipulated so that we look past any temporal conditions to the present. The stylistic effectiveness of a life
history recapitulation would also be one of retardation, where
moments of time are held in their original flow and can, by
contrast, heighten temporal awareness. Here, for awhile, the
seasonal and personal aging process is muted through the additional aid of conversation about future action for Greece.

The opposing pressure of passing, declining time intrudes
by the very introduction of recollection. After the first
break with Alabanda, Hyperion begins to live from their pre-
break days: *"Da ich einst in heitrer Mitternacht die Dioskuren
ihm wies. ... Da ich die Wälder des Ida mit ihm durchstreifte"*
(That once when in clear midnight I showed him the Dioskouroi.
... When I roamed through the forests of Mount Ida with him
[1:61]). Remembering his own past is not simply the basic

feature of Hyperion's writing of the letters; it occurs within
the narrated past at especially those transitional moments when
the temporal quality of life intrudes on the consciousness. I
have discussed how this occurs on the boat after Hyperion leaves
Alabanda; it also marks the passing of spring into summer in
the Diotima period of volume 1, book 2. The act of recollect-
ing is actually initiated by the human objectification of the
seasonal ebb. Alabanda's youth identity fluctuates with its
opposite through association with the Nemesis group, the post-
harvest reapers and plowers *(1:57-59);* politically, humanly,
and seasonally they are *"am Abend unsrer Tage"* (in the evening
of our days *[1:58]),* to avenge the rape of the earth by man but
not to restore it nor partake in its rebirth.

So we are left with the unresolved opposition of a youthful
titan in an aging season of barrenness. Such a polarity is
somewhat analogous to the composition of melancholy, as we have
examined it for the six-day summer period of the next book.
The basic difference is the meditative, visionary aspect of the
summer experience in contrast to the activistic form of this
fall encounter. The basic nexus for the two seasons is the
projecting of an eternal youth existence, with all of the joy
it evokes, over and against the present experiencing of time in
the extreme as death, with all of the sadness that this presen-
timent evokes. A further contrast is that spring love, as a
harmonizing experience, prepares the Diotima summer, whereas,
in direct contrast, the self-centered image of the hero has
shaped the Alabanda fall.

The titan identity of Hyperion is a thwarted aberration
from natural space-time orbiting for the sake of self-determination. At this fall point, the titan notion can be described
as ambivalent: it is an aspect of the Kronos myth and yet it
tends to function counter to the Plato version of the age of
Kronos.[11] The titanic impulse to be law unto oneself, specifically in a period antithetical to the ageless nature of the

titan--namely in the fall and, generally, the present modern
era--evidences signs of what, for Plato, is the feature of the
age of Zeus. Alabanda, with his total faith in the "god within
himself" and his distaste for otherworldly *Schwärmerei* (ecstasy),
can be considered essentially a figure belonging to the Zeus era.
He is introduced, however, in a period of Hyperion's life with
dominant Kronos tendencies and is seen from the Kronos point of
view.

If ever the Kronos inclination of volume 1 approximates the
reality of eighteenth-century Greece, it is in the spring with
Diotima. Most importantly, and simply, Hyperion experiences a
rebirth that is synchronous with that of nature; moreover, the
experience is one of effortless integration in which all forms
of life assume interacting patterns of unity. The picture is
quite different from the wilder, more individuated impression
of the previous spring in Smyrna. On the other hand, it is not
civilized; the human mind has not impressed its own order on it.
The spirit of love is the immanent agent of the harmonization
objectified in nature: *"Und all dies war die Sprache Eines*
Wohlseins, alles Eine Antwort auf die Liebkosungen der entzük-
kenden Lüfte" (And all this was the language of one well-being,
all of it one answer to the caresses of the charming breezes
[1:89]). Hyperion has not had to create this scene of youthful
timelessness in his mind and beyond the present, as he has and
will in the summer, but is obviously conscious of it as a
present reality. Diotima, through the love relationship, will
thereupon embody the human fulfillment of this natural event.

For the first time, Hyperion can feel himself determined
by a force outside himself and feel a self-fulfilling identity
between being determined and determining himself: *"Eine fremde*
Macht beherrschte mich. Freundlicher Geist, sagt ich bei mir
selber, wohin rufest du mich? nach Elysium oder wohin?" (An
alien power ruled over me. Friendly spirit, I spoke to myself,
where are you calling me? to Elysium, or where? [1:89]). So

long as the season lasts, the physical force that draws together
earth and sun is a reconciling guardian spirit of the psyche--
and Hyperion has discovered his Elysium of the Golden Age.[12]

An example of parallelism will point out the distinctness
of this Elysium quality. The entry into spring, as if into a
new world, is made in somewhat mythological fashion: the spatial
passage from one place to another is also a temporal passage
from one world of time to another--specifically, from the world
of temporality to timelessness. Drinking of forgetfulness from
the river Lethe is necessary in transit. The journey from
Smyrna to Tina at the end of volume 1, book 1 was an attempt
at such a rebirth into childhood. An analogous journey introduces volume 1, book 2--from Tina to Kalaurea *(1:86)*:

Ich gab mich hin, fragte nichts nach mir und andern, suchte
nichts, sann auf nichts, liess vom Boote mich halb in Schlum-
mer wiegen, und bildete mir ein, ich liege in Charons Nachen.
O es ist süss, so aus der Schale der Vergessenheit zu trinken.

(I surrendered myself, asked nothing about myself or others,
looked for nothing, had designs on nothing; I let myself be
rocked half to sleep by the boat and imagined I was lying in
Charon's skiff. Oh, it is sweet thus to drink from the cup
of forgetfulness.)

The vast difference in these basically identical moments is
that now the psychic trip is not forced out of the natural cycle
and the awakening is into a present that reflects the childlike
beginnings that the mind needs. Hyperion, in turn, finds timeless present in Diotima: *"Sie aber stand vor mir in wandelloser*
Schönheit, mühelos, in lächelnder Vollendung da. ... Sie war
mein Lethe, diese Seele, mein heiliger Lethe, woraus ich die
Vergessenheit des Daseins trank" (But she stood before me in
unchanged beauty, effortless, in smiling perfection. ... She
was my Lethe, this soul, my sacred Lethe, out of which I drank
the oblivion of life *[1:103-4])*.

Clearly, Hyperion identified Diotima with spring, and as
long as this particular spring lasts neither is viewed from the
aspect of temporality. When Hyperion exclaims: *"Lass allen
Tugenden die Sterbeglocke läuten! ich höre ja dich, dich, dei-
nes Herzens Lied, du Liebe! und finde unsterblich Leben, indessen alles verlischt und welkt"* (Ring the knell for all virtues!
It is you I hear, you, the song of your heart, Beloved! and I
find immortal life while all is extinguished and wilts [1:120]),
we have good reason to recognize the transition from spring to
summer. Lethe is yielding to the awareness of time change in
nature. Early in the spring the narrator had promised a rein-
tegration of the spirit of man into the earth's rhythm of life,
as determined by its orbit around the sun, *"wo uns ist, als
kehrte der entfesselte Geist, vergessen der Leiden, der Knechts-
gestalt, im Triumphe zurück in die Hallen der Sonne"* (where it
seems to us as if the unfettered mind, having forgotten sorrow,
its shape in servitude, were to return in triumph into the halls
of the sun [1:93]). The integration proves only temporary, as
Diotima also discovers when she falls out of the seasonal rhythm
in the summer as the price of her love.

New alignments of the mind-world temporal relationship do,
however, result from this summer experience. A quality of duration can be perceived even in the transience of the moment.
The coming fall of the year will reflect its own beginnings of
the spring. What Hyperion then glimpses in a moment of nature's
time of the wholeness of life, he can generate in the human time
of the present. As he says: *"Ideal ist, was Natur war"* (What
was nature's comes to partake of the ideal [1:112]); or, as
Diotima asserts in a way more appropriate to the creating of
the novel itself: *"Wer jenen Geist hat, ..., dem stehet Athen
noch, wie ein blühender Fruchtbaum. Der Künstler ergänzt den
Torso sich leicht"* (Whoever has that spirit, ..., for him
Athens still stands like a fruit tree in blossom. The artist
easily completes the torso for himself [1:152-53]). Diotima

challenges Hyperion to go into the world and instill new life
in a declining people. Inasmuch as it is her own sense of
mortality in a period of decline that gives rise to her call,
she moves closer to the position that Alabanda had once had
for Hyperion. The intersecting of the two figures' lines is
indicated by a shared allusion in which, for Diotima and Alabanda both, Hyperion is the Pollux who infuses his mortal
brother with the immortality of his spirit: *"Da werd ich
frohlocken, als hättst du mir die Hälfte deiner Unsterblichkeit, wie Pollux dem Kastor, geschenkt"* (Then I will rejoice,
as if you had made me the gift of half of your immortality,
as did Pollux to Kastor [1:159]).[13]

The foreshadowing of Alabanda's reentry into Hyperion's
life through the final scene of volume 1 is of structural consequence. Not only does Hyperion reverse the poles of seasonal
progression from spring in volume 1 to fall in volume 2, but
he also reverses the seasonal identifications of Alabanda and
Diotima for book 1 of volume 2. From Alabanda-fall to Diotima-
spring in volume 1, we proceed in volume 2 to the sequence:
Diotima-fall to Alabanda-spring. The modification of these
reversals in book 2 will result in an even more important
meshing of the opposing tendencies of volumes 1 and 2.

Book 1 of volume 2 begins in the form of a retarded fall
season, a fall which first through memory bears signs of the
previous spring: *"Wir erinnerten uns des vergangenen Mais, ...
so mühelos, so seeligruhig, wie ein Kind, das vor sich hin
spielt, und nicht weiter denkt"* (We remembered the May just
past, ... as effortlessly, as tranquil of soul as a child who
plays and thinks no further [2:4]). It is a rather elegiac
alternation of the previous fall in Smyrna imbued with its
heroic tone. Both fall seasons juxtapose the opposing elements
of youth and decline. But now, by contrast, a calm develops
from an identity of these two poles of time. Both seasons of
spring and fall reflect coincidental aspects of duration and

transience, suspended time and motion *("zögerten wandernde Vögel"* [migrating birds hesitated (ibid.)]) in the fall, and *"so voll unaufhörlichen Wachstums und doch auch so mühelos"* [so full of ceaseless growth and yet so effortless too (ibid.)] for the spring). There is, in fact, a sense of time progression for the spring which was not then evident but has been perceived only in retrospect. The mere perception of differing modes of time in the life process--and then the attempt to reconcile such differences--by way of the recollection of immediate past is a new development for Hyperion, not characteristic of his Alabanda fall.

But spring enters into this season in two directions, into the future as well as from the past. A forward-looking spring is superimposed on the present by Hyperion through the promise of great deeds and of a new political life aroused by Alabanda's letter. Spring is regenerated as a memory and then as a psychic actuality, regardless of the season, by Hyperion's attitude toward battle.

A persistence in resolved ambivalence imbues the winter moment of parting from Diotima. While the symbolic suffering of winter is done justice by their own suffering in separating, Hyperion, soon thereafter in his first letter to Diotima, relates his awakening from the *"Tode des Abschieds"* (death of departure [2:21])--the antipode to a natural winter experience. By the time early spring has arrived, he has long been there mentally. This first letter to Diotima must be thought of as a counterpart to the beginning of his Diotima relationship. For here in distance from her he again experiences rebirth after having passed through a semblance of the river Lethe, living now only in the action of the present: *"Ein Gott muss in mir sein, denn ich fühl auch unsere Trennung kaum. Wie die seligen Schatten am Lethe, lebt jetzt meine Seele mit deiner in himmlischer Freiheit und das Schicksal waltet über unsre Liebe nicht mehr"* (There must be a god in me, for our separation

I hardly feel. As the blessed shades of Lethe, my soul now
lives with yours in heavenly freedom, and fate no longer rules
over our love [2:22]). Here is a double contrast in the identity of the two periods: rejuvenation in the winter rather than
in the spring, and the source of action has now been turned
over to Hyperion rather than being a *"fremde Macht"* (alien
power) as before.

The quality of youth in the winter setting is reinforced
by Hyperion's being back at the same place he visited as a youth
with Adamas--the Peloponnese *(2:22)*--and by his renewed impression that Alabanda is a youth (despite facial features to the
contrary [2:27]). The irony of temporal contrasts is compounded
by Diotima's condition. Her first letter from the spring (the
appropriate time to reintroduce her) betrays a psyche in winter
opposition to both the season and Hyperion. It is only through
memory of the past that she knows the spring experience, so
out of tune is she with the present seasons *(2:31-33)*. For
Hyperion, on the other hand, his springtime at the initial
height of battle seems to actualize what had been only a con-
struct for his mind during the earlier fall with Alabanda; his
soldiers are as titans rising from the earth in armored youth
(2:36-37):

> ... *nach unzähligen Jahren klimmt noch in uns ein Sehnen
> nach den Tagen der Urwelt, wo jeder die Erde durchstreifte,
> wie ein Gott, ... Diotima! mir geschieht oft wunderbar,
> wenn ich mein unbekümmert Volk durchgehe und, wie aus der
> Erde gewachsen, einer um den andern aufsteht und dem Mor-
> genlicht entgegen sich dehnt, ...*

> (... after countless years there still aspires within us a
> longing for the days of the primordial world, in which
> everyone strode through the earth like a god, ... Diotima!
> often I have a wonderful feeling when I walk among my un-
> perturbed people, and one man after another stands up as
> if having grown out of the earth, and stretches toward
> the morning light, ...)

Although Hyperion has had an extra-long spring existence
by virtue of having anticipated the natural spring, the functioning of his own inner tempo also accelerates his inner cycles
in contrast to the natural cycle of life. By what is approximately the end of spring, the fall phenomenon of retardation of
time sets in--expressed in the standstill of indecisive battle.
Moreover, now the second main element from the Alabanda fall
season of volume 1, book 1 is added to the titan aspect, so
that a basically complete projection of that fall is superimposed upon the action of this spring, creating through the identity of the opposing seasons a new image of that season's unresolved polarity. The barren, harvestless earth, previously
associated with Alabanda's Nemesis group, is the late spring
picture left to Hyperion by his plundering soldiers: *"Diese
trauernde Erde! die nackte! so ich kleiden wollte mit heiligen
Hainen, so ich schmücken wollte mit allen Blumen des griechischen Lebens!"* (This sorrowing earth! The naked one! Whom I
wanted to clothe with sacred groves, whom I wanted to adorn
with all flowers of Greek life! *[2:46]*). Full cycle is made
when summer is upon Hyperion and the suicidal wish to die in
battle is uttered in his last letter to Diotima from volume 2,
book 1. The death attempt puts him in obviously diametric
opposition to the natural life cycle.[14]

The two facts: (1) that the period between the last letter
of book 1, from July 4, 1770, to the first letter of book 2
represents a death-birth experience; and (2) that the duration
of unconsciousness was six days, put this summer episode into
a parallel relationship to the previous summer's six-day eclipse-
melancholy period. By contrast, what was then a visionary
experience is here one of reality, where even the inner senses
are eclipsed. Moreover, one of the novel's most fascinating
examples of structuring precision now ensues. Hölderlin here
exploits the unique potential of the epistolary form. By the
simple device of spacing the late letters of Diotima he is able

to constitute a new synchronization of seasonal and psychic
time periods.

When Hyperion is half healed from his sickness it is the
height of fall. From the blessing of his birthlike reawakening
he experiences a new balancing of spring with fall--renewed
youth with fruition. The simultaneity of the opposites of the
life cycle now expresses the changelessness of nature. In
distinction to the previous fall with Diotima--as well as to
the earlier one with Alabanda--the maturation process itself
reflects a timeless spirit of youth; the mind's awakening has
apparently projected into nature, and then found its new consciousness in it, without recourse to an elegiac remembrance
of a past spring *(2:63)*:

*Es war ein grosser, stiller, zärtlicher Geist in dieser
Jahrszeit, und die Vollendungsruhe, die Wonne der Zeiti-
gung in den säuselnden Zweigen umfing mich, wie die er-
neuerte Jugend, so die Alten in ihrem Elysium hofften.
... das kindliche Leben der Welt ... und die selige
Natur war wandellos in ihrer Schöne geblieben.*

(There was a great, quiet, gentle spirit in this season,
and the peace of perfection, the pleasure of the ripening
in the whispering branches embraced me like that renewed
youth the ancients had hoped for in their Elysium.
... the childlike life of the world ... and blessed
nature had remained unchanged in its beauty.)

It is at this moment in nature--the moment of discovering the
timeless in time--that Diotima's first letter of this book ar-
rives. It is in itself a reminder of human time, and specifically of a piece out of Hyperion's lowest moment in the past.
It answers the second-to-last letter written by Hyperion as a
farewell in early summer and received by Diotima in late summer.[15] In it he must relive two kinds of loss, the loss of
the people of Greece as Diotima describes their previous late-
summer visit to the ruins of Athens, and the more personal loss

of purpose in his life which he felt when he had written his
own letter. Consequently, a curious reflex must occur in him
when she understands his decision to give up his own life and
return *"ins heilge, freie, jugendliche Leben der Natur"* (into
the holy, free, youthful life of nature *[2:73]*). On the one
hand, he can understand the meaning which she salvages from
his disaster because he has found fulfillment, unknown to her,
in the present fall season. On the other hand, he is forced
to find that same fulfillment from the perspective of his own
change and loss; this perspective had apparently not played a
role in his present fall condition.

    These factors must affect Hyperion's answer, for he thinks
backward to recapturing the life of spring calm with Diotima,
to retreating into a sylvan, Edenesque haven (with features of
a summer shelter *[2:76-77]*). The effect of this epistolary
retracing of past seasons is to enhance the sense of retarded
time in the present season. The effect of this, in turn, is
gradually to bring the past as relived in the letters into
alignment with the present. The autonomously operating seasonal
clocks of the characters' psyches are being reintegrated into
the natural seasonal movement. The effect shows when the moment
begins to assume more of its true fall shape of a *"Schattenland"*
(land of shadows *[2:78]*); the presence of fallen foliage is
noted more sharply than before *(2:79)*. Diotima and Alabanda,
the representatives of opposing seasons, spring and fall, make
indirect contact in this fall season as they both look to the
end of their cycles in the approaching winter *(2:79-82)*.

    The last, extensive letter of Diotima, answering Hyperion's
last summer suicide letter, is written in the fall and received
in late fall. It thus contributes to the final integration of
the different time periods of the letters, letter-writers, and
letter-receivers. Continuity of time is achieved by this integration of times. We, Alabanda, and Diotima appear at this
point to have gained one vital insight still unabsorbed by

Hyperion. As Alabanda and Diotima reach the present end of the
year with their reflections and with their lives, they also look
forward. What they see is not only the death season of winter
but also a festive dawn; they see the continuation of the regenerative process both in nature and in the spirit of man--an
approximation of a Kronos-Zeus synthesis.[16] The coming vision
of Hyperion in the spring, in conjunction with the act of revis-
iting his life through these letters, remains before he knows
the sense of the rewinding which he has just undergone.

I feel that it is particularly appropriate that Hyperion's
concluding vision, evoked as if by the voice of Diotima, occurs
in spring. Through the course of the first half of the novel
especially, we have been accustomed to associating pensive,
visionary moments in solitude with the melancholic aspect of
summer. The contents of such visions of timeless youth are
now born into time; perceived against the background of nature's
and Diotima's youthful spring beauty and Alabanda's indestruc-
tible spirit, they are seen for the first time by Hyperion to
endure in and through the periodicity of the life cycle.

That the vision is the vehicle of insight *("Worte ...,*
wie des Feuers Rauschen" [words ..., like the roar of fire
(2:122)]) at this concluding moment in the narrated past is
also of particular interest for Hyperion's role in the narrating present. The form of Hyperion's vision is an apt stage of
transition into his artist's role. A final appeal to a Kronos-
Zeus distinction may be useful. We know from Hölderlin's poem
"Natur und Kunst oder Saturn und Jupiter" that Jupiter-Zeus is
the patron of art; it is also a long tradition that Kronos,
in his melancholic aspect, is the god-planet under which divine
madness--that is, poetic inspiration and prophecy--flourishes.
The two faces of the poetic muse are distinct: the prophetic
is the voice of the life of the earth; the artistic is the
projection of the free and conscious mind, operating in the
Zeus world. Diotima introduces the prophetic voice in volume

2, book 2. She was once one with the childlike *"Leben der Natur"*
(2:102), and by having lost this identity and having felt the
tones of changing time, she looks to the eternal composition of
life in which she will continue to exist after death. Consonant
with viewing book 2 of volume 2 as the reconciling of the Zeus
and Kronos worlds, Diotima's role as prophetic muse functions
as a bridge between the two.

She fulfills not only the Melancholia personification in
which Hyperion had seen her two summers before, but she also
challenges Hyperion to reveal--and to give life to--her visions:
*"Hyperion! Hyperion! hast du nicht mich, die Unmündige, zur Muse
gemacht?"* (Hyperion! Hyperion! have you not made me, artless as
I was, your Muse? *[2:71]*).[17] Her last letter describes her role
for Hyperion even more explicitly *(2:96-97)*:

*Eine Kraft im Geiste, vor der ich erschrak, ein innres Leben,
vor dem das Leben der Erd erblasst' und schwand, wie Nacht-
lampen im Morgenrot--soll ichs sagen? Ich hätte mögen nach
Delphi gehn ... eine neue Pythia.*

(A strength in the spirit before which I started up, an inner
life before which the life of earth paled and vanished like
night lamps at dawn--should I say it? I would have liked to
go to Delphi ... a new Pythia.)

The prophetic spirit is moved to speak of the ageless soul of
the world, from which the artist must feed in order to create
the living unity for his world of temporal figures.

It has been well demonstrated that ultimate reconciliation
for Hyperion as artist occurs through the act of present narration of the past.[18] My examination of temporal relationships
in the structuring of the novel must end, for this paper only,
with the presentation of narrated past. It may suffice to say
that the narrating Hyperion does not simply respond--and develop
through his responses--to the time periods as they unfold solely
from his past. He has his own temporal cycles in the present,

which are coordinated in various juxtapositions with the temporal rhythms of the past. Patterns arise in this fashion which are analogous to those already examined: coordination of identical seasons under contrasting aspects, of contrasting seasons under identical aspects. The richness of variation cannot be as great in the present as in the past, especially since the commentary fades markedly in volume 2. Yet much of such narrative reflection as has an anticipatory effect for the past narration proceeds not only from a general temporal overview of the past, but also from the seasonally contrasting perspective of the present to the past moment. The present mode of time can, in its difference from the past mode, establish an increasingly complementary and balanced relationship with the past. There is also some reason to see a modified form of a Kronos-Zeus temporal structure established in the present and in reversed pairing with the temporal structure of the past. The effect is a faint echo of the opposite tendencies of the past being resolved in unity.

Hölderlin's *Hyperion:* A Romantic Novel?

by Lawrence Ryan

I

From the point of view of genre, Hölderlin's novel *Hyperion* cannot easily be placed in the history of the German novel. Its apparently lyrical language has, in fact, led many to deny it altogether the status of a fully formed novel. But this characteristic can well deceive the reader as to the care with which Hölderlin attempted to maintain a consistent narrative perspective through the use of complex temporal layers and an organized, stage-by-stage development of various areas of experience. Thus he attempted not merely to retain the accepted characteristics of the genre, but indeed--in his own words--to venture into a terra incognita in the realm of poetry.[1] We must ask, then, whether a comparison with typical novel forms developed in Germany around 1800, and also with contemporary theories of the novel, can provide us new categories that will do justice both to the historically conditioned and to the more individual features of Hölderlin's conception.

First published in Jochen Schmidt, ed., *Über Hölderlin* (Frankfurt am Main: Insel, 1970), pp. 175-212.

180

In this context, a comparison with the confessional type of first-person novel such as Goethe's *Die Leiden des jungen Werthers* has often been suggested. Indeed, Hyperion has often been regarded as a younger brother of Werther who, instead of committing suicide, turns away from any attempt at worldly fulfillment in order to become a hermit (the subtitle of the novel is *Der Eremit in Griechenland*) and seek absorption into an all-embracing nature. That both novels use the epistolary form and in the main restrict themselves to a single letter-writer, emphasizes this similarity. Their differences, however, are more relevant to our particular question. The most obvious difference is that of narrative perspective, or rather the temporal distancing of the narrator from that which is narrated. Whereas Hyperion looks back on a completed sequence of experience which is recapitulated in his letters, Werther's letters have no real temporal distance from the occurrences they narrate. Thus for Werther reality is to a large extent shaped by his manner of describing it in his letters, and his lack of distancing reflection renders him incapable of surviving the loss of the fulfilled moment. This gives his mortal sickness its ultimate virulence. The lyrical aspect of the work—the lack of distance between narrator and narrated events—determines the essential structure of the book. At the end, the final objectivity can only be provided by an editor, who recounts the last days of Werther's life. It would seem that the term *lyrical novel*, insofar as it is useful at all, can best be applied to *Werther* rather than to *Hyperion*. For the structural principle of Hölderlin's work hinges upon the development and elaboration of precisely that distance between narrator and narrated experience that in *Werther* is only minimally present.

Many characteristics that are present in *Hyperion* but not in *Werther* seem to relate Hölderlin's work to the subgenre of the *Bildungsroman*, that supposedly peculiarly German form of

the novel. Indeed, the hero undergoes a continual progression
and development, in the course of which his original enthusiasm
is sobered by his confrontation with the outside world and with
other human beings. Finally, Hyperion approaches a reconciliation that Hölderlin, in his preface to the novel, describes as
"die Auflösung der Dissonanzen in einem gewissen Charakter"
(the resolution of dissonances in a particular character [1:3]).
(In *Werther*, of course, such a process of development is pre-
cluded from the outset.) The presence of this characteristic
in *Hyperion* makes it pertinent to ask whether the term *Bildungsroman* can be applied to the work.

This subgenre (or genre) is generally classified according
to the hero's goal and the path he takes to reach it (as, for
example, in the definition given by Hans Heinrich Borcherdt).[2]
But this kind of definition according to content does not seem
quite satisfactory, as it is based on other than artistic criteria. Can such aesthetic criteria be found? While Fritz Martini,
for example, has despaired of ever finding a typical formal
structure in the *Bildungsroman*,[3] we should at least wish to
raise the question whether the common content of works of this
genre is not conditioned by a particular narrative form, or
does not at least tend toward such a form. Most such works,
after all, are not narrated by the protagonist in the act of
developing and maturing, but from a superior or retrospective
standpoint--be it that the narrator who can see the plot as a
whole can comment ironically on the youthful aberrations of his
hero (as in Goethe's *Wilhelm Meisters Lehrjahre*), or be it that
the narrator, grown older, looks back upon his earlier life
(as in *Hyperion*). If the *Bildungsroman* has essential characteristics that distinguish it from biography and autobiography,
then its structural principle may perhaps have its origin in
the interplay of knowledge and action, in reflection upon the
nature and the necessity of the course of action followed, in
the representation of individual development as an exemplary

process.   There appear to be sufficient similar characteristics
to justify examining *Hyperion* in this context.

But as the very concept of the *Bildungsroman* seems questionable and its supposed characteristics are hardly meaningful unless further explained in other terms, one must not stop here.
It is perhaps no accident that a constant interplay of narration
and reflection, of creative and critical activity, is characteristic of another conception of the novel which, shortly after
the writing of *Hyperion*, was set forth by Friedrich Schlegel
and illustrated by him most fully in his review of Goethe's
Wilhelm Meister.[4]   The concept of a romantic novel in this sense
has hitherto not been consistently applied to *Hyperion*; but we
shall have to ask whether a comparison with this conception of
the genre categories will not enable us to go some way toward
situating *Hyperion* within the history of the novel.

II

If in *Werther* the very act of letter-writing is in a sense an
essential aspect of the novel, then this is even more clearly
the case in *Hyperion*, where the narration of past experience
becomes an essential part of the plot and even constitutes a
principle of organization that ultimately contains in itself
the sequence of narrated events.   Superficially viewed, nothing
actually happens in the course of the book, except that Hyperion
recounts the story of his previous life; but as he narrates it
he gains a totally new relationship to the events he describes,
in that he perceives in them a continuity and necessity of
which he had been unaware.   In this sense the narration of the
past may be seen as a continuation of the plot of the letters,
creating at the same time a second level that allows the narrator continually to reflect on the relationship of past to
present.

This kind of structure demands that the reader distinguish

between those passages that reproduce thoughts or feelings of
the earlier Hyperion and those that reflect the views of the
more mature narrator. It is deceptive, for example, to regard
the last letter of the book as the final standpoint of the
letter-writer. Here Hyperion is inspired by the visionary
appearance of Diotima at a celebration of nature, in whose
harmony all *"lebendige Töne zusammenstimmen"* and the *"Dissonanzen der Welt"* are resolved.[5] This seems to constitute a
confirmation of Hyperion's opening commitment to the life of
a hermit, integrated into the eternal cycle of nature. But
the passage is, in fact, merely a quotation of a previous stage
of development *("So dacht ich"* [So I thought *(2:124)]*): he does
not remain at the end resigned to his solitary fate, but is
ready to go forth as a priest of nature, an incipient poet
("die dichterischen Tage keimen dir schon" [already your days
as a poet are germinating *(2:104)]*).

It is to this readiness to go forth that Hölderlin refers
when he describes in his preface the intention of the novel as
"die Auflösung der Dissonanzen in einem gewissen Charakter."
Just as in the *Bildungsroman* the erring of the protagonist
constitutes a constructive formal element, so Hölderlin sees
the development of his hero in terms of *Irren* (error) and
Zurechtgewiesenwerden (correction). Hyperion's vacillation
between these two poles--the development Hölderlin describes
elsewhere to be *"die exzentrische Bahn"* (the eccentric path)--
largely determines the sequence of events.[6] Unlike the *Bildungsroman*, however, it is not the individual in his confrontation with the world, but an inner dividedness of man himself,
who vacillates between self-centered consciousness on the one
hand and a feeling of belonging to the wholeness of life on
the other. The self-glorification of the individual is seen
as *Irren*, because he thus cuts himself off from the wholeness
of nature; but nature herself corrects this one-sidedness by
directing him back to the uniting center of things from which

he had fallen away. Thus the compound loss, first of his
friend Alabanda, then of his beloved Diotima, is seen as a
personal blow of fate that plunges Hyperion into despair and
causes him to withdraw from the world. In the course of his
letter writing, however, he becomes able to accept separation
and loss as part of life itself: division and unity are seen
dialectically as aspects of an overriding whole.

What interests us here is that this change of emphasis is
not motivated solely by the actual course of events described,
but very much also by the act of letter-writing, which enables
the more mature Hyperion to distance himself from his earlier
experiences and to view them from a more objective vantage
point. Thus the vacillation between hope and despair is
matched by a constant interplay between the narrated experiences and the later reflections on them; previous attitudes
are repeatedly examined, modified, and taken up into a new view
of things as a whole, as the letter-writer progresses toward
the resolution of what had seemed to be dissonances into a complex unity that includes a principle of differentiation within
itself. Thus the novel, rather than returning to its starting
point as it at first appears to do, consists of a development
on two time planes, which become, however—in terms of the
gradual reduction of opposition to dialectical unity—a single
sequence, a kind of infinite progression toward a more comprehensive unity.

III

Returning to our analysis of the various forms of the novel,
we find two characteristics of *Hyperion* that diverge from the
customary scheme of the *Bildungsroman*. First, the more individual and empiric starting point of this genre—the young man
who develops through confrontation with the world—differs from
what one might call the transcendental orientation of *Hyperion*.

This orientation--as Friedrich Schlegel says in another con-
text--is intimately connected *"mit einer Reflexion über das
Verhältnis des Idealen und des Realen"* (with reflection on the
relation between the ideal and the real) and thus portrays not
so much the development of an individual into an integrated
member of society, as rather the relationship of nature to
consciousness in general.[7] Second, *Hyperion* not only retains
the distance between narrator and narrated experience that we
have characterized as a formal principle of the *Bildungsroman,*
but develops it in a far more differentiated way: Hölderlin
creates here a continuity of experience and narration, a constantly changing interplay of the two such as is hardly possible in a third-person novel and which even in the first-person
novel does not usually attain such paramount formal and thematic
significance. We may ask, therefore, whether these two characteristics suffice to enable us to assign *Hyperion* to a different
category of the novel.

As it happens, Goethe's paradigmatic novel *Wilhelm Meisters
Lehrjahre* was treated by Friedrich Schlegel in a review in which
he also sketched out his own conception of the romantic novel.
It may be useful to characterize here the main features of this
conception, which approaches the novel in such a way that new
connections become apparent. In particular, we shall have to
discuss the categories of progressivity, universal poetry,
irony, and the romantic novel as they apply first to Goethe's
novel, then to Hölderlin's.

It should be noted that Schlegel attributes to the individual maturation process on which Goethe's work happens to focus
only a subordinate significance:

*Nicht dieser oder jener Mensch sollte erzogen, sondern die
Natur, die Bildung selbst sollte in mannigfachen Beispielen
dargestellt, und in einfache Grundsätze zusammengedrängt
werden.*[8]

(Not this or that person ought to be educated, but rather
nature and culture themselves ought to be represented in
a multiplicity of examples and summarized in simple axioms.)

Even the portrayal of the theater in *Wilhelm Meister* is *"nicht
bloss, was wir Theater oder Poesie nennen"* (not merely what we
call theater or poetry), but *"das grosse Schauspiel der Menschheit selbst und die Kunst aller Künste, die Kunst zu leben"*
(the great play of humanity itself and the art of all arts,
the art of living); he speaks in this connection of *"der Weltgeist des Werks"* (the universal spirit of the work).[9] This
"Weltgeist" manifests itself not only in the superior view of
the narrator, but also in the structure of the work and in the
manner in which it begins with what Schlegel calls the most
circumscribed, but shows this to be a small part of the infinite world. Schlegel emphasizes that the novel, which starts
out on a small scale, gradually expands outward; each part of
the novel is on the one hand a *"System für sich"* (self-contained
system), but at the same time a preparation for what follows,
each part surpassing the preceding part in breadth and depth.
This development of the work Schlegel does not, however, regard
merely as a manifestation of the author's creative will, but
also as a reflection of a development inherent in nature itself:
he sees the novel as *"die Darstellung einer sich wie ins Unend-
liche immer wieder selbst anschauenden Natur"* (the portrayal
of a nature reflecting upon itself again and again, as if into
infinity).[10]

   The relationship of this conception to other statements
made by Schlegel is apparent, as can be shown by a comparison
with the famous "Athenäums-Fragment" No. 116, on *"progressive
Universalpoesie."*[11] In this fragment Schlegel shows that the
goal of progressive poetry is a unity that combines all themes
and all poetic forms, all levels of consciousness and all forms
of life. The impelling principle of this unity is poetic reflection, on whose wings universal poetry *"kann ... zwischen*

dem Dargestellten und dem Darstellenden, ... in der Mitte schwe-
ben, diese Reflexion immer wieder potenzieren und wie in einer
endlosen Reihe von Spiegeln vervielfachen" (can ... hover in
the middle between that which is portrayed and him who portrays
it, ... raise this reflection to an ever higher exponent and
multiply it as in an infinite series of mirrors). The progressive element refers to what Schlegel calls *Ironie:* the *"Unmög-*
lichkeit und Notwendigkeit einer vollständigen Mitteilung"
(impossibility and necessity of complete communication). The
concept of irony designates both the relationship of the work
to an absolute goal and the irrevocable distance that separates
it from its goal; in essence, it is a kind of infinite approximation.[12]

    We must ask, however, whether in Goethe's novel the prin-
ciple of progressivity is, in fact, perfectly maintained.
Schlegel points out that while Wilhelm Meister himself gains
in maturity and insight, he is still portrayed *"leicht und*
launig" (lightheartedly and capriciously) by the author, and
mentioned *"fast nie ohne Ironie"* (almost never without irony).[13]
But in contradistinction to Schlegel's analysis, it would seem
that the narrator also maintains an ironic distance from the
members of the *Turmgesellschaft.* This is manifested by the
inability of the latter, for all its seeming wisdom, to understand Mignon and the *Harfner;* and only Felix's bad habit of
drinking from the bottle instead of from the cup saves him from
death by poisoning and averts the threat emanating from the
harp player. In the final scenes it becomes evident that the
Turmgesellschaft does not even see the ramifications of its
own affairs as a totality, but imagines itself involved in an
apparently insoluble dilemma when Wilhelm's courtship of Therese
seems to place an obstacle in the way of her marriage to Lotha-
rio. In the last analysis there remains a subtle ambivalence
which resists any reduction to simpler terms.

    In respect to the reflection on the relation between the

ideal and the real, it would seem, then, that *Hyperion* comes
closer than *Wilhelm Meister* to Schlegel's model. One important
formal difference between the two novels is, however, that in
Hyperion the narrator and the protagonist are one and the same.
This means that the transition from the aberrations of the individual caught up in his own experiences to the knowledge of the
narrator, who sees his own life as a totality and projects it
against the distancing background of nature as a whole, can be
developed with much greater continuity. Whereas in Goethe's
novel there is an irreducible distance between narrator and
protagonist, Hölderlin's more self-contained method of presentation realizes more consistently the systematic intent of
Schlegel's review.

If the concept of progressivity implies an infinite approximation to a totality, it can be shown that the final stage
reached by Hyperion the narrator may indeed be so described.
The last words of Hölderlin's novel: *"Nächstens mehr"* (More
soon [2:124]), are no mere flourish of the letter-writer, nor
are they an indication of any planned continuation of the novel,
but rather they are an integral part of the narrative fiction,
in that they indicate the incomplete and incompletable nature
of narrative reflection.

There is another sense in which *Hyperion* corresponds more
exactly to Schlegel's concepts than does *Wilhelm Meisters
Lehrjahre*. In his review Schlegel speaks of the *Weltgeist*
of Goethe's novel and of nature reflecting upon itself; but
it never becomes clear why nature should so reflect, nor why
the novel should develop toward *Geist*. The novel contains no
reflection upon the relationship between the ideal and the
real that would throw light on such development. Such reflections do, however, take up considerable space in Hölderlin's
novel. The reflecting narrator gradually learns to see the
death of his beloved in its necessity, as the projection of
the divine into the temporal, and as a condition of the self-

revelation of totality. The self-oriented reflection of the
narrator recapitulating his own past coincides with the philosophical reflection concerning not only unity and separation,
but also the basis of unity and separation. In this sense the
novel realizes the early romantic demand for a union between
philosophy and poetry through the connection of poetic portrayal
with transcendental reflection.

IV

With respect to its double aim--the uniting of poetry with phi-
losophy--*Hyperion* may be compared with yet another contemporary
novel which, according to its author, was to expand into an
infinite realm, but which even in its fragmentary form realizes
the transcendental approach referred to--Novalis's *Heinrich
von Ofterdingen*. Whereas in the first part of this novel the
progress of a developing young man is the central focus, it
becomes apparent at least in the beginning of the second part
that Heinrich's development to poetic mastery also involves
the transformation of the world as a whole to poetry. In this
sense, the double formula: *"Die Welt wird Traum, der Traum
wird Welt"* (World becomes dream, dream becomes world [N 1:319])
is valid for the whole of the novel. Similarly, as another
passage puts it, *"jede Handlung des Meisters ist zugleich Kund-
werdung der hohen, einfachen, unverwickelten Welt--Gottes Wort"*
(every action of the master is at the same time a proclaiming
of the sublime, simple, uncomplicated world--God's word [N 1:
331-32]). Thus Novalis wished Heinrich's *Lehrjahre* to be
understood as *"Übergangsjahre vom Unendlichen zum Endlichen"*
(years of transition from the infinite to the finite).[14] But
this is the questionable point about the work. Heinrich's
path does not lead him through errors and suffering but is
rather a constant, conflict-free expansion of what is already
within him; the *Geist der Dichtkunst* is from the outset his

companion, making all Heinrich's fellow travelers function un-
noticed as its voices. The tension between the narrator and
the narrated action is hardly an explicit feature of the novel's
structure. The transcendental point of view is the overriding
one throughout, and this almost entirely excludes the tensions
and sufferings of empirically conditioned experience. One
constantly has the feeling that what is happening has already
happened long before, so that the dimension of time is largely
excluded. Not without reason did Novalis claim that the novel
should go over into the *Märchen;* this is exactly what happens
in *Heinrich von Ofterdingen.*

It seems, therefore, that Hölderlin's *Hyperion* has a certain right to be designated as an example of the romantic novel.
Of course, one cannot claim that it fulfills all of Schlegel's
criteria; but the fact that a perfect novel would have to be a
far more romantic work than *Wilhelm Meister*—or, for that matter, than *Hyperion*—is unimportant.[15] The very nature of such
a conception of the novel is that it is more an abstract requirement than an attainable goal, more a tendency than a fulfillment. But, more than the other novels we have discussed
here, *Hyperion* fulfills the requirement of reflection on the
relationship between the ideal and the real and illustrates
the theory of *progressive Universalpoesie.* Instead of regarding it as a first-person novel in the tradition of *Die Leiden
des jungen Werthers,* we can with some justification see in
Hyperion—rather than in *Heinrich von Ofterdingen*—the romantic
counterpart to *Wilhelm Meisters Lehrjahre.*

Lyrical Creativity and Schizophrenic Psychosis as Reflected in Friedrich Hölderlin's Fate

by Helm Stierlin

I

The year 1770--separated from the present by 200 years--witnessed the birth of three seminal personalities, all Germans: Georg Wilhelm Friedrich Hegel, Ludwig van Beethoven, and Friedrich Hölderlin. Yet while the genius of Hegel and of Beethoven was soon recognized, that of Hölderlin had to await its time in order to receive its due echo. Today, however, Hölderlin's star shines brightly, as many Germans have come to consider him their country's greatest lyrical poet. No other poet writing in German has become the subject of a similar renaissance or, perhaps more correctly, discovery. This discovery was made possible through some of the most painstaking philological research ever devoted to any writer. Once discovered, Hölderlin has fascinated authors with diverse backgrounds--Martin Heidegger (who devoted a volume of essays to Hölderlin), Bertolt Brecht, Paul Celan, Karl Jaspers, Theodor Adorno, Walter Benjamin, to name only a few.[1]

The reasons for the increasing interest in Hölderlin are certainly many. Should I be asked to name the main one, I

would single out his *timeless modernity*, using a paradoxical
phrase of the kind of which Hölderlin has coined so many. It
is, above all, the works of his late creative period--spanning
approximately the years from 1800 to 1806--that reflect this
quality of timeless modernity. And it is also these late works
that had to wait longest--more than 150 years--before their
extraordinary quality could be appreciated.

The term *late works* must, however, be qualified. For
Hölderlin, who lived to the age of seventy-three, was only in
his mid-thirties when he wrote these late works. We speak here
of late works because Hölderlin, during his final, incredibly
creative, period, became mad--and stayed mad until the time of
his death thirty-six years later. Following a year in a psychiatric hospital (the Autenriethsche Klinik in Tübingen) he led
a restricted life in a tower in the same city from 1807 until
1843, cared for by a carpenter by the name of Ernst Zimmer.
Hölderlin wrote only a few, relatively short, poems during
these last thirty-six years of his life. In their seemingly
childlike simplicity they would never suggest to the uniniti-
ated that they were written by one of Germany's greatest lyric
poets.

Hölderlin's madness has unanimously been diagnosed as a
form of schizophrenia. The concept *schizophrenia* (split mind)
as a diagnostic term has remained tainted by controversy.
Still there can be no doubt that Hölderlin was deeply disturbed
mentally, if not deranged, and that the label of schizophrenia
best fits his disturbance. From 1802 on he became irritable
and prone to uncontrollable rages. Later he appeared withdrawn
and subdued. He seemed unable to focus his attention for any
length of time; he was manneristic, servile in a mocking, exaggerated way; and he referred to himself by different names such
as Scardanelli, or Scaliger Rosa. It is doubtful, however,
whether he had any extensive delusional ideas. Neither is it
certain that he hallucinated.

In the following essay I want to consider some aspects of
the ways in which the development of Hölderlin's mental disturbance may have interlocked with his lyrical creativity. I
do so with trepidation, however. For, in attempting to link
what appears as psychopathology with creative achievement, I
must cope with two dangers. First, there is the danger of
becoming impoverishingly overexplanatory. Here I speak of the
temptation to explain in psychiatric or psychodynamic jargon
what by its nature cannot be explained through psychiatric
concepts--those qualities that make any creative work outstanding and unique. Such psychiatric overexplanations easily become another instance of what Whitehead has called "the fallacy
of misplaced concreteness" or, in blunter terms, of an irreverent, as well as inappropriate, reductionism. On the other
side, there is the danger of becoming overawed by the genius
and everything that pertains to him. This, then, can induce
an undue idealization of many aspects of his work and life.
Freud, in his essay on Leonardo da Vinci, has exemplified how
a biographic study can avoid these twin dangers. While bringing to light important aspects of da Vinci's life and works
through a psychoanalytic interpretation, he also has carefully
delimited the validity of this interpretation.[2]

Regarding the dangers just mentioned, Hölderlin had, I
believe, little luck with his psychologically inclined biographers. While his psychiatric pathographers--such as Lange,
Treichler, but also Jaspers--have tended to investigate him
with outdated reductionist models of psychopathy and schizophrenia in their minds, his nonpsychiatric biographers have
tended to view his personality and personal relation through
rose-colored, idealizing glasses. In their need to find in or
near him only the sublime, the heroic, the loving, and the
positive, these scholars have often closed their eyes to many
negatively tainted features that are important from a humane
and psychological point of view, such as the intrapsychic and

interpersonal drama of hatred, jealousy, ambivalence, and destructiveness with which Hölderlin, no less than other persons of creative genius, confronts us.[3] I shall try here to do justice to the positive as well as to the negative features of the poet's life and work--as much as the limited intent of this paper will permit. But before taking up these features, I must briefly reflect on some aspects of schizophrenia that seem relevant to my topic.

This cannot be the place to review the many complex and, to a large extent, still unresolved issues pertaining to the concept of schizophrenia. Suffice it to say that we have good cause to view schizophrenic disorders as the outcome of a life process which--contrary to views held by Jaspers and by many other European psychiatrists--can be understood. In this process we see, from the moment of birth and even before, an individual disposition interacting with a given human environment. This life process is circular insofar as disposition and environment affect and modify each other on ever new levels, thereby creating ever new transactional configurations which, in turn, imply changing dispositions and changing environments.

Although from this theoretical vantage point it appears problematical to use the concepts *disposition* and *environment* in an unqualified (that is, undialectical) manner, let us do so for a moment and consider separately these two ingredients in any human, and hence also potentially schizophrenic, development.

Regarding the disposition for schizophrenia, most available evidence suggests that it is relatively weak and unspecific. We must think of it at present as a rather common vulnerability to a wide range of stresses out of which a wide range of disorders might develop. For these latter the term *schizophrenic spectrum disorders* has been suggested. These disorders include not only cases of bona fide schizophrenia, but also character disorders, so-called inadequate personal-

ities, schizoid states, and others. In monozygotic twin pairs
with one schizophrenic member, we find a probability of only
25 to 45 percent that the co-twin--who supposedly has the same
hereditary endowment--will some day also be diagnosed as schizophrenic.[4] Yet further: careful studies of biologic and adoptive
relatives of schizophrenics, which were carried out in the
United States and abroad, suggest in addition that the same
disposition that may give rise to these schizophrenic spectrum
disorders may also--and this seems important in our present
context--give rise to creativity. For example, L. Heston, an
American researcher, compared two groups of approximately fifty
adopted children who had grown into adulthood. One group came
from biologic parents of whom at least one parent had been
diagnosed as schizophrenic. The other group of adoptees came
from biologic parents without any diagnosis of schizophrenia.
Among the children from schizophrenic parents Heston found five
cases of schizophrenia and, in the control group, none; however,
in the group of subjects who had schizophrenic parents, he also
found a sizeable number of individuals with an artistic and
unconventional bent and life style. In contrast, the individuals in the control group appeared uniformly mundane and conventional.[5]

Observations such as these make us ask: Can we discern
also in Hölderlin a disposition that harbors the potential for
creativity *and* schizophrenia? Can we find in him clues as to
how the ingredients for creativity and schizophrenia may become
perhaps inextricably mixed? I believe we can, although, admittedly, these clues are crude and provide at best circumstantial
evidence. So let us, with this question in mind, briefly look
at the personality of the poet as it has been described to us
by him and by persons who knew him well.

In a letter to his mother that Hölderlin wrote after he
had broken off his engagement to his first girl friend Luise
Nast, he resisted his mother's wishes that he marry and settle

down as a Protestant minister. In this letter we also find
him reflecting on his peculiar character, on his whims, on his
penchant for unrealizable projects, on his ambition and, above
all, on his fear of anything, any position or relationship,
that might tie him down.[6] From Hölderlin's adolescence on we
find many further references--by himself and by others--to his
mood swings, to his lacking joy in life, to his loneliness,
and to his eternal melancholic worrying. His fellow students
at the Tübinger Stift (theological seminary at Tübingen) noticed
his suspicious recalcitrance and called him *Holz* (wood). Hölderlin described himself in those days as a *Klotz* (blockhead).
But some of these same fellow students have also transmitted
an altogether different portrait of Hölderlin, that of a charming youth of incredible radiance and amiability. In Christoph
Theodor Schwab's Hölderlin biography we read (7:399):

*Die Freundschaft mit Hölderlin gewann schon durch seine
körperliche Schönheit etwas Idealisches; seine Studienge-
nossen haben erzählt, wenn er vor Tische auf und abge-
gangen, sei es gewesen, als schritte Apollo durch den Saal.*

(Friendship with Hölderlin gained an ideal quality by
his physical good looks alone; his schoolmates told of
how, when he would walk up and down before their table,
it seemed as if Apollo were passing through the room.)

We are made aware of the young poet's tender imagination, of
his passion for heroic metaphor, of his enthusiasm for all
that is truly great--here we remind ourselves that the etymol-
ogical origin of the word *enthusiasm* lies in Greek *en theos*
"the God in us"--and, perhaps most important, of his compulsion
constantly to objectify, to express, and to reflect on his
inner experiences, experiences which often seem to have baffled
him. Note, for example, the piece of self-reflection from his
early twenties in which he writes that he is sitting between
his dark walls, and calculates how abysmally poor he is in

terms of inner joys, and that he admires his resignation.[7]

We thus get a glimpse of completely intermixed personality traits and, judging from our present enlightened perspective, it seems fair to assume that they reflect a disposition to become a poet and/or a schizophrenic. Our next question, then, must direct itself to the second ingredient in the circular process I mentioned earlier: the human environment with which Hölderlin interacted during the formative and crucial periods of his life. This human environment consists, first, of his family and, second, of those important persons outside his family who engaged him while he seemed to be reaching a crossroads in his artistic and psychological development. Let me briefly comment on this environment and begin with his family.

Hölderlin, who was born into a small-town, middle-class milieu, lost his father at the age of two. His mother remarried two years later. Her new husband, the poet's stepfather, died of pleurisy when Hölderlin was nine years old. As an adolescent Hölderlin described movingly how much this death had shaken him. He had one sister who was two years, and one half brother who was six years younger. He corresponded with both siblings rather frequently but irregularly up to the time of his madness. His most important family tie was clearly that to his mother. Four times during his adult life he returned to her--at least twice abruptly--when for one reason or another he had failed to establish himself professionally. After his last return home, his mother arranged for his institutionalization as a psychiatric patient. Unfortunately we know little concerning what his mother was like, since only a few documents from her own hand--such as one letter written to the poet after her final will--have been transmitted to us. We know, however, a good deal about how Hölderlin reacted to her, as he wrote her numerous letters of which many are extant. On the next page I present the only preserved letter to the poet from his mother, which reads as follows (HW 6:371-72):

Allerliebster Sohn!
Ob ich schon nicht so glücklich bin auf mein wiederholtes
Bitten auch einige Linien von Dir mein Lieber zu erhalten,
so kann ich es doch nicht unterlassen, Dich manchmal von
unserer vordauernden Liebe und Andenken zu versichern. Wie
sehr würde es mich freuen und erheitern, wenn Du mir nur
auch wieder einmal schreiben wolltest, dass Du die l. Dei-
nige noch liebst und an uns denkest. Vielleicht habe ich
Dir ohne mein Wissen und Willen Veranlassung gegeben, dass
Du empfindlich gegen mich bist, und so bitter entgelten
lässest, seie nur so gut, und melde es mir, ich will es
zu verbessern suchen. ....
Besonders aber bitte ich Dich herzlich, dass Du die
Pflichten gegen unser l. Gott und Vater im Himmel nicht
versäumest. Wir können auf dieser Erde keine grössere
Glückseligkeit erlangen, als wenn wir bei unseren l. Gott
in Gnaden stehen. Nach diesem wollen wir mit allem Ernst
streben, dass wir dort einander wieder finden, wo keine
Trennung mehr sein wird.
Ich sende Dir anbei ein Wämesle und vier Paar Strümpf
und ein Paar Handschuh als einen Beweis meiner Liebe und
Andenken, ich bitte Dich aber, dass Du die wollene Strümpfe
auch trägst. ... Nebst unserm allerseitigen herzlichen Gruss
und Bitte, dass Du mich auch wieder mit etwas erfreust und
bald schreibst, schliesse ich mit der Versicherung, dass
ich unverändert verharre.
Nürtingen   *Deine*
d. 29. Oktober 1805   *getreue M. Gockin.*

(My dearest Son:
Although I am not so happy as to receive even a few lines
from you, after begging you repeatedly, my dear one, I
cannot help assuring you how much I love you and think of
you all the time. How joyous and delighted I would be if
only once again you would write me that you still love and
remember me, your dear mother. Maybe I have, without my
knowledge or intent, given you reason for being so easily
hurt and so bitterly vengeful. If this should be the case,
please let me know and I shall try to improve matters. ...
   Most of all I beseech you with all my heart not to become
amiss in your duties toward our dear God and Father in
heaven. We can on this earth obtain no greater bliss than
to stand in the grace of our dear God. Toward this God
let us strive with mighty seriousness so that we shall
find each other again in the Beyond where there shall be
no more separation.
   Enclosed I am sending you a woolen undershirt and four
pairs of socks and a pair of gloves as proof of my love
and thought of you. Yet please--do not forget to wear the
woolen socks after I have sent them to you. ... In adding

my most heartfelt regards and the request that you will
again make me a little happy and write me soon, I am closing with the assurance that I remain unchanged as ever.
  Nürtingen,   Your
October 29, 1805   faithful M. Gockin)

    This letter has touched many readers because of its seem-
ing childlike simplemindedness (which comes out even better in
the German original than in my slightly streamlined German
translation). Yet in order to grasp some of the psychological
impact and implications of this letter for Hölderlin, we must
remind ourselves that it was written when the poet was thirty-
five years old, when he had already been intermittently disturbed and had been in deepest emotional turmoil. (It was only
a short time later that he was institutionalized for good.)
To judge from this letter, the mother seems to have been unable
to acknowledge, and empathize with, her son's emotional disturbance. Instead, she views his silence vis-à-vis her as evidence
that he--her son--wants to hurt her and wants to take his re-
venge on her. She projects a picture of herself as the one who
is being unjustly slighted but who continues to love and to
forgive. Yet in so doing she clearly induces guilt in her
correspondent. At the same time she admonishes him to believe
in God according to her own narrow fundamentalist notions. The
reward for such belief will be their--mother's and son's--re-
union in heaven.

    Certainly there is the danger that we make too much of
this one extant letter written by the mother. In reading it
and trying to put myself into the poet's situation at the time
it was written, however, I could not help being struck by its
imperviously binding, possessive, and guilt-inducing qualities.

    And yet on the basis of Hölderlin's own extant letters to
her and on other grounds, we have reason to believe that there
existed also many positive elements in this mother-son relationship. In my book *Conflict and Reconciliation: A Study in*

Human Relations and Schizophrenia (Garden City, N. Y.: Doubleday, Anchor Books, 1969) I have tried to speculate on those features of an early mother-child relationship that may give rise to a creative variety of schizophrenia. I have there reflected on that often strange mixture of responsive tenderness and imperviousness, of rich, maternal giving and tyrannical, guilt-inducing enslavement that--sometimes!--seem to be at the root of simultaneous schizophrenia and creativity. Most of the mother-child interaction, crucial from this perspective, seems to occur during what I have called the *dawn of knowing individuation:* that is, during the child's first three years of life, when he is still most symbiotically enmeshed with his mother, most dependent, most moldable, and hence most receptive to the good as well as to the bad that comes to him from her. I shall later have more to say about how Hölderlin eventually, in trying to return to his (internalized) mother, overreached himself and became schizophrenic.

The loss of two husbands in short succession seems to have further channeled the mother's binding love on her oldest son, increasing her importance to him. Thus while the image of the mother--in all its contradictory intensity--became strongly implanted in the poet, that of his father (or fathers) seems to have been more shadowy. As models for identification, these fathers must have seemed only precariously available. As Oedipal rivals they must have appeared weak and vulnerable. His two younger siblings, in contrast, appeared to offer the poet, relatively speaking, the most unambivalently enduring family relationships available to him. This may be the reason for the apparently, and again relatively, conflict-free nature of Hölderlin's association with his peers throughout his life. Outside his family circle I can mention here as his perhaps most important friends only such significant figures as the philosophers Hegel and Schelling; further, Neuffer, Magenau, and Sinclair; Schiller, his mentor in Jena; and, perhaps most important of all, Susette Gontard, his fateful experience in love.

Having thus outlined the two ingredients of the inter-actional process which may result--and in Hölderlin's case may have resulted--in schizophrenia *and* creativity, I had origi-nally intended to trace this process to and through the poet's last creative period. But the more I immersed myself in the period, the more I felt compelled to give up my plan because of the sheer richness and complexity of the material. In order to stay within the bounds of a paper I had to restrict my focus. I finally settled on one theme which presents one aspect of the transactional process just mentioned--the seemingly inextri-cable interlocking of self-destructive and self-healing proces-ses in certain creative persons of whom Hölderlin appears as a prime example. This theme does not necessarily imply the simultaneous presence of creativity and schizophrenia in all creative persons. On the contrary. However, in Hölderlin's case at least, the schizophrenic disorder seems to have cast into unusually clear relief how that which may destroy us may also save us, and vice versa.

II

Lyric poets more than other artists have, I believe, alerted us to such tragic dilemmas. Many of them tend to demonstrate through their lives that the very same intrapsychic or inter-personal configuration that allows creativity to flourish also seems to promote the creator's eventual destruction. Such, for example, seems to be the case with Dylan Thomas, whose exuberant, apparently inexhaustible, orally-tainted productivity of earlier years appeared to interlock with the alcoholism that finally killed him.

When we reflect on the kind of configuration that specifi-cally underlies lyrical creativity, adolescent sensitivity and proneness to conflict appear as important prerequisites. In lyric poets who have been creative throughout their adult lives, such as Goethe, for example, a repeated renaissance of adolescence has been noted. But many and perhaps most great people, we notice at once, have not been as fortunate and successful as Goethe who—admittedly amidst frequent crises—could integrate an ever-renewed adolescence into a richly unfolding and maturing life. For most of these poets either died young, or their inner sources of inspiration dried up after they had reached a certain age. Keats, Shelley, Novalis, Trakl, Pushkin died young, to name only a few. And their biographers have in many instances produced good evidence for suspecting a self-destructive bent in their lives which contributed to such early death. Rimbaud stopped writing poetry in his late teens and then disappeared in the jungle, and Wordsworth, Hölderlin's exact contemporary, seemed to lose his lyrical inspiration about the same time that Hölderlin became mad.

Creativity in the lyric poet frequently implies, however —and this seems important here—not only a tendency toward self-destruction but also one toward self-healing. And for longer or shorter periods of time the creator's fate may hang in the balance as to whether the self-healing or the self-destructive forces will win out.

The notion of self-healing through creativity is, of course, not new. This notion implies that creativity—and lyrical creativity in particular—is the creative person's royal and only road to solving unbearable personal conflicts and dilemmas. It becomes then a by-product of his uniquely personal attempts at conflict resolution that this person creates new meanings and gestalten, possibly a new consciousness and new sensibility, and very possibly a new vision of man's inner and outer worlds. Let us now look more closely at four of the elements inherent in lyrical creativity that paradoxically may link together the creator's self-healing and self-destructive tendencies.

III

The principle of attempted salvation through creation implies, first, that the creative effort is frequently so total and so exclusive that it thrives only at the expense of almost every-thing else. Nietzsche once said that any great talent tends to turn into a vampire: it feeds on everything--on friends, on the family, on the artist's physical and mental health. For this reason the world in which creative persons move often becomes a human disaster area. It is strewn with the wreckage of ruined and exploited lives and hopes. From this point of view it can rightly be said, and has been said by Philip Weiss-man, among others, that creativity is neither constructive nor adaptive in a conventional sense. The creative drive does not align itself with an ego that obeys a so-called reality princi-ple, but seems, rather, captive to an unusually exacting and idiosyncratic superego which disregards what may seem most important for survival as well as most elementary in human decency.[8]

Such self-healing through creation seems, second, frequently to thrive on precarious life situations and human relationships which the artist himself did not want or could not control. Bertolt Brecht is a case in point. Again and again this author --who was great as poet *and* as playwright--decried the cold competitive climate of capitalist America. He called it his misfortune that he had to live in the States when the advent of Nazism and the outbreak of World War II left him no choice. But it was exactly in the oppressed loneliness of his American days that he created some of his most important plays--*Leben des Galilei*, *Mutter Courage und ihre Kinder*, *Der kaukasische Kreidekreis*--and poetry. In Communist East Germany, in con-trast, where he was put in charge of an excellent theater and was acclaimed (at least publicly) as that country's most distin-guished author, he produced no major play but wrote only syco-phantic rhymes in praise of Stalin and the regime.

Third, the poet, in order not to allow his creative inspiration to dry up, must again and again expose himself to the
spontaneous life within and outside himself which, by its very
nature, is full of danger and conflict. This seems tied to the
needed renaissance of adolescence mentioned earlier. Yet in
such exposure to life the artist's ego might become overwhelmed.

Should he finally succeed in his effort—and this is a
fourth point—he may strike such an immediate and powerful chord
in his contemporaries that he can feel confirmed. But often
such reception remains for a long time in the balance. The
poet's contemporaries may be repelled by, or insensitive to,
the truth and power of his creations. They need time to catch
up with his ideas. Only later generations can then begin to
appreciate his works—if he is lucky enough to have his works
preserved. Such a fate implies that there is little or no
feedback to the creator that could boost his self-esteem,
relieve his loneliness, and sustain his vision. Lacking such
feedback, the self-healing potential inherent in his creative
attempts will be further negated.

IV

Let me now take up these four points with Hölderlin as my
specific focus.

First, the totality of Hölderlin's creative effort seemed
to conflict ever more sharply with the demands for adaptive
survival, this conflict reaching its crescendo and climax in
his last five productive years. Most of the elegies and hymns
on which his fame as a timeless modern rests were written
between 1800 and 1806. This was clearly the most unsettled
period of the poet's life, the period when he showed increasing
signs of schizophrenic disturbance. He seemed less and less
able to work as a tutor in well-to-do households, after his
earlier plans to start a literary journal had failed. The

exact reasons for his failure in this and related enterprises
are unclear. We can plausibly assume, however, that he became
so obsessed with his creation that few, if any, energies were
left for ordinary living.[9] The only matter that really counted
to him seemed to be to reach ever higher levels or artistic
precision, construction, and craftsmanship. All else seems
to have faded into insignificance. When composing the hymn
"Der Rhein," one of Hölderlin's latest completed works, for
example, he jotted down in the margin of the manuscript (2:722):

Das Gesetz dieses Gesanges ist, dass die zwei ersten Parthien
der Form nach durch Progress und Regress entgegengesetzt,
aber dem Stoff nach gleich, die zwei folgenden der Form nach
gleich dem Stoff nach entgegengesetzt sind die letzte aber
mit durchgängiger Metapher alles ausgleicht.

(It is the principle of this poem that its first two parts,
in terms of progression and regression, are opposed to each
other as regards their form, while they are alike in content;
the two following parts are alike in form but opposed in
content; while the last part reconciles everything in pervasive metaphor.)

He appears to have feverishly written one version after another
of a given poem, never seeming really satisfied with the end
result. While he was being driven to ever more complex self-
expression as a poet, the inner as well as the outer foundations
of his life seemed to crumble. His ego seemed to break down
almost visibly under the strain of having to reach ever higher
degrees of artistic reconciliation. He seemed to implore his
God, as in Empedokles' last great soliloquy (4:138):

O Geist, der uns erzog, der du geheim
Am hellen Tag und in der Wolke waltest,
. . . . .
Nun nicht im Bilde mehr, und nicht, wie sonst,
Bei Sterblichen, im kurzen Glück, ich find
Im Tode find ich den Lebendigen
Und heute noch begegn' ich ihm, ...

> (O Spirit, you that reared us, secretly
> Both in the cloud and in the bright noon govern,
> . . . .
> No longer in the image now, nor yet
> As formerly, with mortals, in brief joy,
> No, but in death I find the Living One
> And this day shall confront him, ...)

Yet, despite his metaphysical anxiety, he seems to have been unable to seek his salvation in any other way than through his creative work.

It is therefore not difficult to find the taint of schizophrenia in Hölderlin's late poetry, as this poetry suggests a loosening of associations and a breakdown of the hierarchical organization of thought processes which Eugen Bleuler considered central to the schizophrenic disturbance.[10] Hölderlin tended more and more--as has been noted by Friedrich Beissner, Michael Hamburger, and others--to shake together different historical periods, different associative contexts, different things near and distant.[11] This makes for the frequently terse and dissonant quality of his later poetry and for a seemingly disjointed multilevel complexity. But also, I believe, this makes for the modernity of his poetry. When reading Hölderlin's late poems we feel--despite their frequent references to ancient gods and mythologies and their frequently elevated style--much closer to the world of Arnold Schoenberg, Anton von Webern, or James Joyce, than to that of Goethe, Schiller, or even Beethoven, who were his contemporaries.

While Hölderlin thus introduces us to a dissonant, multilevel complexity, he also opens our eyes to the new harmonies, new lyrical patterns, and new modes of reconciliation that seem feasible and necessary to cope with this complexity. He not only gives us glimpses of the pristine chaos in us, but also points out the way this chaos--through a singular devotion to craftsmanship--can in unorthodox ways be harmonized without being squelched.

Second, we have to focus on the precarious and transitional state of related unrelatedness that seems to underlie Hölderlin's most intensely creative efforts, and particularly his late works. We notice here that Hölderlin tended to become most productive after he had broken off an important relationship, yet when he--and this seems important--could still feed on this relationship creatively. This holds true, above all, for his latest creative period which, from the viewpoint here presented, must also be considered his latest phase of related unrelatedness.

In order to document this viewpoint of mine, I must briefly turn to Hölderlin's fateful love relationship with Susette Gontard, the wife of the Frankfurt banker, whose children he served as tutor. He held this tutorial position from 1796 to 1798, but continued a clandestine correspondence with Susette throughout the following two years. Susette became immortalized as Diotima (named after Plato's priestess of love in *Symposion*) in Hölderlin's poetry and paramountly in his novel *Hyperion*. As far as we know, the relation between Hölderlin and Susette remained sexually unconsummated, but was for both partners of an incredible emotional intensity. The sudden separation of the lovers in 1798 seems to many Hölderlin scholars to be the event that set the poet on the road to final emotional wreck and madness. This may be so, but we cannot overlook the immense sense of liberation that Hölderlin seems to have experienced-- for a while, at least--when circumstances finally had forced him to give up his love; a sense of liberation which, I think, sustained the near-frantic productivity of his late period. Note, for example, these lines from the elegy "Menons Klagen um Diotima," which express his strange bliss in the midst of deepest suffering (2:75-76):

Festzeit hab ich nicht, doch möcht ich die Locke bekränzen;
Bin ich allein denn nicht? aber ein Freundliches muss

Fernher nahe mir sein, und lächeln muss ich und staunen,
Wie so selig doch auch mitten im Leide mir ist.

(Cause I have none to be festive, but long to put on a green
    garland;
  Am I not quite alone? Yet something kind now must be
Close to me from afar, so that I smile as I wonder
  How in the midst of my grief I can feel happy and blessed.)

    Thus, while there can be no doubt that Hölderlin grieved
deeply over his loss, as an artist he seems to have benefited
from this loss in at least three ways: (1) he underwent the
kind of emotional experience that allowed him to drench his
elegies with his life's blood, as it were; (2) having obtained
a respite from a deeply entangling relationship, he could
devote himself anew and totally to his work to the extent that
he, as indicated earlier, disregarded his everyday survival;
and (3) this loss seems to have induced the kind of ego growth
that Freud must have had in mind when he referred to the ego
as the precipitate of past object losses. The ego, according to
this view of Freud's, can erect the lost person as a part
within itself and can, as Hölderlin's case seems to indicate,
become stronger and richer in ways that make for heightened
creativity. However--and this seems important--we deal here
at best with an uneven, one-sided ego growth which does not
necessarily enhance one's chances for a happy life or even
simple everyday survival.
    Now to my third point: the poet must expose himself to
life's most conflict-ridden currents with suspended defenses
--and in so doing he must risk being torn asunder by them. In
the following passage of the letter to Böhlendorff of December
4, 1801, Hölderlin seems to show how aware he is of the extent
to which he was subject to this dilemma (6:426):

Denn das ist das Tragische bei uns, dass wir ganz stille in
irgendeinem Behälter eingepackt vom Reiche der Lebendigen

hinweggehn, nicht dass wir in Flammen verzehrt die Flamme
büssen, die wir nicht zu bändigen vermochten.

(For this is the tragic element in our lives: that we, completely silenced, packed away in some container, depart from
the realm of the living; rather than that we, consumed by
flames, atone for the very flames we were unable to tame.)

And in a letter to his friend Neuffer, written November 12,
1798, we read (6:290; No. 167):

... weil ich alles, was von Jugend auf Zerstörendes mich traf,
empfindlicher als andre aufnahm, und diese Empfindlichkeit
scheint darin ihren Grund zu haben, dass ich im Verhältnis
mit den Erfahrungen, die ich machen musste, nicht fest und
unzerstörbar genug organisiert war. Das sehe ich. Kann es mir
helfen, dass ich es sehe? Ich glaube, so viel. Weil ich
zerstörbarer bin als mancher andre, so muss ich um so mehr
den Dingen, die auf mich zerstörend wirken, einen Vorteil
abzugewinnen suchen, ...

(... because from youth on I have reacted more sensitively
than other people to what could destroy me, and this sensitivity seems to have to do with the fact that I, considering
the experiences I had to endure, was not organized solidly
and indestructibly enough. So much I see. But will the fact
of seeing it help me? To this extent, I believe: because I
am more easily destroyed than other persons, I must try all
the harder to obtain an advantage from those things which
have a destructive influence on me, ...)

What, then, were the things that were destructive to Hölderlin and that, nonetheless, he had to seek out in order to
realize himself as an artist? In the letter to Neuffer just
quoted he was not too specific about it. I, for my part, am
inclined to find these destructive influences chiefly in the
realm of his inner, subjective experiences, as these had come
to be shaped by his past and reactivated in his present human
relationships. And because family associations are so centaal,
it is, above all, these on which we must focus in order to

understand what may have been destructive--as well as conducive
to creation--in his subjective experience.

Our family relationships, and among them specifically our
long dependence on our mother, we cannot help carrying with us
through our lives even after we have left home or our parents
have died. And when we engage in new human contacts it has to
be through that inner mold and matrix of conflicts and expectations that our parents have bequeathed to us. In my book
Conflict and Reconciliation and elsewhere I have dealt with
the complex dynamics which here come into play. At this point
I can only touch on a few of those dynamics in Hölderlin's
inner experience that seem most relevant here.

I have in mind the perhaps deepest conflict which seems
rooted in the poet's early psychic ties with his mother and
which, to some extent, became reactivated through his later
relationships. This conflict constitutes, I believe, a part
of those aforementioned experiences that Hölderlin felt he had
to undergo, although he doubted whether he was (as he expressed
it in the letter to Neuffer) *"fest und unzerstörbar genug organisiert"* (organized solidly and indestructibly enough) not to
be harmed by them (that is, he doubted whether his ego was
strong enough to stand them).

This most central conflict seems inherent in Hölderlin's
ever-recurring wish and longing to return to a mother earth
who promises to gratify and protect him totally, while he
simultaneously fears that any such return will destroy him.
This, of course, is the schizophrenic's core conflict in a
nutshell. Both sides of this conflict appear richly elaborated
in Hölderlin's late work. There is hardly another poet who
has so intensely evoked the nourishing, peace-giving, enliven-
ing aspects of the earth--which he expressly linked with the
image of the mother. The expression *Mutter Erde* occurs, according to Pierre Bertaux, more than one hundred times in the
late work (after March 1799).[12] Passages like the following

two, both taken from his play *Der Tod des Empedokles*, seem
typical. In the first passage we hear Empedokles in his great
opening soliloquy in the fragmentary third version (4:122):

> *Und wenn ... ihren Arm*
> *Die Mutter um mich breitet, o was möcht*
> *Ich auch, was möcht ich fürchten.*

> (And when ... the Mother
> With her own arms enfolds me, O what could I,
> What could I fear.)

In the second passage, from the same late version, Empedokles'
faithful companion Pausanias addresses him (4:129):

> *Und wagtest dich ins Heiligtum des Abgrunds,*
> *Wo duldend vor dem Tage sich das Herz*
> *Der Erde birgt und ihre Schmerzen dir*
> *Die dunkle Mutter sagt, o du der Nacht*
> *Des Aethers Sohn! ich folgte dir hinunter.*

> (Daring to tread the sanctum of the abyss
> Where, patient, Earth conceals her heart from day
> And the dark Mother will confide to you
> Her sufferings, her griefs, O son of Night,
> Of Aether, even then I'd follow you down.)

We note in this context that Hölderlin has chosen the
pre-Socratic philosopher Empedokles of Akragas as the hero of
his only play--the same Empedokles who tried to save mankind
and himself by throwing himself into the volcano Etna. But,
also in the "Thalia-Fragment" of *Hyperion*, in the definitive
novel, as well as in a large number of his poems we find passages that strikingly reflect his longing for death through
reunion with the mother. (We have heard how Hölderlin's actual mother, in the letter quoted earlier, hoped for a reunion
with her son in heaven.) How much it must have tempted but
also terrified Hölderlin when the woman who had stirred up

the deepest layers of passion and conflict in him, namely
Susette Gontard--Diotima--expressed from her side a longing
for a reunion through mutual death. For example, we read in
one of Susette's last letters to Hölderlin, written at the end
of December 1799:

> *Ich musste gestern noch viel über Leidenschaft nachdenken,*
> *------ . Die Leidenschaft der höchsten Liebe findet wohl*
> *auf Erden ihre Befriedigung nie! ------ Fühle es mit mir:*
> *diese suchen wäre Torheit ------ . Mit einander sterben!*
> *------ Doch still, es klingt wie Schwärmerei und ist doch*
> *so wahr ------ , ist die Befriedigung.*[13]

> (Yesterday I had to think a lot about passion, ------ .
> The passion of the highest love will probably never find
> its fulfillment on earth! ------ Feel it with me: to seek
> this would be folly ------ . To die united! ------ Yet
> stop, it sounds like a romantic wish and yet is so true
> ------ , it is fulfillment.)

Critics have also speculated on a possible prophetic significance attaching to the death of Diotima in volume 2 of *Hyperion,*
especially since Hölderlin, in one of his very few extant letters to Susette, apologizes to her for letting the heroine of
the novel die.[14] We have next to no evidence on how this
development in *Hyperion* affected Susette, unless indeed the
letter just quoted be construed as pertinent evidence. But I
am willing to believe that it must have shaken Hölderlin deeply
and stirred up unconscious guilt in him when Susette died in
1802 after seemingly having wasted away in her frustrated
passion.

But--and this brings into focus the other side of Hölderlin's perhaps deepest ambivalence--while he sought to be reborn
through death and through his return to the mother earth, he
seems to have become increasingly aware that such death would
not necessarily mean blissful union and rebirth, but would
rather mean madness, nothingness, or both. I know of no poem

in Hölderlin's oeuvre that develops this point so movingly as his hymn "Mnemosyne"--the last hymn he ever completed--of which I quote the concluding stanza in the wording of the third and final version (2:198):

> *Am Feigenbaum ist mein*
> *Achilles mir gestorben,*
> *Und Ajax liegt*
> *An den Grotten der See,*
> *An Bächen, benachbart dem Skamandros.*
> *An Schläfen Sausen einst, nach*
> *Der unbewegten Salamis steter*
> *Gewohnheit, in der Fremd, ist gross*
> *Ajax gestorben,*
> *Patroklos aber in des Königes Harnisch. Und es starben*
> *Noch andere viel. Am Kithäron aber lag*
> *Elevtherä, der Mnemosyne Stadt. Der auch, als*
> *Ablegte den Mantel Gott, das Abendliche nachher löste*
> *Die Locken. Himmlische nämlich sind*
> *Unwillig, wenn einer nicht die Seele schonend sich*
> *Zusammengenommen, aber er muss doch; dem*
> *Gleich fehlet die Trauer.*

(Beside the fig-tree
My Achilles has died and is lost to me,
And Ajax lies
Beside the grottoes of the sea,
Beside brooks that neighbour Scamandros.
Of a rushing noise in his temples once,
According to the changeless custom of
Unmoved Salamis, in foreign parts
Great Ajax died,
Not so Patroclus, dead in the King's own armour.
And many others died. But by Cithaeron there stood
Eleutherae, Mnemosyne's town. From her also
When God laid down his festive cloak, soon after did
The powers of Evening sever a lock of hair. For the
        Heavenly, when
Someone has failed to collect his soul, to spare it,
Are angry, for still he must; like him
Here mourning is at fault.)

We are indebted to Beissner for having alerted us to the ways in which this extraordinary poem, right through its various versions with their many rich and overdetermined images, expresses a despair beyond despair--that is, that state of mind which, so it seems, allows only for suicide or massive schizophrenic disintegration and retreat.[15]

Hölderlin invokes here, among many other things, the futility of heroic enterprises and heroic death; the despair, madness, and suicide of Ajax; the end of friendships; the failure of reconciliation between gods and mortals; the pointlessness of artistic efforts; and, perhaps most frightening, the end of all memory.

After this last hymn there followed only fragments before his madness (almost) silenced him.

I can be brief about my fourth and last point: of all artists who were misunderstood in their own time, Hölderlin probably fared worst. Yet the fate he feared most, as indicated in these last lines, that his work would be totally wiped out and forgotten, has not materialized--yet. He seems rather to have provided proof for the truth of what he stated in one of his best-known lines: *"Was bleibet aber, stiften die Dichter"* (But what is lasting the poets provide [2:189]).

PART III

Translators

Heidelberg

Lange lieb ich dich schon, möchte dich, mir zur Lust,
  Mutter nennen, und dir schenken ein kunstlos Lied,
    Du, der Vaterlandsstädte
      Ländlichschönste, so viel ich sah.

Wie der Vogel des Walds über die Gipfel fliegt,
  Schwingt sich über den Strom, wo er vorbei dir glänzt,
    Leicht und kräftig die Brücke,
      Die von Wagen und Menschen tönt.

Wie von Göttern gesandt, fesselt' ein Zauber einst
  Auf die Brücke mich an, da ich vorüber ging,
    Und herein in die Berge
      Mir die reizende Ferne schien,

Und der Jüngling, der Strom, fort in die Ebne zog,
  Traurigfroh, wie das Herz, wenn es, sich selbst zu schön,
    Liebend unterzugehen,
      In die Fluten der Zeit sich wirft.

Quellen hattest du ihm, hattest dem Flüchtigen
  Kühle Schatten geschenkt, und die Gestade sahn
    All ihm nach, und es bebte
      Aus den Wellen ihr lieblich Bild.

Aber schwer in das Tal hing die gigantische,
  Schicksalskundige Burg nieder bis auf den Grund,
    Von den Wettern zerrissen;
      Doch die ewige Sonne goss

Ihr verjüngendes Licht über das alternde
  Riesenbild, und umher grünte lebendiger
    Efeu; freundliche Wälder
      Rauschten über die Burg herab.

Sträuche blühten herab, bis wo im heitern Tal,
  An den Hügel gelehnt, oder dem Ufer hold,
    Deine fröhlichen Gassen
      Unter duftenden Gärten ruhn.

Heidelberg

Long have I loved you and for my own delight
 Would call you mother, give you an artless song,
  You, of all the towns in our country
   The loveliest that ever I saw.

As the forest bird crosses the peaks in flight,
 Over the river shimmering past you floats
  Airy and strong the bridge,
   Humming with sounds of traffic and people.

Once, as if it were sent by gods, enchantment
 Seized me as I was passing over the bridge
  And the distance with its allure
   Shone into the mountainscape,

And that strong youth, the river, was rushing on down
 To the plain, sorrowing-glad, like the heart that overflows
  With beauty and hurls itself,
   To die of love, into the floods of time.

You had fed him with streams, the fugitive, given him
 Cool shadow, and all the shores looked on
  As he followed his way, their image
   Sweetly jockeying over the waves.

But into the valley hung heavy the vast
 And fate-acquainted fort, by lightnings torn
  To the ground it stood on; yet
   Eternal sun still poured

Its freshening light across the giant and aging
 Thing, and all around was green with ivy,
  Living; friendly woodlands ran
   Murmurous down across the fort,

Bushes flowered all down the slope to where,
 In the vale serene, with hills to prop them, shores
  For them to cling to, your small streets
   Mid fragrant garden bowers repose.

Vulkan

Jetzt komm und hülle, freundlicher Feuergeist,
 Den zarten Sinn der Frauen in Wolken ein,
  In goldne Träum und schütze sie, die
   Blühende Ruhe der Immerguten.

Dem Manne lass sein Sinnen, und sein Geschäft,
 Und seiner Kerze Schein, und den künftgen Tag
  Gefallen, lass des Unmuts ihm, der
   Hässlichen Sorge zu viel nicht werden,

Wenn jetzt der immerzürnende Boreas,
 Mein Erbfeind, über Nacht mit dem Frost das Land
  Befällt, und spät, zur Schlummerstunde,
   Spottend der Menschen, sein schröcklich Lied singt,

Und unsrer Städte Mauren und unsern Zaun,
 Den fleissig wir gesetzt, und den stillen Hain
  Zerreisst, und selber im Gesang die
   Seele mir störet, der Allverderber,

Und rastlos tobend über den sanften Strom
 Sein schwarz Gewölk ausschüttet, dass weit umher
  Das Tal gärt, und, wie fallend Laub, vom
   Berstenden Hügel herab der Fels fällt.

Wohl frömmer ist, denn andre Lebendige,
 Der Mensch; doch zürnt es draussen, gehöret der
  Auch eigner sich, und sinnt und ruht in
   Sicherer Hütte, der Freigeborne.

Und immer wohnt der freundlichen Genien
 Noch Einer gerne segnend mit ihm, und wenn
  Sie zürnten all, die ungelehrgen
   Geniuskräfte, doch liebt die Liebe.

Vulcan

Come, friendly spirit of fire, and wrap
 In cloud the sensitive minds of women,
  Swathe them in golden dreams and shield
   Their flowerlike peace, they are all kindness.

And men, let them take pleasure in planning and trade,
 Candlelight, day that is still to come,
  Let not vexation be too much,
   Let ugly care be not multiplíed,

When now the north wind, always angering, my
 Arch-enemy, blows attacking the land
  With frost overnight, and late, at sleeptime,
   Sings, deriding men, his terrible song,

Makes havoc with town walls and the fence we rigged
 With much toil, ripping the quiet orchard apart,
  Troubles me, even in the middle of
   A poem, Boreas the Blighter, spoiling it all,

And in wild rampage spills over the gentle stream
 His black cloud, the valley swirls and
  Seethes with it, big rocks like leaves
   Plummeting down as a hill bursts open.

Yes, man is religious, more so than any
 Other being; yet when hell breaks loose
  Outside, he sits tight indoors, more his own man
   Than ever, thinking, safe, and born free.

And one friendly spirit always does like
 To live with him, and bless him; let them rage,
  All the untutored spirit powers:
   Love still is and still does love.

Griechenland

O ihr Stimmen des Geschicks, ihr Wege des Wanderers!
Denn an der Schule Blau,
Fernher, am Tosen des Himmels
Tönt wie der Amsel Gesang
Der Wolken heitere Stimmung, gut
Gestimmt vom Dasein Gottes, dem Gewitter.
Und Rufe, wie Hinausschauen, zur
Unsterblichkeit und Helden;
Viel sind Erinnerungen. Wo darauf
Tönend, wie des Kalbs Haut,
Die Erde, von Verwüstungen her, Versuchungen der Heiligen,
Denn anfangs bildet das Werk sich,
Grossen Gesetzen nachgehet, die Wissenschaft
Und Zärtlichkeit und den Himmel breit lauter Hülle nachher
Erscheinend singen Gesangeswolken.
Denn fest ist der Erde
Nabel. Gefangen nämlich in Ufern von Gras sind
Die Flammen und die allgemeinen
Elemente. Lauter Besinnung aber oben lebt der Aether. Aber
      silbern
An reinen Tagen
Ist das Licht. Als Zeichen der Liebe
Veilchenblau die Erde.

Greece

O you voices of fate, you
             Pathways of man
                    Traveling!
   For the unruffled mood
Of clouds, like blackbird song, sounds
         From afar, in the blueness
      Of the school, in the rushing
              Of the sky, tuned
To harmony by storm that is
           God's being-there.

   And shouts, like
       Lookings-out toward
Immortality and heroes;
             Manifold
   Memories are, to which a vibrance
Clings, of earth, as to a drumskin, from
       Destructions,
          Temptations of saints,
     For the work shapes itself
In the beginning, obeys
       Great laws, and afterward
Choral
   Clouds appear, singing
      Knowledge, tenderness, the sweep
Of sky--all
     Integument.

   For fixed and firm is
The earth navel. Shores of grass
      Batten down
       The flames and universal
Elements. But pure
   And utter consciousness
          Aither lives above. The light
Yet
   On clear days is
       Silver. Signifying love,
Earth is violet.

Zu Geringem auch kann kommen
Grosser Anfang.
Alltag aber wunderbar zu lieb den Menschen
Gott an hat ein Gewand.
Und Erkenntnissen verberget sich sein Angesicht
Und decket die Lüfte mit Kunst.
Und Luft und Zeit deckt
Den Schröcklichen, dass zu sehr nicht eins
Ihn liebet mit Gebeten oder
Die Seele. Denn lange schon steht offen
Wie Blätter, zu lernen, oder Linien und Winkel
Die Natur
Und gelber die Sonnen und die Monde,
Zu Zeiten aber,
Wenn ausgehn will die alte Bildung
Der Erde, bei Geschichten nämlich,
Gewordnen, mutig fechtenden, wie auf Höhen führet
Die Erde Gott. Ungemessene Schritte
Begrenzt er aber, aber wie Blüten golden tun
Der Seele Kräfte dann, der Seele Verwandtschaften sich zusammen,
Dass lieber auf Erden
Die Schönheit wohnt und irgend ein Geist
Gemeinschaftlicher sich zu Menschen gesellet.

Süss ists, dann unter hohen Schatten von Bäumen
Und Hügeln zu wohnen, sonnig, wo der Weg ist
Gepflastert zur Kirche. Reisenden aber, wem,
Aus Lebensliebe, messend immerhin,
Die Füsse gehorchen, blühn
Schöner die Wege, wo das Land

Here the fragment breaks off.--Ed.

Grand beginnings, too,
Can come to little. But day in, day out
        God wears a garment
Wonderfully for the favor of man.
            And his face hides
    From cognizance, and robes
            The air with art.
And air and time
        Robe God the Terrifier, lest
One thing love him
            Overmuch, or the soul do. For nature
    Was always news, an open book
To learn from, or lines
                And angles, yellower the suns,
                    Yellower the moons,

        But times do come
When the old shaping imageries
        Of earth launch forth--
    In histories,
                Happenings past, brave
        Battlings, when God
Leads earth from height
    To height. But he sets
                A limit to the stride unchecked
By measure, then
        The soul's powers and
        Affinities draw in tight,
            As golden blossoms do, together,
So that beauty may dwell on earth
More fondly, and a spirit of some kind
        Makes commoner cause with men.

    Sweet then it is to dwell
Sunnily in the tall
        Shade of tree and hill, where
            There is a paved path goes to the church.
But for travelers, with whom
    The feet comply, moving in measure, on and on
For love of life,
        The pathways flower, lovelier yet,
    Where the countryside

Translated by Christopher Middleton

Heimkunft

An die Verwandten

1

Drin in den Alpen ists noch helle Nacht und die Wolke,
  Freudiges dichtend, sie deckt drinnen das gähnende Tal.
Dahin, dorthin toset und stürzt die scherzende Bergluft,
  Schroff durch Tannen herab glänzet und schwindet ein
    Strahl.
Langsam eilt und kämpft das freudigschauernde Chaos,
  Jung an Gestalt, doch stark, feiert es liebenden Streit
Unter den Felsen, es gärt und wankt in den ewigen Schranken,
  Denn bacchantischer zieht drinnen der Morgen herauf.
Denn es wächst unendlicher dort das Jahr und die heilgen
  Stunden, die Tage, sie sind kühner geordnet, gemischt.
Dennoch merket die Zeit der Gewittervogel und zwischen
  Bergen, hoch in der Luft weilt er und rufet den Tag.
Jetzt auch wachet und schaut in der Tiefe drinnen das Dörflein
  Furchtlos, Hohem vertraut, unter den Gipfeln hinauf.
Wachstum ahnend, denn schon, wie Blitze, fallen die alten
  Wasserquellen, der Grund unter den Stürzenden dampft,
Echo tönet umher, und die unermessliche Werkstatt
  Reget bei Tag und Nacht, Gaben versendend, den Arm.

2

Ruhig glänzen indes die silbernen Höhen darüber,
  Voll mit Rosen ist schon droben der leuchtende Schnee.
Und noch höher hinauf wohnt über dem Lichte der reine
  Selige Gott vom Spiel heiliger Strahlen erfreut.
Stille wohnt er allein und hell erscheinet sein Antlitz,
  Der ätherische scheint Leben zu geben geneigt,
Freude zu schaffen, mit uns, wie oft, wenn, kundig des Masses,
  Kundig der Atmenden auch zögernd und schonend der Gott
Wohlgediegenes Glück den Städten und Häusern und milde
  Regen, zu öffnen das Land, brütende Wolken, und euch,
Trauteste Lüfte dann, euch, sanfte Frühlinge sendet,
  Und mit langsamer Hand Traurige wieder erfreut,
Wenn er die Zeiten erneut, der Schöpferische, die stillen
  Herzen der alternden Menschen erfrischt und ergreift,
Und hinab in die Tiefe wirkt, und öffnet und
    aufhellt,
  Wie ers liebet, und jetzt wieder ein Leben beginnt,
Anmut blühet, wie einst, und gegenwärtiger Geist kömmt,
  Und ein freudiger Mut wieder die Fittige schwellt.

Homecoming

To My Kinsmen

1

Within the Alps it is still bright night, and the clouds,
　Creating joy, cover the yawning valley within.
This way, that way, the playful mountain air tumbles and falls,
　Abrupt through fir-trees a ray of light flashes downward and
　　disappears.
Chaos, shuddering with joy, hurries slowly and struggles,
　Young in form, though strong, it celebrates loving strife
Among the rocks, it swells and staggers in its eternal bounds,
　For within, more Bacchantic, the morning ascends.
For the year grows more endlessly there, and the sacred
　Hours and the days are more boldly ordered and mixed.
Yet still the bird of the storm marks the time, and between
　The mountains high in the air he soars and proclaims the day.
In the depths within, the village also awakens now and looks
　Upward below the summits, fearless, familiar with heights,
Sensing growth, the the ancient waterfalls already descend
　Like lightning, the ground steams beneath the falls,
Echo resounds everywhere, and dispensing gifts,
　By day and night the immeasurable workshop flexes its arm.

2

The silvery heights meanwhile gleam in silence above,
　Up there the flashing snow is already filled with roses.
And higher still, above the light, dwells the god,
　Pure and blissful, rejoicing in the play of the sacred rays.
Silently he dwells alone and brightly shines his countenance,
　Aetherial, he seems inclined to give forth life,
To create joy, as often, with us, when aware of limits
　And also aware of those who breathe, hesitant and sparing,
He sends good fortune and true to cities and homes, and mild
　Rain, to open the land, brooding clouds and you,
Intimate breezes, you, mild seasons of spring,
　And with a slow hand brings joy again to the sad,
When he renews the times, the creative one, refreshes
　And seizes the silent hearts of aging men,
And downward into the deep directs his power, opens and
　　brightens,
　As he loves to do, and now life begins again,
Grace blossoms, as before, and all-present the Spirit comes,
　And a joyous mood once more spreads its wings.

3

Vieles sprach ich zu ihm, denn, was auch Dichtende sinnen
  Oder singen, es gilt meistens den Engeln und ihm;
Vieles bat ich, zu lieb dem Vaterlande, damit nicht
  Ungebeten uns einst plötzlich befiele der Geist;
Vieles für euch auch, die im Vaterlande besorgt sind,
  Denen der heilige Dank lächelnd die Flüchtlinge bringt,
Landesleute! für euch, indessen wiegte der See mich,
  Und der Ruderer sass ruhig und lobte die Fahrt.
Weit in des Sees Ebene wars Ein freudiges Wallen
  Unter den Segeln und jetzt blühet und hellet die Stadt
Dort in der Frühe sich auf, wohl her von schattigen Alpen
  Kommt geleitet und ruht nun in dem Hafen das Schiff.
Warm ist das Ufer hier und freundlich offene Tale,
  Schön von Pfaden erhellt, grünen und schimmern mich an.
Gärten stehen gesellt und die glänzende Knospe beginnt schon,
  Und des Vogels Gesang ladet den Wanderer ein.
Alles scheinet vertraut, der vorübereilende Gruss auch
  Scheint von Freunden, es scheint jegliche Miene verwandt.

4

Freilich wohl! das Geburtsland ists, der Boden der Heimat,
  Was du suchest, es ist nahe, begegnet dir schon.
Und umsonst nicht steht, wie ein Sohn, am wellenumrauschten
  Tor und siehet und sucht liebende Namen für dich,
Mit Gesang, ein wandernder Mann, glückseliges Lindau!
  Eine der gastlichen Pforten des Landes ist dies,
Reizend hinauszugehn in die vielversprechende Ferne,
  Dort, wo die Wunder sind, dort, wo das göttliche Wild
Hoch in die Ebnen herab der Rhein die verwegene Bahn bricht,
  Und aus Felsen hervor ziehet das jauchzende Tal,
Dort hinein, durchs helle Gebirg, nach Como zu wandern,
  Oder hinab, wie der Tag wandelt, den offenen See;
Aber reizender mir bist du, geweihete Pforte!
  Heimzugehn, wo bekannt blühende Wege mir sind,
Dort zu besuchen das Land und die schönen Tale des Neckars,
  Und die Wälder, das Grün heiliger Bäume, wo gern
Sich die Eiche gesellt mit stillen Birken und Buchen,
  Und in Bergen ein Ort freundlich gefangen mich nimmt.

5

Dort empfangen sie mich. O Stimme der Stadt, der Mutter!
  O du triffest, du regst Langegelerntes mir auf!
Dennoch sind sie es noch! noch blühet die Sonn und die Freud
    euch,
  O ihr Liebsten! und fast heller im Auge, wie sonst.

3

Much did I speak to him, for whatever poets may think
  Or sing, it pertains most often to the angels and him,
Much did I request, for love of my homeland, so that the Spirit
  Not descend all at once, unrequested, upon us;
Much also for you, who in the homeland have cares,
  To whom, smiling, sacred thanks brings fugitives,
For you, my countrymen! meanwhile the lake rocked me,
  And the boatman sat quietly and praised the journey.
Far out on the water's surface there was one joyous swell
  Filling the sails, and now the city blossoms and brightens
There in the early day, our boat well-guided comes
  From the shady Alps and rests now in the harbor.
The shore is warm here and friendly the open valleys,
  Brightened by paths, flourish beautifully and shimmer for me.
Gardens stand together and the gleaming buds begin to burst,
  And the song of birds invites the traveler home.
All things seem intimate, even hurried greetings
  Seem to show friendship, every face seems akin.

4

But of course! it is your native land, the ground of your home,
  What you are seeking is near, already confronts you.
And not in vain a well-traveled man stands, like a son,
  At your doorway, washed by waves, and sees you and seeks
Loving names for you through song, O Lindau, blessed by fortune!
  This is one of the gates of the land, hospitable,
Enticing to set forth into the promising distance,
  To that place where miracles are, where the divine beast,
High up, the Rhine, forces his devious path downward into the
      plains,
  And forth from the rocks leads the jubilant valley,
In there, through the bright mountains, to travel toward Como,
  Or downward, as the day goes, on the open lake;
But for me more enticing, you consecrated gateway!
  To go homeward, where the blossoming paths are well-known to me,
There to visit the land and the beautiful valleys of the Neckar,
  And the forests, the green of sacred trees, where the oak
Gladly stands alongside silent birches and beech,
  And a place in the mountains, friendly, takes me captive.

5

There they welcome me. O voice of my city, voice of my mother!
  How they move me, renew in me what I learned long ago!
And yet they are still the same! still the sun blooms and
      joy,
  O dearest ones! and almost more brightly than ever in your eyes.

Ja! das Alte noch ists! Es gedeihet und reifet, doch keines,
  Was da lebet und liebt, lässet die Treue zurück.
Aber das Beste, der Fund, der unter des heiligen Friedens
  Bogen lieget, er ist Jungen und Alten gespart.
Törig red ich. Es ist die Freude. Doch morgen und künftig,
  Wenn wir gehen und schaun draussen das lebende Feld
Unter den Blüten des Baums, in den Feiertagen des Frühlings
  Red und hoff ich mit euch vieles, ihr Lieben! davon.
Vieles hab ich gehört vom grossen Vater und habe
  Lange geschwiegen von ihm, welcher die wandernde Zeit
Droben in Höhen erfrischt, und waltet über Gebirgen,
  Der gewähret uns bald himmlische Gaben und ruft
Hellem Gesang und schickt viel gute Geister. O säumt nicht,
  Kommt, Erhaltenden ihr! Engel des Jahres! und ihr,

6

Engel des Hauses, kommt! in die Adern alle des Lebens,
  Alle freuend zugleich, teile das Himmlische sich!
Adle! verjünge! damit nichts Menschlichgutes, damit nicht
  Eine Stunde des Tags ohne die Frohen und auch
Solche Freude, wie jetzt, wenn Liebende wieder sich finden,
  Wie es gehört für sie, schicklich geheiliget sei.
Wenn wir segnen das Mahl, wen darf ich nennen, und wenn wir
  Ruhn vom Leben des Tags, saget, wie bring ich den Dank?
Nenn ich den Hohen dabei? Unschickliches liebet ein Gott nicht,
  Ihn zu fassen, ist fast unsere Freude zu klein.
Schweigen müssen wir oft; es fehlen heilige Namen,
  Herzen schlagen und doch bleibet die Rede zurück?
Aber ein Saitenspiel leiht jeder Stunde die Töne,
  Und erfreuet vielleicht Himmlische, welche sich nahn.
Das bereitet und so ist auch beinahe die Sorge
  Schon befriediget, die unter das Freudige kam.
Sorgen, wie diese, muss, gern oder nicht, in der Seele
  Tragen ein Sänger und oft, aber die anderen nicht.

Yes! it is still the same! It grows and ripens, but nothing
  Which lives and loves there abandons its loyalty.
But the best, the treasure, which is found beneath the rainbow
  Of sacred peace, is saved for young and old.
I talk like a fool. It is my joy. But tomorrow and in future,
  When we go out and behold the living field
Beneath the blossoms of the trees, in the festivals of spring,
  Much shall I talk and hope about it, O loved ones, with you.
Much have I heard about our great father and long
  Have I kept silence about him, who in the heights above
Renews the time as it passes and rules over the mountains,
  He soon will provide us with heavenly gifts and call
For brighter song and send many good spirits. Delay no longer,
  Come, you preservers! angels of the year! and you,

6

Angels of the house, come! May the power of heaven spread
  Through all the veins of life, bringing joy to all at once!
Ennoble! Renew! So that nothing of human goodness, so that no
  Single hour of the day be without the joyful and that also
Such joy be suitably sanctified, as now,
  When loved ones are reunited, as they should be.
When we bless the meal, whom shall I name, and when we
  Rest from the life of day, tell me, how do I offer thanks?
Should I name the highest? A god does not love what is unsuitable,
  Our joy is almost too small to grasp him.
Often we must be silent; sacred names are lacking,
  Hearts beat and yet speech fails?
But poetic song lends its tones to every hour,
  And brings joy perhaps to the heavenly who approach.
Let that be made ready, and so this care also will almost be
  Removed, which arose in the midst of our joy.
Such cares as these, whether gladly or not, a singer must
  Bear in his soul, and often, but not the others.

Translated by Cyrus Hamlin

Hölderlin's Elegy "Homecoming": Comments

by Cyrus Hamlin

Poetry may be defined as that mode of discourse which cannot be translated from its own language into another. If we grant the validity of such a statement, then it follows that every attempt to translate poetry must fail. Hölderlin's mature poems, in all their enormous complexity, provide sufficient proof. Yet a translator has the privilege of choosing his particular kind of failure. The limitations and distortions of a translation may be made to serve the motives of the endeavor. In this way the results are redeemed in part by a measure of self-determination. With such thoughts in mind concerning my own translation of "Homecoming," I would like to describe the circumstances and motives that led me to attempt it. I hope also to suggest how I understand the original poem and what it is above all that I have tried to recapture from it in my English version.

My initial pretext for translating Hölderlin was purely practical. I wanted to include several of his poems in an undergraduate course at Yale, "German Romanticism in Its European Context," for students with no knowledge of the language. Existing translations were inadequate for the kind of interpretation I wanted to make. I thus began translating with a desire to be exact, leaving nothing out and adding as little as possible,

232

changing the structural relationships of the language only where
it was necessary in order to make sense in English. It became
apparent, however, that exactitude in the translation of poetry
is useless without a degree of eloquence and that for a translation eloquence must involve the imitation of effects achieved
by the original poem. Two important criteria also had to be
abandoned in order not to lose control of my own language. The
first criterion was meter. "Heimkunft" is written in the meter
of the classical elegy, the elegiac distich. In contrast to
German, where such meter was used by poets from Klopstock on,
English has no valid tradition in this form. The distich inevi-
tably sounds forced and awkward. It also became apparent to me
that the meter could only be imitated at the expense of syntax.
Much too liberal a rearrangement of poetic structure was required.
I thus adopted a loose approximation (based on the practice of
Richmond Lattimore in translating Homer), consisting of a long
line with a norm of six stresses and a varying system of one or
two unstressed syllables between stresses and the occasional
juxtaposition of stressed syllables. Such a procedure achieves
a reminiscence of the distich without being subject to its strict
rule. It has also been possible in this way to recreate some
of the rhythmic effects of the original poem.

The second criterion to be abandoned was the strict imitation of syntax. German is notoriously more flexible in syntax
than English, due primarily to its extensive inflection. Hölderlin's usage in his later poems even goes beyond the normal
limits of German syntax (to the extent that Theodor Adorno has
proposed the term *parataxis* as a descriptive alternative).
Particularly frequent in Hölderlin's language are elaborate
inversions and suspensions, complicated by a multiple frame of
reference. Hölderlin's syntax also achieves important rhythmic
and rhetorical effects, which contribute significantly to his
unique poetic style. English cannot allow itself such freedom
of syntax, especially in the use of inversion. I have therefore

adopted a procedure of simplification, attempting to achieve an acceptable structure in English while maintaining the most crucial rhythmic and rhetorical configurations of the original. These two concerns were not always reconcilable. At times I have done violence to English for Hölderlin's sake; at other times syntactical patterns from the original which may be important to Hölderlin's style were omitted in order to make sense in English.

Several aspects of "Homecoming" that seem to me particularly important for understanding the poem were uppermost in my mind in making the translation. I wish to comment briefly on these, with regard especially to the biographical background and to the inner structure of the poet's statement.

The elegy was composed in 1801 and was occasioned by Hölderlin's return to Nürtingen from Switzerland. The title thus refers to this event. The dedication is similarly specific, indicating the members of his immediate family who welcomed him at his mother's home. The elegy describes his journey from the Alps across Lake Constance to Lindau, from there by foot northward to the Neckar valley, and finally to Nürtingen. All-pervasive to the poem is a festive mood which the poet brings with him, proclaiming his joy in anticipation of a new era about to commence for all his countrymen. We may interpret this mood in Hölderlin to be a response to the Treaty of Lunéville, signed in February of the same year, which the poet believed would inaugurate a great era of peace for Germany and for all of Europe. Evidence for such a response, apart from such a poem as "Friedensfeier," may be found in Hölderlin's letters, notably in the following statement written to his half brother just before Hölderlin left for Switzerland at the end of 1800 (6:407; No. 222):

... *dass unsere Zeit nahe ist, dass uns der Friede, der jetzt im Werden ist, gerade das bringen wird, was er und nur er bringen konnte; denn er wird vieles bringen, was viele hoffen, aber er wird auch bringen, was wenige ahnden.*
.... *dass der Egoismus in allen seinen Gestalten sich beugen wird unter die heilige Herrschaft der Liebe und Güte, dass*

Gemeingeist über alles in allem gehen, und dass das deutsche
Herz in solchem Klima, unter dem Segen dieses neuen Friedens
erst recht aufgehn, und geräuschlos, wie die wachsende Natur,
seine geheimen weitreichenden Kräfte entfalten wird, dies mein
ich, dies seh und glaub ich, ...

(... that our time is near, that the peace which is now in the
making will bring us just that which it alone can bring; for
it will bring many things that many hope for, but it will also
bring what only a few suspect.
   ... that egotism in all its forms will bow down before the
sacred rule of love and goodness, that a Common-Spirit will
move all in all, and that in such a climate the German heart
will open up in the bliss of this new peace, and soundlessly,
like organic nature, the mysterious, all-pervading powers of
this peace will unfold, this I think, this I see and believe,
....)

   What Hölderlin claims in "Homecoming" is a peculiar privilege
which his journey into the Alps has established for him. He
returns to Württemberg to bear witness to the emerging powers of
divinity within the world, which he asserts to have been perceived in the landscape of the Alps. This event is depicted in
the poem through a metaphor of natural renewal, which includes
both the coming of day and the coming of spring. It occurs as a
dispensation from God, who dwells above the light of heaven in
the ethereal realm. The poet has spoken with this God, intimately and directly; and above all he has requested that this
gift of grace, this cosmic mood of joy, be extended to the citi-
zens of his homeland. Confident that his request will be granted
--for evidence of the coming festival is apparent to him in every
aspect of the season and the day--Hölderlin is reunited with his
loved ones, sharing his joy with them as he proclaims that higher
joy which soon they shall find like treasure beneath the rainbow
of sacred peace. With such conviction he calls directly to the
earthly representatives of the God, his messengers--the angels
of the year and the angels of the house--that they come and reveal
themselves, bringing joy, ennobling and renewing everyone and
everything within the great Common-Spirit of the divine festival

of peace. The poet also hopes to participate himself in the
festival as a singer, celebrating the revealed powers of divinity by name, offering up his thanks through an appropriate song,
which shall bring joy even to the gods who approach the realm
of mankind.

Such a paraphrase represents the essential situation of
the poem, the poet's fundamental attitude, and his ultimate
purpose in writing of his homecoming to his kinsmen. But the
elegy achieves far more than such a paraphrase can indicate.
I believe that Hölderlin's poetic language also prefigures in a
highly sophisticated and articulate manner that festival event
that he proclaims for the coming renewal of time. Throughout
the poem, in other words, Hölderlin establishes the mood of the
festival as a poetic reality. The song that he hopes to sing
at the festival--this is the paradox of the poem, which must be
understood--is already achieved here with this elegy as an event
of the poetic imagination. This event is acknowledged to be no
more than a prefiguration--a prophetic vision or dream--but it
is communicated to the poet's audience (and we, of course, may
include ourselves among those kinsmen to whom he speaks) as an
authentic aesthetic experience that takes place in and through
the poem. If we can discern how such an experience is achieved
even for us as readers, then we shall comprehend Hölderlin's
true status as a poet. The fact that his prophecy of peace was
wrong--for the expected era did not occur, as history shows--
becomes quite unimportant for an evaluation of the poem. The
only true reality for such a universal peace--whether or not
Hölderlin would have agreed at the time when he composed the
elegy--is found in poetry, within the realm of art and myth.

This mythical reality (if so troubled a term as *myth* can
still be used) is established above all through the dynamic
structural interrelationships of Hölderlin's language. These
interrelationships--which may be described with a phrase from
Hölderlin's "Anmerkungen zur Antigonae" as *"Der Rhythmus der*

Vorstellungen" (the rhythm of representation [5:265])--have been
reconstructed as far as possible in my translation. To outline
in detail the structures that I have in mind would require an
exhaustive explication, inappropriate to the present occasion.
It may be helpful, however, to mention at least two of the elements that contribute to this structural process in Hölderlin's
poem. I have in mind, for one, all references to temporal and
spatial relationships and the dimensions defined for both within
the poem. Equally important, for the other, are references to
those who participate in the poem as dialogue, to the poet as
first person and to the various recipients of his statement in
the second person. The particular location of both these kinds
of references determines in large measure the inner structure
of the elegy. I shall survey this structure in brief, keeping
also in mind the external architectonics to which Hölderlin has
so masterfully submitted his statement. The elegy consists of
six stanzas, each containing nine distichs. Some trace may also
be found of a principle of further subdivision, used in both
"Stutgard" and "Brod und Wein," where each stanza is subdivided
into three units of three distichs each. The individual distich
also serves as the basic component of Hölderlin's statement,
imposing its particular demands upon the movement of the language;
but such an external criterion of form is also frequently ignored
or complicated for rhythmic and rhetorical purposes (as mentioned
earlier) through syntactical disruptions, enjambement, suspension,
and inversion.

In the opening stanza it is significant that no reference
occurs to either the first or second person. The poet's statement is strictly objective, directed to a process that is described as an immediate dramatic event, taking place within the
Alps. All temporal reference is focused upon this dramatic
present tense. We witness the event with the poet as it happens.
Spatial distinctions of height and depth become important within
the stanza, though only gradually. At first the entire landscape

is presented at rest by night, covered with a blanket of cloud. Then gradually a force begins to assert itself, involving the play of breezes and the flash of a ray of light. A chaos of activity gradually builds into the bacchantic procession of morning as it ascends. All at first is boldly ordered and mixed, both the processes of time and the dimensions of space. But the eagle soars upward, thus asserting the vertical focus of the stanza, into the approaching light of day to proclaim the event with his cry. In apparent response to this call, the village deep down below the summits awakens and looks upward. What the inhabitants perceive is growth, involving the renewal of nature, apparently in response to the approaching light, whereby the waterfalls descend like lightning and the entire realm of earth, regarded metaphorically as the workshop for the day labor of the world, flexes its arm. Do we not perceive a pervading mythical association of the earth with a titanic figure that is, at first, asleep, then stirs in response to the coming light and finally arises to meet the new day? There is also a purposeful prefiguration of the poet's role of proclaiming the approaching festival of peace to his kinsmen, namely in the flight of the eagle into the dawn and his call to the village below.

In the second stanza the temporal frame of reference is sustained as a dramatic present. The here and now of renewal is reaffirmed at the end. But the range of spatial reference is greatly increased, and spatial relationships become more prominent. The stanza moves in an arc of ascent (upward beyond the peaks and the light to the dwelling place of the God) and descent (following the path of the God's influence downwards as he asserts his creative powers through the rain, the clouds, the breezes, and the spring generally). A purposeful generality of reference is introduced in the long subordinate clause (stanza 2, lines 7-16), which describes the processes whereby the God creates life and joy. Dramatic immediacy is reestablished (at stanza 2, line 16 "now"), as the stanza culminates in an affir-

mation of the universal Spirit which now emerges within the human
realm and solicits an appropriate response of joy. We note the
delicate use of the first-person plural pronoun in a preposi-
tional phrase (stanza 2, line 7 "with us"), indicating a community with which the poet associates himself and which is directly
affected by the creative power of the God. This is presumably
the community of all mankind. The poet also addresses directly,
using the second-person pronoun, the various agents in nature
that mediate these powers to the human realm. Here Hölderlin
purposefully anticipates the climax of the elegy at the end of
the fifth stanza and at the beginning of the sixth, where these
same agents are invoked as the messengers of the God--the angels
of the year and the angels of the house. It would thus appear
by the dramatic quality of Hölderlin's language in these opening
stanzas that the central mythical event of the elegy has already
been achieved as a reality in the poem. This is quite true; and
it is crucial that we perceive it as such. But this event,
though it now exists for the poem, has not yet been comprehended
by the poet as the proclamation of joy that he seeks to communi-
cate to his kinsmen through his homecoming. The event does not
yet exist *for him*, even less so *for us*. It is to this process
of assimilation that the elegy now turns.

   In the third stanza the poet enters the poem, speaking of
himself in the first person for the first time. He establishes
a specific relationship between himself and the God (with whom
he has spoken) and between himself and his countrymen (on whose
behalf he spoke). An expansion of the temporal framework also
occurs backward in time to this past experience of communication.
This experience preceded the writing of the poem, as it also
presumably preceded the process of renewal described in the
opening stanzas in the present tense. Beginning with the word
"meanwhile" in the middle of stanza 3, line 7, there is a seemingly abrupt introduction of a narrative account, initially in
the past tense, of the poet's journey across Lake Constance to

Lindau. A dramatic present is quickly reestablished, however, as the poet enters the city (stanza 3, lines 10-11):

> jetzt blühet und hellet die Stadt
> Dort in der Frühe sich auf, ...

>   (and now the city blossoms and brightens
>   There in the early day, ...)

His description of the place and his response to it, also of his meeting with the people there, is once again given in the present tense, as if all this too were taking place within the poem as an immediate event. The only complication of the narrative occurs in the final lines of stanza 3, where the poet acknowledges that his assessment of the situation depends upon his own surmise--as indicated by the threefold use, in lines 17-18, of the verb *scheinen* "to seem" (roman and italic types are here added for emphasis):

Alles scheinet *vertraut, der vorübereilende Gruss auch*
    Scheint *von Freunden,* es scheint *jegliche Miene verwandt.*

(All things *seem* intimate, even hurried greetings
    Seem to show friendship, every face *seems* akin.)

The fourth stanza begins with an exclamation that indicates a heightening of self-reflection on the poet's part in response to the situation just described as it appears to him. He addresses himself in the second person through an internal dialogue. The language here achieves an act of recognition that is crucial to the homecoming. The return is affirmed to be a meeting with the object of the poet's search. The full significance of this meeting, here intuited by recognition, comprehends the entire poem. Abruptly, however, the poet's discourse shifts its focus from himself to the city of Lindau, the gateway to his homeland. The poet is now referred to in the third person--"*wie ein Sohn*

... *ein wandernder Mann"* (a well-traveled man ... like a son
[stanza 4, line 3])--and the city is invoked, in line 5, directly
in the second person: *"glückseliges Lindau!"* (O Lindau, blessed
by fortune!). The remainder of the stanza consists of an elaborate description, sustaining a spatial frame of reference that
expands in two opposite horizontal directions: outward away from
the homeland and inward through the gateway to the home itself.
This description serves, both to recapitulate the part of the
poet's journey that lies behind him--through a backward glance
as it were--and to survey the journey still ahead of him, all in
such a way that the completion of the journey is achieved through
this survey as an imagined event, an event which thereby assumes
a poetic reality in the final lines of the stanza. On the one
hand, the poet's outward glance fixes upon the paths that have
been cut through the mountains by the rivers, notably by the
Rhine (here called a "divine beast"--as in the hymn to the river,
composed at approximately the same time as "Homecoming," it is
called a "demigod"). Not by accident, the poet's homeward journey has followed these paths, but has done so in a direction
that for him is opposite: neither southward toward Como nor
westward--"as the day goes" (stanza 4, line 12)--along Lake
Constance. Turning inward, on the other hand, his vision moves
northward along familiar paths in bloom toward the valley of the
Neckar and the forests with their sacred trees--the oak, the
birches, and the beech--and the mountains of the Swabian Alps
which contain the town of Nürtingen, where the poet is taken
into friendly captivity.

    The poet's homecoming is thus achieved in fact at the begin-
ning of the fifth stanza. He is received by the voice of the
city and of his mother--the two presumably identical in the
opening line of the stanza, at least. Throughout the stanza
the spatial frame of reference is fixed upon the home. The
range of temporal reference is purposefully expanded, however,
through recollection backward to the poet's childhood and

through anticipation forward to the coming festival of peace.
In this way Hölderlin establishes between himself and the place
of his home an intimate relationship to which is joined the
approaching God. Through such recollections the poet affirms
the enduring value of his home--"*das Alte noch ists*" (it is still
the same [stanza 5, line 5]); it is the same as ever, faithful
and true in all aspects of its life. Through his anticipation
of the coming festival, however, the poet also emphasizes that
the best is yet to come. Here for the first time in the elegy
a predominantly future mode is introduced, looking ahead to
events that are acknowledged to be as yet unachieved. In the
latter section of the stanza the poet refers to the coming feast
days of the spring when he will walk with his kinsmen through
the living fields and talk at length with them about the true
object of his joy. What he will say pertains directly to what
he heard high up in the Alps when he received the word from the
God of heaven, "*vom grossen Vater*" (our great father [stanza 5,
line 13]). Stanza 5 is also sustained by the poet's dialogue
with his kinsmen, whom he addresses directly in the second person throughout the stanza. This mode of discourse reestablishes
a sense of dramatic immediacy to the poem; but here--in contrast
to the earlier sections--the poet's audience is included in the
intimacy of this situation. Time and time again members of this
audience are directly invoked: "*O Stimme der Stadt, der Mutter!*"
(O voice of my city, voice of my mother! [stanza 5, line 1]);
"*O ihr Liebsten!*" (O dearest ones! [ibid., line 3]); "*ihr Lieben!*"
(O loved ones [ibid., line 12]). There is a charming directness
to the poet's language, ranging from the confusion and embarrass-
ment of his joy (stanza 5, line 9) to the intimacy and trust in
his conversation (ibid., lines 9-12). The final lines of the
stanza return once more to the God of heaven, describing in
briefest terms his mode of operation within the earthly realm
and all the heavenly gifts that he will soon grant and the
beneficent spirits whom he will send. This statement reminds

us, as readers of the poem, that the event here referred to in
the future tense has already been achieved within the poem as
a dramatic reality in the present tense (that is, in stanzas 1
and 2). It is crucial for the meaning of the elegy that we
recognize this.

Upon the authority of this affirmation of the coming God,
which is both a recollection for the poet and a prophecy for
his kinsmen, the messengers of the God--the angels of the year
and the angels of the house--may be directly invoked. The poet
calls upon them to reveal themselves within the homeland and to
rejuvenate the Common-Spirit for all who dwell there. This
triumphant invocation, running from stanza 5, line 17 through
stanza 6, line 6, and involving the sole example of inter-stanzaic
enjambement in "Heimkunft," I take to be the climax of the entire
poem:

O säumt nicht,
Kommt, Erhaltenden ihr! Engel des Jahres! und ihr,

6

Engel des Hauses, kommt! in die Adern alle des Lebens,
* Alle freuend zugleich, teile das Himmlische sich!*
Adle! verjünge! damit nichts Menschlichgutes, damit nicht
* Eine Stunde des Tags ohne die Frohen und auch*
Solche Freude, wie jetzt, wenn Liebende wieder sich finden,
* Wie es gehört für sie, schicklich geheiliget sei.*

(Delay no longer,
Come, you preservers! angels of the year! and you,

6

Angels of the house, come! May the power of heaven spread
  Through all the veins of life, bringing joy to all at once!
Ennoble! Renew! So that nothing of human goodness, so that no
  Single hour of the day be without the joyful and that also
Such joy be suitably sanctified, as now,
  When loved ones are reunited, as they should be.)

The poet's mode of statement here is futurity; his plea is directed forward in time toward a fulfillment which he anticipates but which has not in fact yet come. Within the poem, however, the force of this invocation affirms the reality of those spirits who are invoked by the poet, as it also affirms the reality of the poet's initial vision of renewal within the Alps (which is the necessary precondition for the emergence of these spirits within the homeland). More important: the poetic vision of the festival of peace has now been communicated by the poet to his audience, both to his kinsmen and to us as his readers. Although it remains an event for the future, the poem has established an objective validity for this event; that is to say, the poet has affirmed his vision as something more than a subjective dream. The festival of peace has been established in and through the poem—regardless of what may or may not be achieved in the world—as a poetic or mythical reality.

The conclusion of "Homecoming" in the last six distichs of stanza 6 pursues further implications of the poet's promise for his kinsmen and for himself. In a series of questions directed as much to himself as to the others (stanza 6, lines 7-12), the poet considers what his role will be at the festival. He is concerned about his ability to celebrate the God by name and to offer adequate thanks. He fears that at the moment of highest joy his language may fail him. But language itself, specifically poetic song, provides the only possible answer to his questions (stanza 6, lines 13-14):

Aber ein Saitenspiel leiht jeder Stunde die Töne,
* Und erfreuet vielleicht Himmlische, welche sich nahn.*

(But poetic song lends its tones to every hour,
  And brings joy perhaps to the heavenly who approach.)

Hölderlin here expresses a profound faith in the powers of poetry to celebrate the highest God. And what further proof for such

faith do we need than the successful completion of the song that
he has here been singing? Faith in his vocation as poet provides reassurance, so that the care that here intruded upon the
joy of his homecoming is almost removed. But such care is
apparently necessary to the poet--so the final lines of the
elegy remind us. The poet must remain always aware of the
superhuman task that his song endeavors to fulfill ever anew.

Patmos

Dem Landgrafen von Homburg

   Nah ist
Und schwer zu fassen der Gott.
Wo aber Gefahr ist, wächst
Das Rettende auch.
Im Finstern wohnen
Die Adler und furchtlos gehn
Die Söhne der Alpen über den Abgrund weg
Auf leichtgebaueten Brücken.
Drum, da gehäuft sind rings
Die Gipfel der Zeit und die Liebsten
Nah wohnen, ermattend auf
Getrenntesten Bergen,
So gib unschuldig Wasser,
O Fittige gib uns, treuesten Sinns
Hinüberzugehn und wiederzukehren.

So sprach ich, da entführte
Mich schneller, denn ich vermutet,
Und weit, wohin ich nimmer
Zu kommen gedacht, ein Genius mich
Vom eigenen Haus. Es dämmerten
Im Zwielicht, da ich ging,
Der schattige Wald
Und die sehnsüchtigen Bäche
Der Heimat; nimmer kannt ich die Länder;
Doch bald, in frischem Glanze,
Geheimnisvoll
Im goldenen Rauche, blühte
Schnellaufgewachsen,
Mit Schritten der Sonne,
Mit tausend Gipfeln duftend,

Mir Asia auf, und geblendet sucht
Ich eines, das ich kennete, denn ungewohnt
War ich der breiten Gassen, wo herab
Vom Tmolus fährt
Der goldgeschmückte Paktol
Und Taurus stehet und Messogis,
Und voll von Blumen der Garten,

Patmos

For the Landgrave of Homburg

 Up close,
That hard to hold fast, is God.
But it is also in danger
That rescue grows live.
Eagles live in the
Dark, and the Alps' sons
Go their ways, fearless over the chasm
On lightly-built bridges.
There--since round us emerge
The peaks of time, and our well-loved
Live near and weary on
The farthest mountains--
Now give innocent waters,
Yes, give us wings for crossing over
In faith, and for the returning.

I was saying this, when a genius
Led me, faster than I thought it,
And far, where I had never
Dreamed of going--right from
My own house. Shadowed
Woods glimmered as I went
In twilight,
And the longing brooks of the home
Country--these were not countries I knew--;
But soon in a brilliance fresh
As mystery
In golden smoke
Quickly sprung up
With the sun's steps and
Fragrant with a thousand mountain-

Peaks: Asia burst into blossom before me, and
Blinded, I looked for a sight I knew for feeling
Lost on the broad avenues where
From Tmolos, the gold-jeweled
Paktolos comes tumbling down,
And there stand Taurus, Messogis, and
Full with flowers the garden,

Ein stilles Feuer, aber im Lichte
Blüht hoch der silberne Schnee,
Und Zeug unsterblichen Lebens
An unzugangbaren Wänden
Uralt der Efeu wächst und getragen sind
Von lebenden Säulen, Zedern und Lorbeern,
Die feierlichen,
Die göttlichgebauten Paläste.

Es rauschen aber um Asias Tore
Hinziehend da und dort
In ungewisser Meeresebene
Der schattenlosen Strassen genug,
Doch kennt die Inseln der Schiffer.
Und da ich hörte,
Der nahegelegenen eine
Sei Patmos,
Verlangte mich sehr,
Dort einzukehren und dort
Der dunkeln Grotte zu nahn.
Denn nicht, wie Cypros,
Die quellenreiche, oder
Der anderen eine
Wohnt herrlich Patmos,

Gastfreundlich aber ist
Im ärmeren Hause
Sie dennoch
Und wenn vom Schiffbruch oder klagend
Um die Heimat oder
Den abgeschiedenen Freund
Ihr nahet einer
Der Fremden, hört sie es gern, und ihre Kinder,
Die Stimmen des heissen Hains,
Und wo der Sand fällt, und sich spaltet
Des Feldes Fläche, die Laute,
Sie hören ihn und liebend tönt
Es wider von den Klagen des Manns. So pflegte
Sie einst des gottgeliebten,
Des Sehers, der in seliger Jugend war

Gegangen mit
Dem Sohne des Höchsten, unzertrennlich, denn
Es liebte der Gewittertragende die Einfalt
Des Jüngers und es sahe der achtsame Mann
Das Angesicht des Gottes genau,

That silent fire. Still, in light, high
Up, blossoms the silver snow;
And witness to undying life
On walls you and I cannot climb
Ancient the ivy grows, and by living
Pillars: cypresses, laurels, the festive
The god-built
Palaces are carried.

   But there around Asia's doorway,
Stretching far and all over
The perilous waves, unshaded
Seaways surge in abundance.
Yet a boatman will know the islands.
And as I heard that
One of the nearby ones was supposed to
Be Patmos,
I wanted very much
To take rooms there, and there to
Approach the dark grotto.
For it is not as Cyprus,
Wealthy with fountains, or
Any of the others that
Patmos lives in splendor,

Though even in her more modest
House she will play you hostess
Regardless.
And should a stranger come to her, from
Shipwreck, or mourning after
His country or a
Friend who departed--
She is glad to hear it, along with her children,
Voices of the heat-filled grove, and
Where the sand falls and the earth's
Crust cracks they hear him,
These voices, and it's with a love,
The way the place echoes the man's woes. That's how she
Once nursed the godly-beloved,
The Seer, who in blessed youth had

Walked with
The Son of the Highest: inseparably, for
The Thunderbearer loved the clarity
In the Disciple. And that observant man saw
Minutely the countenance of God

Da, beim Geheimnisse des Weinstocks, sie
Zusammensassen, zu der Stunde des Gastmahls,
Und in der grossen Seele, ruhigahnend den Tod
Aussprach der Herr und die letzte Liebe, denn nie genug
Hatt er von Güte zu sagen
Der Worte, damals, und zu erheitern, da
Ers sahe, das Zürnen der Welt.
Denn alles ist gut. Drauf starb er. Vieles wäre
Zu sagen davon. Und es sahn ihn, wie er siegend blickte,
Den Freudigsten die Freunde noch zuletzt,

    Doch trauerten sie, da nun
Es Abend worden, erstaunt,
Denn Grossentschiedenes hatten in der Seele
Die Männer, aber sie liebten unter der Sonne
Das Leben und lassen wollten sie nicht
Vom Angesichte des Herrn
Und der Heimat. Eingetrieben war,
Wie Feuer im Eisen, das, und ihnen ging
Zur Seite der Schatte des Lieben.
Drum sandt er ihnen
Den Geist, und freilich bebte
Das Haus und die Wetter Gottes rollten
Ferndonnernd über
Die ahnenden Häupter, da, schwersinnend,
Versammelt waren die Todeshelden,

Itzt, da er scheidend
Noch einmal ihnen erschien.
Denn itzt erlosch der Sonne Tag,
Der Königliche, und zerbrach
Den geradestrahlenden,
Den Zepter, göttlichleidend, von selbst,
Denn wiederkommen sollt es,
Zu rechter Zeit. Nicht wär es gut
Gewesen, später, und schroffabbrechend, untreu,
Der Menschen Werk, und Freude war es
Von nun an,
Zu wohnen in liebender Nacht, und bewahren
In einfältigen Augen, unverwandt
Abgründe der Weisheit. Und es grünen
Tief an den Bergen auch lebendige Bilder,

Doch furchtbar ist, wie da und dort
Unendlich hin zerstreut das Lebende Gott.
Denn schon das Angesicht

That time when over the vine's mystery they
Sat together at the banquet hour,
And with death in the great soul, quietly feeling
It coming, the Lord spoke of it and the last love, for
He'd never had enough words
On goodness, and not then, nor to cheer up
--Once he saw it--the world's rage.
Because everything is good. That's how he died. A lot could be
Said on that subject. And for a last time the friends
Saw as he glanced victory, him of the ultimate joy,

   And yet they mourned, now that it
Had turned evening, astonished,
For in their souls the men were storing decisions
Bigger than life, while they loved living
Under the sun and would not part
With the Lord's face,
Or with home. Driven in, that was,
As fire is into iron, and their adored
Shadow walked along by their side.
That's why he sent them the
Ghost, and of course, the house
Shook and God's thunderclouds rolled
Far-rumbling over
Their dawning minds as heavy of heart,
Heroes in death, they were gathered

When he in farewell
Appeared to them once more.
For now the light of day,
The Royal One, went out, and smashed
The head-on radiant
Sceptre, in godly suffering, by himself:
Because when the time was right it was
Bound to return. It would not have been good
Later, in abrupt breaking-off, disloyally,
Of the work of men; and it was a joy
From then on
To dwell in the loving night and to conserve
Unlinked, in guileless glances,
Ravines of wisdom. And then deep in the
Mountains living reflections grow green,

Still it is fearsome how at random
And miles on end God disperses the living.
For this meant as much as leaving

Der teuern Freunde zu lassen
Und fernhin über die Berge zu gehn
Allein, wo zweifach
Erkannt, einstimmig
War himmlischer Geist; und nicht geweissagt war es, sondern
Die Locken ergriff es, gegenwärtig,
Wenn ihnen plötzlich
Ferneilend zurück blickte
Der Gott und schwörend,
Damit er halte, wie an Seilen golden
Gebunden hinfort
Das Böse nennend, sie die Hände sich reichten--

    Wenn aber stirbt alsdenn,
An dem am meisten
Die Schönheit hing, dass an der Gestalt
Ein Wunder war und die Himmlischen gedeutet
Auf ihn, und wenn, ein Rätsel ewig füreinander,
Sie sich nicht fassen können
Einander, die zusammenlebten
Im Gedächtnis, und nicht den Sand nur oder
Die Weiden es hinwegnimmt und die Tempel
Ergreift, wenn die Ehre
Des Halbgotts und der Seinen
Verweht und selber sein Angesicht
Der Höchste wendet
Darob, dass nirgend ein
Unsterbliches mehr am Himmel zu sehn ist oder
Auf grüner Erde, was ist dies?

Es ist der Wurf des Säemanns, wenn er fasst
Mit der Schaufel den Weizen,
Und wirft, dem Klaren zu, ihn schwingend über die Tenne.
Ihm fällt die Schale vor den Füssen, aber
Ans Ende kommet das Korn,
Und nicht ein Übel ists, wenn einiges
Verloren gehet und von der Rede
Verhallet der lebendige Laut,
Denn göttliches Werk auch gleichet dem unsern,
Nicht alles will der Höchste zumal.
Zwar Eisen träget der Schacht,
Und glühende Harze der Aetna,
So hätt ich Reichtum,
Ein Bild zu bilden, und ähnlich
Zu schaun, wie er gewesen, den Christ,

The sight of friends dear to you and
Going far over the mountains
Alone, where doubly
Recognized the celestial
Spirit sang unison; nor did it come prophesied: it
Gripped you by the forelocks, right on the spot,
When suddenly
Dashing far off the God glanced
Back at them, and chanting
For him to stop as though bound from that moment
Golden with ropes
They named the evil and reached one another their hands--

But if right then he dies:
Whom beauty embraced
The strongest, so that miracle clung
To that form, and from heaven they made their
Sign on him; and when as eternal riddle for
One another, they who lived
Together in the mind now cannot
Reach one another; and he rips away not
Just the beach or the meadow, and he shakes the
Temples as the cult of
The demigod and of his own
Die out; and if the Supreme One turns
His face away
So that no immortal
Can be seen any longer, either in heaven or
On the green earth--*What is this?*

It is the sower's throw, when he scoops the
Wheat up with his shovel,
And flings it sunward, chasing it over the threshing floor.
Chaff falls at his feet, but
The kernel comes in the end,
And it's no tragedy if a few
Are lost and the living sound from
The sermon dies away,
For the work of gods is much like our own.
Not that the Highest wants all action told.
But if mine shafts bear ores,
And the Etna its resinous fires,
Then I should have riches
To sculpt my image and see him in
Likeness of what he had been, the Christ;

Wenn aber einer spornte sich selbst,
Und traurig redend, unterweges, da ich wehrlos wäre,
Mich überfiele, dass ich staunt und von dem Gotte
Das Bild nachahmen möcht ein Knecht--
Im Zorne sichtbar sah ich einmal
Des Himmels Herrn, nicht, dass ich sein sollt etwas, sondern
Zu lernen. Gütig sind sie, ihr Verhasstestes aber ist,
Solange sie herrschen, das Falsche, und es gilt
Dann Menschliches unter Menschen nicht mehr.
Denn sie nicht walten, es waltet aber
Unsterblicher Schicksal und es wandelt ihr Werk
Von selbst, und eilend geht es zu Ende.
Wenn nämlich höher gehet himmlischer
Triumphgang, wird genennet, der Sonne gleich,
Von Starken der frohlockende Sohn des Höchsten,

Ein Losungszeichen, und hier ist der Stab
Des Gesanges, niederwinkend,
Denn nichts ist gemein. Die Toten wecket
Er auf, die noch gefangen nicht
Vom Rohen sind. Es warten aber
Der scheuen Augen viele,
Zu schauen das Licht. Nicht wollen
Am scharfen Strahle sie blühn,
Wiewohl den Mut der goldene Zaum hält.
Wenn aber, als
Von schwellenden Augenbraunen,
Der Welt vergessen
Stilleuchtende Kraft aus heiliger Schrift fällt, mögen,
Der Gnade sich freuend, sie
Am stillen Blicke sich üben.

Und wenn die Himmlischen jetzt
So, wie ich glaube, mich lieben,
Wie viel mehr Dich,
Denn Eines weiss ich,
Dass nämlich der Wille
Des ewigen Vaters viel
Dir gilt. Still ist sein Zeichen
Am donnernden Himmel. Und Einer stehet darunter
Sein Leben lang. Denn noch lebt Christus.
Es sind aber die Helden, seine Söhne,
Gekommen all und heilige Schriften
Von ihm und den Blitz erklären
Die Taten der Erde bis itzt,

But then if some man spurred himself on
And on the road, where I would be unarmed, attacked
Me with mournful tongue, that I should gape while that
Lackey might render the portrait of God--
That's how I once saw the lords of heaven in
Blooded scorn: not that I was to be anything, but
To learn. They are kind, and what they despise
Above all, while ruling, is falseness, a time when
Nothing human counts among men any more.
For they don't govern; it's never-dying
Fate that does the governing, and their influence
Walks abroad by itself, and hurries on to its end.
For see, every time the triumphal procession of
Heaven ascends even higher, then by the Powered,
Sunlike, the Dancing Son of the Highest is named

   A password; and here is the baton
Of song, giving the beat earthward,
For none is unworthy. Now he wakes
The dead, whom crudity
Has not yet spoiled. But many wait
With bashful glances
To behold the light. They'd rather not
Flourish in strong sunlight,
Though that golden harness holds their lust.
But when, as from
Swollen eyebrows and in the
Forgetting of this world,
Silent light falls in strength from sacred scripture, then
Celebrant of that grace they
May rehearse quiet vision.

And if in heaven now
They love me as I believe it,
Then how much more you,
For I do know one thing,
Namely that the eternal
Father's will has always meant
Much to you. His sign is calm
On the thundering sky. And someone shall stand
Under it his life long. For Christ lives today.
Only by now the heroes, his sons,
Have come, all of them, and holy writings
As well; and it's the lightning that
The world's deeds announce to this moment--

Ein Wettlauf unaufhaltsam. Er ist aber dabei. Denn seine
    Werke sind
Ihm alle bewusst von jeher.

Zu lang, zu lang schon ist
Die Ehre der Himmlischen unsichtbar.
Denn fast die Finger müssen sie
Uns führen und schmählich
Entreisst das Herz uns eine Gewalt.
Denn Opfer will der Himmlischen jedes,
Wenn aber eines versäumt ward,
Nie hat es Gutes gebracht.
Wir haben gedienet der Mutter Erd
Und haben jüngst dem Sonnenlichte gedient,
Unwissend, der Vater aber liebt,
Der über allen waltet,
Am meisten, dass gepfleget werde
Der feste Buchstab, und Bestehendes gut
Gedeutet. Dem folgt deutscher Gesang.

One relentless track race. And he attends it. For his works
    have been
Known to him all along.

All too long now the cult of
Celestials has not been in evidence.
That's because they all but have to lead us
By the fingers, and a power
Tears at our hearts for sheer meanness.
Look: all in heaven demand offerings,
And any time but one of them was slighted
It's never yet brought any good.
We have borne service to our Mother the Earth
And have recently also served the Sun God
--In ignorance--; but the Father who rules
Over the whole world
Prefers above all that the fixed letter
Be attended, and that what exists be
Worthily treated of. This German poetry fulfills.

Translated by Emery E. George

Hölderlin's Hymn "Patmos": Comments

by Emery E. George

The five late poems presented in translation in this closing
section include the ode "Vulkan," the elegy "Heimkunft," and
the hymn "Patmos" as representative examples from that portion
of Hölderlin's oeuvre that most unmistakably identifies him as
an early modern. Between 1800 and 1804, the closing period of
his lucid career, the three classical lyric forms of the ode,
the elegy, and the Pindaric hymn all but completely absorbed
the energies he devoted to original poetic creation. Especially
in a series that includes six of the last great odes--"Chiron,"
"Tränen," "An die Hoffnung," "Vulkan," "Blödigkeit," "Ganymed"[1]--
six elegies--"Menons Klagen um Diotima," "Der Wanderer," "Der
Gang aufs Land," "Stutgard," "Brod und Wein," "Heimkunft"--and
twelve hymns--"Wie wenn am Feiertage," "Der Mutter Erde," "Am
Quell der Donau," "Die Wanderung," "Der Rhein," "Germanien,"
"Friedensfeier," "Der Einzige," "Patmos," "Andenken," "Der Ister,"
"Mnemosyne"--the poet attained a degree of lyric expression and
craftsmanship reached by very few poets, either before or after
Hölderlin. It is in these twenty-four poetic documents perhaps
more than anywhere else that Hölderlin demonstrates his paradoxical ability to break away from the Greeks in order to become
one of them in the truer sense. Certainly, in both elegy and

258

hymn Hölderlin is often said to have staked out new formal boundaries within which to accommodate a virtually limitless spiritual energy. If I may pursue the metaphor, the texts of the new poems are maps of the new countries of the mind Hölderlin discovered. We have every right to feel, if we wish, that "Heimkunft" and "Patmos," the most exquisitely engraved maps, may well represent the most marvelous of these new countries--in other words, that these two poems are the most perfectly constructed examples of Hölderlin's elegiac and hymnic art that we have.

I, for one, feel that "Heimkunft" and "Patmos" *are* two of Hölderlin's crowning works. But even if this were a matter of universal agreement--and I am aware that it is not--we could well feel that so exclusive a concentration on the elegiac and hymnic corpus between 1800 and 1804 tends to slight equally wonderful works of that period, notably odes like "Chiron" and "Ganymed," the puzzling short poem "Hälfte des Lebens," or the angular Pindar and Sophokles translations. Despite this, I must go one step further and suggest an even clearer and more painful separation. For it is not even in the elegies so much as in the late hymns, the body of controlled free verse inspired by the example of Pindar's epinikian odes, that Hölderlin most successfully transmuted the Greek poetic experience into a creative moment that bears Hölderlin's stamp and no one else's. The fact that in the field of hymnic expression Hölderlin began by experimenting with Pindar's strict metrical scheme, the so-called responsion, is amply attested in his sole experimental text, "Wie wenn am Feiertage"; and the hymn following it in the *Grosse Stuttgarter Ausgabe,* "Der Mutter Erde," shows that Hölderlin was also fascinated by possibilities of individual and choric response in hymnic poetry (a fascination possibly inspired by the choruses of Greek tragedy, and very possibly worked out definitively in the language of "Friedensfeier"). Both "Wie wenn am Feiertage" and "Der Mutter Erde" were left unfinished.

It was in the ten poems that followed that it was given to Hölderlin to speak, in his new mobility and freedom, of the concerns always nearest to him: of the life of the man of genius, of the immediacy of mythic religious experience, of the reconciliation of opposed cultural traditions, of the poet's indispensable role in bringing to men the message of divinely sponsored universal peace. This is not to say that "Wie wenn am Feiertage" does not reflect some of these concerns. But the feeling of community and the choric attitude that prevail in this early experiment soon give way to that characteristic confrontation with the self, to that experience of brilliant, even frightening aloneness without which the poet's self-image, especially in "Der Rhein," "Patmos," and "Mnemosyne," would not be what it is.

Many critics and scholars, not the least among them Edwin Muir and C. M. Bowra, have written illuminatingly on "Patmos," and it is not my intention here to attempt to discuss or evaluate what they have said. Nor do I wish to continue, in the present connection, the textual and stylistic studies on "Patmos" that I have undertaken elsewhere. In the following my remarks will be almost purely of a personal bent. I would like to go back to what first attracted me to the poem; to what made me read it many times, study it systematically, and finally to what made me translate it. The structure of my comments will be the approximate reverse of that of Professor Hamlin's, in that I would first like to talk about conceptual, then about linguistic matters. Finally, I should like to defend (if a defense is needed) the validity of the kind of translation I attempt, especially in view of the fact that previous translations of "Patmos" into English known to me have now come to number in the vicinity of one dozen separate offerings.[2]

I

My first acquaintance with Hölderlin's hymn "Patmos" goes back
to the summer of 1959 at Michigan, when I first participated in
Martin Dyck's graduate seminar on the life and works of the poet.
It was read to me in that class by the Italian-American critic
Glauco Cambon, who had accepted an invitation to give a guest
lecture. Although Professor Cambon used a very modest text for
the occasion--the Hölderlin volume in the Goldmanns Gelbe Taschenbücher series[3]--and, in addition, limited his reading and explication to stanza 1 of the hymn, I remember having been deeply
impressed. I felt even then that this moment was an important
beginning in my understanding of a great poet, and this feeling
was encouraged by the poem's obscure title, its forbidding opening lines, and by its discoursing on danger among mythical mountain peaks, on crossing over and returning above the world's
waters. Later, as I read the entire hymn (and I recall that it
seemed, on that first unabridged reading, interminably long,
but strange and disturbing as well) and gradually came to famil-
iarize myself with its every detail, my initial feeling on the
level of spiritual energy in the poem came to be confirmed.
First of all, the hushed silence pervading the poem seemed as
inescapable to me then as it does now. It seemed to be a silence
having to do with distance and time, a silence of initial noncom-
prehension and suspecting and of subsequent learning and illumination. A year or so later, after I had become quite comfortable
with the poem's length and architecture and had begun to understand something of its demonstrable content, I recall that the
issue of silence did not disappear but only became more insistent.
For then, after everything that could be written on Hölderlin's
debt to such sources as the Bible and Klopstock had been written
down, and after "Patmos" had become the subject of several important interpretations (by that time I had read Edwin Muir's
essay, as well as Alice Gladstone's interpretation of "Patmos"
in the special Hölderlin issue of the *Quarterly Review of Liter-*

ature),[4] I still felt that I had not touched on that center of
the poem that the disturbing silence was being silent about.

A second important stage of my understanding of Hölderlin's
creative act was reached, I think, when I realized that the poet's
dreadful silence within the poem runs simultaneously with his
creation of poetic language--out of nothing. It is certainly
no deep critical insight to suggest that, if "Patmos" is a philosophical poem (and it has been called that time and time again),
it bears no resemblance to any of Schiller's so-called philosophical poems. Also, it may seem provocative, although surely far-
fetched at first, to compare Hölderlin's severely restrained
diction with the understatement that marks the poetic language
of Hemingway. Yet if Schiller and Hemingway somehow seem inappropriate as bases for direct comparison, perhaps no styles can
serve us better than theirs in our immediate, common-sense effort
to assess the magnitude of Hölderlin's achievement. For it was
the noise, the empty grandiloquence of Schiller's hymnic language
from which Hölderlin eventually felt he had to get away (and
"Patmos" was conceived at just about the time Schiller finally
stopped answering Hölderlin's highly ambivalent letters), and
it is in the silence of the exquisitely wrought poetic prose of
such an author as Hemingway that, whether we are fully aware of
it or not, we may well discover some of the silence Hölderlin
has to offer. At least I speak for myself (and I suspect for
many of my contemporaries) when I say that both Hemingway and
Schiller (occasioned by different needs, to be sure) had become
important reading to me by the time I discovered Hölderlin. The
temporal proximity between background and discovery helped me
soon to understand how very much unlike his own contemporary
(Schiller) and how much like ours (Hemingway) Hölderlin really
is. And already in those earlier days (including the spring of
1962, when I began translating "Patmos") it was not the semantic
concerns of the poet that made me grateful to know his work, but
rather his unique conception of language, involving especially

the strange and wonderful entente Hölderlin effects between
language and silence.

II

Wherein does this silence reside and how do we grasp it? How
do we come to have a guarantee of its poetic usefulness? The
poem "Patmos" is about a journey from the present to the past,
and back again to the present; and that, to judge from previous
commentaries as well as my own individual reading, is the substance of my immediate interpretive understanding of it. The
journey is the conceptual substance of the poem, it is its *message*, and the poem is the journey itself. This all seems true
and compelling enough. Yet it is well to remember that by the
time Hölderlin began to copy out into the fair his dedication
copy of "Patmos" for the fifty-fifth birthday of Heinrich Ludwig,
Landgrave of Hessen-Homburg (January, 1803), he, the poet, had
already taken this journey many times in his mind.[5] In the
process of writing down his poetic document the poet must, I
think, be thought of as taking his journey simultaneously in
its every moment. One of the most important clues to this is
that, in the overall architecture of the poem, it is at two of
its most crucial points that the poet sees to it that language
fail him--and us. The first point comes at stanza 6, lines
13-14:

Denn alles ist gut. Drauf starb er. Vieles wäre
Zu sagen davon.

(Because everything is good. That's how he died. A lot could be
Said on that subject.)

And the poet leaves it at that; he does not enter into the secret
of that *"Vieles."* A lot could be said on that subject--that is

all we are told. It is notable that, immediately preceding this
passage (stanza 6, lines 9-11):

Aussprach der Herr und die letzte Liebe, denn nie genug
Hatt er von Güte zu sagen
Der Worte, ...

             (the Lord spoke of it and the last love, for
He'd never had enough words
On goodness, ...)

the Lord speaks, and immediately after, silence, the language
of the eye, dominates: *"wie er siegend blickte"* (as he glanced
victory [stanza 6, line 14; ibid., line 15 in the translation]).
The second crucial point on the limitations of language occurs
at the end of stanza 12 and the beginning of stanza 13:

Wenn nämlich höher gehet himmlischer
Triumphgang, wird genennet, der Sonne gleich,
Von Starken der frohlockende Sohn des Höchsten,

   Ein Losungszeichen, ...

(For see, every time the triumphal procession of
Heaven ascends even higher, then by the Powered,
Sunlike, the Dancing Son of the Highest is named

   A password; ....)

Celebrant naming constitutes, for Hölderlin, a nuclear act of
language; here it is all the more telling that the Christ, now
dancing in his triumph across the firmament of the mind, can
yet be grasped by no more than a formula, a mere password.
Words in the meaningful texture of language fail us in the
presence of the divine.
     This is the intent of the great invocation of the hymn,
of its beginning:

Nah ist
Und schwer zu fassen der Gott.

(Up close
That hard to hold fast, is God.)

This opening, silent gnome contains the proportional statement:
"The nearer God is, the harder it is to grasp him," and he is
close to the poet now, if he ever was. But this very closeness
of the God represents a danger; the poet finds himself in the
mountainous landscape of myth, and knows that if he were to
reach out and could not take a secure hold of the God he is
reaching for, he would lose balance and tumble down into the
abyss. The situation is fraught with danger and the gnome is
silent; language is not yet there for the poet to use.[6] The
soul's obscure yearning remains unexpressed, however, for but
a moment; rescue follows on the danger with speed. In an incredible image the poet sees eagles and men cross over between
peaks of the Alps (stanza 1, lines 5-8):

Im Finstern wohnen
Die Adler und furchtlos gehn
Die Söhne der Alpen über den Abgrund weg
Auf leichtgebaueten Brücken.

(Eagles live in the
Dark, and the Alps' sons
Go their ways, fearless over the chasm
On lightly-built bridges.)

and he has caught the hint that the invisible numinous presence
had given him (stanza 1, lines 9-12):

... gehäuft sind rings
Die Gipfel der Zeit, und die Liebsten
Nah wohnen, ermattend auf
Getrenntesten Bergen, ...

(... round us emerge
The peaks of time, and our well-loved
Live near and weary on
The farthest mountains ....)

He now knows: he must undertake a journey across the waters of
time, back into sacred history, and back through curved time to
the present again. And the poem, which is the journey itself,
is to contain those "peaks of time"; the secret of the success
of the allegorical journey about to be undertaken is that the
"peaks of time" are the peaks of the poem, and "our well-loved"
is to be interpreted as precisely those insights on the functioning and failure of poetic language that the poet must visit
and pass over in search of spiritual enlightenment and direction.

Hölderlin's insight in "Patmos" is that time, like space,
is curved and, if we return to the earlier cartographic metaphor
for but a moment, we may reflect that the poem's text, the map
of the journey, may appear flat like a world map in Mercator
projection. However that may be, world maps must show continents, and the map of "Patmos" certainly shows five great continents in an unmistakable and courageous way. But what are
these continents? The poet starts out from and returns to
Europe; *"Asia"* (Asia Minor, the Greece of the islands) is his
immediate goal (stanza 3, line 1; stanza 4, line 1); these are
only two; semantic interpretation breaks down. The real continents of the poet's travel through the world of his poem are the
five great groups of stanzas, or *triads*, of which the poem is
composed.[7] One recalls Hölderlin's very helpful manuscript note
to "Der Rhein," like "Patmos" constructed of five great triads
of stanzas, and wonders whether the *"Gesetz"* (law) of poetic
form drafted in this note is applicable to the structure of the
later hymn. The note reads (2:722):

*Das Gesetz dieses Gesanges ist, dass die zwei ersten Parthien
der Form nach durch Progress und Regress entgegengesetzt,
aber dem Stoff nach gleich, die zwei folgenden der Form nach*

gleich dem Stoff nach entgegengesetzt sind die letzte aber
mit durchgängiger Metapher alles ausgleicht.

(It is the principle of this poem that its first two parts,
in terms of progression and regression, are opposed to each
other as regards their form, while they are alike in content;
the two following parts are alike in form but opposed in
content; while the last part reconciles everything in pervasive metaphor.)

This principle suggests that semantic and formal realization in
the poem are governed by its division into its triads of stanzas,
and by one final grouping of these triads in a pattern of two
triads, followed by another two triads, followed by a single
triad (2 + 2 + 1). In our listening to the poem's progress it
is helpful to assume that the poet wanted to make his pattern
(2 + 2 + 1) audible by incorporating into the poetic texture
crucial features at the ends of triads II and IV--that is, at
the ends of stanzas 6 and 12. And indeed it is here that we
find those unmistakable hints on the breakdown of language that
I pointed to earlier; first at stanza 6, lines 13-14:

                          Vieles wäre
Zu sagen davon.

                        (A lot could be
Said on that subject.)

then at stanza 13, line 1: *"Ein Losungszeichen"* (A password).
Although considerations of *"Form"* (here I borrow from the termi-
nology of Hölderlin's note) would seem to belong in the realm of
language, and of this I shall speak presently, a suggestion on
the realization of the principle in control of "Der Rhein" in
the hymn "Patmos" on both the semantic and formal planes might
look like this (by *"Stoff"* I mean narrative content; by *"Form,"*
the moods and stances of poetic diction):

Triad	*"Stoff"*			*"Form"*		
I	Asia	}	like	hushed	}	unlike
II	Asia			everyday		
III	Gospel	}	unlike	hushed	}	like
IV	present			hushed		
V	*"Der feste Buchstab"*			mixed	→	balanced

This is of course a greatly simplified diagram. On the level of
"Stoff" the poet's fivefold progression takes him through the
journey to *"Asia"*; to his residence there (on Patmos); to his
recalling sacred history immediately following the Passion; to
the Passion itself and through it; to the return of the poet to
the present; and finally to the life of the past in the present
through the cultivation of *"der feste Buchstab"* meaning the fixed
letter of human record--that is, first and foremost of scripture
and of the poetic word.

After the initial invocation of stanza 1 (which should be
understood as being enclosed in quotation marks) the crossing
over to *"Asia"* is accomplished in mystery, in hushed silence,
in the feeling of the simultaneous freshness and agelessness of
the world. In its great richness of imagery, stanza 3 makes
this feeling secure and triumphantly closes the opening triad.
But triad II, although it sustains the theme of the Asian journey, immediately turns away from the blinding Byzantine splendor
of preceding lines and concentrates on splendor of a different
order. The poet must now seek the "more modest house" of the
island of Patmos, of the John of Revelation, a desolate place
of grotto and (stanza 5, lines 9-11):

> *des heissen Hains,*
> *Und wo der Sand fällt, und sich spaltet*
> *Des Feldes Fläche, ...*

```
        (of the heat-filled grove, and
Where the sand falls and the earth's
Crust cracks ....)
```

But it is precisely here that the poet, following the example
of John, tries to recapture his image of the Christ. It seems
clear that, no less than at the beginning of the hymn, here at
the end of stanza 6 Hölderlin is still praying for the clarity
that "the Thunderbearer loved ... in the Disciple," so that with
its aid he too might see, if but for a moment, "minutely the
countenance of God" (stanza 6, lines 3-5). The words *victory*
and *joy* in the final line of triad II I take to be important
hints--fruitful later in the poem--that the poet's wish has been
granted him and that his trip to *"Asia,"* a persistently recurring image and spiritual destination in Hölderlin's late poetry,
has up to this first resting point in "Patmos" accomplished its
purpose.

The second group of triads (III and IV) opens with the word
"Doch" (and yet [stanza 7, line 1]), an important pivoting particle
in Hölderlin's late compositional rhetoric. The poet is still
in *"Asia,"* but he has effected yet another transition. He has
transported himself back into the past related in the Gospels
and the Acts: into the story of the first Pentecost, of the
supper at Emmaus, of the tragic dispersal of the disciples, and
finally--in a tour de force that shatters the triad boundary
between III and IV--of the Passion itself. Characteristically
for Hölderlin's uncompromising asymmetrical technique in this
hymn, the strict stanza-by-stanza organization of the material
runs parallel with the mixed chronology; from stanzas 7 through
10, we have: Pentecost, Emmaus, dispersal, Passion. But the
stanza on the Passion (which, narratively, is the least important part of Hölderlin's Christology in this poem) performs,
between the materially *unlike* triads III and IV, an authoritative
pivoting role; the question *"Was ist dies?"* (*What is this?* [stanza
10, line 16, my italics]) is answered on the level of the pivoting

itself. It is a chiastic experience. The incomprehension and
noncommunication with which the latter half of stanza 10 is concerned point back to stanza 9, to lines 3-6:

> *Denn schon das Angesicht*
> *Der teuern Freunde zu lassen*
> *Und fernhin über die Berge zu gehn*
> *Allein, ...*

> (For this meant as much as leaving
> The sight of friends dear to you and
> Going far over the mountains
> Alone, ...)

while the concern of the first lines of stanza 10, the beauty
of the dying Christ, points ahead to the passionate affirmation
of stanza 11, lines 11-15:

> *Zwar Eisen träget der Schacht,*
> *Und glühende Harze der Aetna,*
> *So hätt ich Reichtum,*
> *Ein Bild zu bilden, und ähnlich*
> *Zu schaun, wie er gewesen, den Christ, ...*

> (But if mine shafts bear ores,
> And the Etna its resinous fires,
> Then I should have riches
> To sculpt my image and see him in
> Likeness of what he had been, the Christ; ....)

and the poet is right back in the midst of his contemporary
time; once again, it is a central position. On the other side
of his mountain, his Etna with "its resinous fires," we see the
image of the sower's throw, as Hölderlin says elsewhere, of
"die notwenige Willkür des Zeus" (the necessary arbitrariness
of the God [4:269]). For (stanza 11, lines 6-8):

> *nicht ein Übel ists, wenn einiges*
> *Verloren gehet und von der Rede*
> *Verhallet der lebendige Laut, ...*

(And it's no tragedy if a few
Are lost and the living sound from
The sermon dies away, ...)

as the time is coming for a more secure and lasting affirmation
of the divine. Far more potentially tragic is the danger to be
feared in modern times from idolaters and falsifiers of art,
active at times when "nothing human counts among men any more"
(stanza 12, line 9). The poet can guard against them in two
ways: by being a lifelong disciple of divine truths (stanza 12,
lines 6-7):

> *nicht, dass ich sein sollt etwas, sondern*
Zu lernen.

> (not that I was to be anything, but
To learn.)

and by reaffirming once again the essential oneness of religious
experience, Greek and Christian.

　　And this union Hölderlin accomplishes in "Patmos" in the
most central way possible. Our clue to this mystical wedding of
the Greek and the Christian is the poet's image of Mount Etna
with its fiery resins, out of which he will scoop molten riches
to sculpt, to cast, his new image of the Christ. In doing this
he knows that his raw material will be the living substance,
the fiery flesh and blood, of the ancient healer and teacher
Empedokles, who in this act of recreation will return to become
the brother, the identical twin, we might say, of the living
Christ. Even the assertion made in "Der Einzige" that Christ
is a brother to Herakles and Dionysos cannot compare in subtlety
and beauty with the silent suggestion in "Patmos" that the
pre-Socratic philosopher who proclaimed himself a god (see the
first version of Hölderlin's drama *Der Tod des Empedokles* [4:
3-85]) and the Hebrew prophet who said, "I am Alpha and Omega" (Rev.
22:13) are, on the level of world mythology, one and the same

numinous personage. This silent suggestion invites me also to
speculate--although a speculation it must very likely remain--
that *"der frohlockende Sohn des Höchsten"* (the Dancing Son of
the Highest) named in the closing line of triad IV may also
reach out his hand to another dancing god in Eastern religion,
to the destructive and regenerative force in the Hindu pantheon,
Siva Nataraja, the Lord of the Dance.[8]

He is named "a password," as we learn at the beginning of
triad V. He is named an isolated word, a secret word, an emblem-
atic word meaningful in a given context of the divine. Uttering
it will admit one to the presence of language and silence at
once. And indeed, in the pervasive metaphor of triad V we are
back with the wonderful silent diction of the beginning of the
poem, where every point along the locus of points constituting
the poet's realm is now central to his purpose: to attend the
fixed letter, to cultivate the tradition of the divine and the
truly human in those acts of interpretation of which only poets
are capable--*"Dem folgt deutscher Gesang"* (This German poetry
fulfills).

III

At the end of the foreword to his translation of the *Iliad*,
Richmond Lattimore thanks "all those friends who have sustained
me in the belief that this work was worth doing, and refrained
from asking: 'Why do another translation of Homer?'; a question
which has no answer for those who do not know the answer already."[9] I must confess I have moments when I feel very much
like Lattimore, not because I dare compare my translation with
his, but because I have worked on this translation of "Patmos,"
off and on, for the past nine years, and all along it has been
a labor of love. Originally I only listened to the strange music
of Hölderlin's hymn, and then I began writing down what I heard,
but only for myself, if I may quote, "not that I was to be

anything, but to learn." But not too long after that beginning
I also began to feel, after many listenings, that what I was
hearing was Hölderlin's true voice, rather than something foreign or subjectively imagined, and from that point on I felt
that it was legitimate for me to work on what I hope emerges
here as a poetic translation.

Reading "Patmos" aloud is an experience in the living word;
and it is only by such rigorous self-training over a long period
of time that the aspiring poet-translator can hope to catch the
refinements of phrase, rhythm, prosody, and overall contour that
constitute the inner life of the poem. The problem of rendering
the opening two lines illustrates this oral-aural principle in
merciless clarity. The lines:

> *Nah ist*
> *Und schwer zu fassen der Gott.*

are two of the most difficult in all of German poetry. For the
translator bent on anything approaching literal accuracy they
have represented an impassable obstacle; it is simply not possible to preserve the prosodic and visual shapes of the two
starkly contrasting lines and at the same time strike a sound
that matches the enormous difficulty of the poet's conception.
The closest I came (and it is a solution I have not seen anywhere else) was:

> Near
> And hard to grasp. That's God.

But a solution like this offers other problems, and I felt that
neither the syntactic break in line 2 nor, in this particular
setting, the contraction "that's" was quite appropriate to the
Pindaric gnome that so palpably constitutes Hölderlin's utterance. Only a willingness to make sacrifices on one level, the
visual, would bring me closer to the results desired on the

other level, the aural. The slowness and hardness of *"Nah ist,"* implemented by the length of the vowel in *"Nah"* and by the glottal stop preceding *"ist,"* could possibly be approached by two English words so juxtaposed that their consonantal juncture would necessarily slow them down. Thus I ventured "Up close," an equivalent no doubt much closer to Hölderlin's original in the spirit than in the letter.

Another level of linguistic energy is carried in the poem by inter-stanzaic enjambement, and here one has to be equally careful. I have seen translations that simply put a period at the end of a stanza merely because the end of the given stanza coincides with an end-point in syntactic structure. But Hölderlin makes it an important point of technique, and not only in "Patmos," to run the utterance on between stanzas and even triads of a long poem; and if we look at "Patmos" closely we find that only six of its fifteen stanzas end on a full stop. Even more important, the first three of these are distributed over the first four triads (stanzas 1, 3, and 10). In addition, sensitive handling of the striking inter-stanzaic enjambement between stanzas 2 and 3 seems imperative; it is at this point in his journey that the poet obtains first glimpse at his Asia, and the word *"Asia"* must come through with every bit as much force and wonder as in the German, where too it is delayed by one syllable: *"Mir Asia auf."* It is at this moment of grace that I felt it justifiable to enrich the diction by a phonic repetitive feature not present in the German (stanza 3, lines 1-2):

> Asia *b*urst into *b*lossom *b*efore me, and
> *Bl*inded, ...

as well as by a rhythmic energy that the poem picks up for the first time at this point.

Although the presumable metrical structure of the late hymns has often been commented on and at times analyzed with more vigor than success, I believe there is a sensible approach to this

problem, one that does not obligate us to any rigorously systematic view. We can observe that the prosodic matrix of the Pindaric free verse has embedded in it important and clearly audible
vestiges of the metrical systems—elegiac, odic, iambic—within
which Hölderlin had worked earlier. While making no attempt to
transplant the vestigial patterns of the original line by line,
I did feel justified, once again in the Hölderlinian spirit of
perceptive practice, in giving certain important passages considerable metric and rhythmic aplomb. Thus (whatever the original
sounds like *at this particular point*), I was happy to be able
to conclude triad III in strong dactylic-anapestic meter:

> and chanting
> For him to stop as though bound from that moment
> Golden with ropes
> They named the evil and reached one another their hands—

Something very similar happens at the end of triad IV, where the
insistent rhythm seems to be the music of the procession itself:

> For see, every time the triumphal procession of
> Heaven ascends even higher, then by the Powered,
> Sunlike, the Dancing Son of the Highest is named ....

One could continue at length pointing out prosodic features
by means of which the translator hopes he has captured something
of his poet's energy. There remains everywhere in "Patmos" the
awesome range of diction between the hushed and holy and the
jarring and downright journalistic, between naïve exultation and
serious understatement. Structurally, there remain the line
lengths, the struggle of syntax against line and stanza, the
powerful enjambement effects. These the attentive reader will,
I hope, recognize and delight in as being at least reminiscent
of Hölderlin's intent. But particulars aside, in the end, one
other, overriding principle must be heard as well. And that is
that the translator must ultimately take a poem and give a poem

in return. I know of no theory of translation that surpasses
this one, either in simplicity or in difficulty. Whether or
not my translation of "Patmos" is a poem I must leave to others
to judge. I would like to close my remarks by expressing thanks
to previous translators, to masters like Vernon Watkins and
Michael Hamburger, who in a multiplicity of ways have shown me
how to look and listen more effectively than I could look and
listen before. In so doing, they have also been among those
who have helped me understand Hölderlin, a poet who, better than
most poets in any age, ancient or modern, has shown us that a
life in the spirit is the life most truly worth living.

Notes

Unless noted otherwise (as, e.g., in the paper by Fiedler), all references to Hölderlin's works and letters by volume and page alone are to the standard quarto edition—the *Grosse Stuttgarter Hölderlin-Ausgabe:* Hölderlin, *Sämtliche Werke,* vols. 1-5 ed. Friedrich Beissner; vols. 6-7 *(Briefe, Dokumente)* ed. Adolf Beck (Stuttgart: Kohlhammer, Cotta, 1943—). Italic volume and page reference is to the first printing of *Hyperion,* in keeping with the practice in vol. 3 of the *Grosse Stuttgarter Ausgabe.* The spelling of all Hölderlin quotations, in the text as in the notes, is that of the shortened octavo edition *(Kleine Stuttgarter Ausgabe):* Hölderlin, *Sämtliche Werke,* vols. 1-5 ed. Friedrich Beissner; vol. 6 ed. Adolf Beck (Stuttgart: Kohlhammer, Cotta, 1946-59).

The following abbreviations are used throughout the book:

CL   *Comparative Literature*

DuV   *Dichtung und Volkstum*

DVLG   *Deutsche Vierteljahrsschrift für Literaturwissenschaft und Geistesgeschichte*

F   Sigmund Freud, *Gesammelte Werke,* ed. Anna Freud, 18 vols. (London: Imago, 1940-52).

GR   *The Germanic Review*

GRM   *Germanisch-Romanische Monatsschrift*

H   Hölderlin, *Werke,* ed. Marie Joachimi-Dege, 2 vols. (Berlin: Bong, n.d. [1908]).

HöJb   *Hölderlin-Jahrbuch*

HW   Hölderlin, *Sämtliche Werke,* ed. Norbert v. Hellingrath, Friedrich Seebass, and Ludwig v. Pigenot, 6 vols., 2d ed. (Berlin: Propyläen, 1922-23).

JDSG   *Jahrbuch der Deutschen Schiller-Gesellschaft*

JEGP   *Journal of English and Germanic Philology*

MLR	*Modern Language Review*
N	Friedrich v. Hardenberg [Novalis], *Schriften*, ed. Paul Kluckhohn and Richard Samuel (Stuttgart: Kohlhammer, 1960--).
OGS	*Oxford German Studies*
PEGS	*Publications of the English Goethe Society*
PMLA	*Publications of the Modern Language Association of America*
QRL	*Quarterly Review of Literature*
R	Rainer Maria Rilke, *Sämtliche Werke*, ed. Ernst Zinn, 6 vols. (Frankfurt am Main: Insel, 1955-66).
RB	Rainer Maria Rilke, *Briefe*, ed. Karl Altheim, 2 vols. (Wiesbaden: Insel, 1950).
S	Friedrich Schlegel, *Kritische Schriften*, ed. Wolfdietrich Rasch, 2d ed. (Munich: Hanser, 1964).
T	Georg Trakl, *Dichtungen und Briefe*, ed. Walther Killy and Hans Szklenar, 2 vols. (Salzburg: Otto Müller, 1969).
W	Josef Weinheber, *Sämtliche Werke*, ed. Josef Nadler and Hedwig Weinheber, 5 vols. (Salzburg: Otto Müller, 1953-56).
ZfgNP	*Zeitschrift für die gesamte Neurologie und Psychiatrie*

Introduction

1. Lawrence J. Ryan, *Hölderlins Lehre vom Wechsel der Töne* (Stuttgart: Kohlhammer, 1960), p. 7.

2. This statement by Stephen Koch is quoted in Egon Schwarz, "Hermann Hesse, the American Youth Movement, and Problems of Literary Evaluation," *PMLA* 85 (1970): 981.

3. Pierre Bertaux, *Hölderlin und die französische Revolution* (Frankfurt am Main: Suhrkamp, 1969).

4. *PMLA* 85:978.

5. One need not, of course, go so far as not to celebrate at all, as the French largely did not, on November 9, 1968, the fiftieth anniversary of the death of Guillaume Apollinaire. More understandable was the near-silence on Hölderlin in America in 1970. To my knowledge, major Hölderlin bicentennial observances in the Western Hemisphere were limited to two events: the Ann Arbor Symposium was matched, earlier in the year, by a similar occasion in Buenos Aires.

6. Robert T. Clark, Jr., *Herder: His Life and Thought* (Berkeley and Los Angeles: University of California Press, 1955), p. 423.

7. M. B. Benn, *Hölderlin and Pindar* (The Hague: Mouton, 1962), p. 96.

8. See only the numerous references in the late poetry and the last drafts and fragments, from the elegy "Stutgard" an, to such medieval and late-medieval figures as: Barbarossa, Columbus, Conradin, Henry IV, Luther, Shakespeare, Ugolino. See also Wilhelm Böhm, *Hölderlin,* 2 vols. (Halle: Niemeyer, 1928-30), 2:494-504, and the introduction to Hölderlin, *Selected Verse,* ed. Michael Hamburger (Baltimore: Penguin, 1961), pp. xxv-xxvi.

9. Alex Preminger, ed., *Encyclopedia of Poetry and Poetics* (Princeton: Princeton University Press, 1965), p. 521.

Herbert Barrows

1. Will Vesper, ed., *Hölderlins Leben in seinen Briefen und Gedichten* (Berlin: Deutsche Bibliothek, n.d. 1915).

2. Edwin Muir's poem "Hölderlin's Journey" was first published in Muir's volume of poems *Journeys and Places* (London: Dent, 1937); Stephen Spender's "Hoelderlin's Old Age" was included in his book *The Still Centre* (London: Faber and Faber, 1939). Some of the references to Hölderlin, but by no means all, which helped to create a characteristic awareness of him among the readers of literary periodicals (as distinguished from professional students of German literature) during the thirties and forties may be listed here. In *New Verse,* edited by Geoffrey Grigson and published in London from January 1933 until May 1939, there is no mention of Hölderlin until 1938. In January 1938 W. H. Auden, reviewing Laurence Housman's *Memoir* of A. E. Housman, quotes the second stanza of "Sokrates und Alcibiades" without identifying it: in the second line, a misprint replaces *"Jugend"* with *"Tugend."* Hölderlin is invoked in Frederic Prokosch's "Ode" in March 1938:

> Walkers in cities, invalids, Hölderlin and the
> Sublime Racine. To these I listened ....

Edwin Muir's essay "Hölderlin," announced for an earlier number of *New Verse,* was published in No. 30, Summer 1938. In the same number appeared Dent's advertisement for David Gascoyne's *Hölderlin's Madness:* "These free renderings of a selection of the poems of the German romantic, Hölderlin, convey the startling intensity of mood and mania which made his tragic life and work so influential."

　In Cyril Connolly's *Horizon,* published in London from January 1940 to December 1949, there also appeared a number of Hölderlin items, beginning in October 1943 with Stephen Spender's lucid and incisive article "Hoelderlin, Goethe and Germany" (8: 273-80). The same periodical published translations of four poems by Hölderlin in April 1944 (9:222-27), two of them by Vernon Watkins ("Hyperions Schicksalslied" and "Hälfte des Lebens") and

two by Frederic Prokosch ("Sokrates und Alcibiades" and "Da ich
ein Knabe war"), together with the German texts. In February
1945 *Horizon* published Vernon Watkins's translation of "Die
Heimat" (11:85). The 1944 translations had been accompanied
by a brief statement quoted from the New York *Nation*, and dated
December 1943, concerning the current interest in Hölderlin in
Germany *(Horizon* 9:227).

The early forties also saw the publication of influential
volumes of translations, both in England and in the United States.
Michael Hamburger's bilingual *Poems of Hölderlin* began its continuing career in London in 1943, with the translations in verse
twice more, in the 1952 and 1967 editions,and once in "plain prose"
in the Penguin selection of 1961. J. B. Leishman's *Selected Poems
of Friedrich Hölderlin* was published in London by The Hogarth Press
in 1944, with a new edition coming out in 1954. Frederic Prokosch's
volume *Some Poems of Friedrich Hölderlin* was published by New
Directions in 1943, and was the subject of some striking reviews
in American periodicals. Paul Rosenfeld wrote about it in *The
Nation*, in the June 12, 1943 number, under the title "The Noblest
German of Them All," and Klaus Mann, in *The Saturday Review of
Literature* (January 8, 1944, pp. 8-9), writing from Camp Crowder,
Missouri, called his review "Hölderlin in the Barracks," ending
it with quotations from "Hyperions Schicksalslied" and "Andenken."

Vernon Watkins's cycle of poems "The Childhood of Hölderlin"
appeared in his volume of poems *Affinities* (London: Faber and
Faber, 1962), although parts of that cycle had already appeared
in *QRL* (10 [1959]: 14-22). Nor should one overlook the concerted
and intelligent attempt to introduce Hölderlin to an English-
speaking audience that was made by *QRL* in its special Hölderlin
Issue (vol. 10 [1959], nos. 1 and 2), which presented in translation a great variety of fundamental material: poems by Hölderlin, excerpts from *Hyperion*, an excerpt from one of Hellingrath's
1915 lectures, "An Essay on Hölderlin" by Stefan George (one of
the *Lobreden)*, a translation of Rilke's poem "An Hölderlin," and
Heidegger's essay "Hölderlin and the Essence of Poetry."

Hölderlin continues to be the subject of glancing allusion
in the work of modern poets, as for example in one of the poems
in Lawrence Ferlinghetti's *A Coney Island of the Mind* (New York:
New Directions, 1968).

3. W. H. Auden, *The Collected Poetry of W. H. Auden*, 20th printg.
(New York: Random House, 1966), pp. 174-75.

4. Ronald Peacock, *Hölderlin* (London: Methuen, 1938), p. 175.

5. It is not easy to win assent to *any* assumption about the nature
of romanticism, even the assumption of its existence. Practically, however, criticism continues to operate on the basis of
such assumptions: for example, in such statements as the following from Rudolf Wittkower's *Art and Architecture in Italy: 1600-
1750*, 2d rev. ed. (Baltimore: Penguin, 1965): "Annibale [Carracci]
handed down to his school the Renaissance method of slow and systematic preparation, and it is probably not too much to say that
it was mainly through his agency that the method remained in
vogue for the following 200 years. It broke down only in the
Romantic era, when it was felt that such a tedious process of

work hampered inspiration" (p. 38), or a similar statement concerning the falling into disrepute of the Renaissance tradition of "eclecticism" when it came into conflict "with the adulation of the *naïveté* of genius in the Romantic era" (ibid., p. 33).

6. Lilian R. Furst, *Romanticism in Perspective: A Comparative Study of Aspects of the Romantic Movements in England, France and Germany* (New York: St. Martin's Press; London: Macmillan, 1969).

7. Alessandro Pellegrini, *Hölderlin: Storia della critica* (Florence: Sansoni, n.d. [1956]), p. 14. See also Pellegrini's history of Hölderlin scholarship in the recent, revised and expanded German translation: Alessandro Pellegrini, *Friedrich Hölderlin: Sein Bild in der Forschung*, trans. Christoph Gassner (Berlin: de Gruyter, 1965).

8. Herbert Read, *The True Voice of Feeling: Studies in English Romantic Poetry* (London: Faber and Faber, 1953), pp. 52-53.

9. As quoted by Read, p. 53. *The Prelude*, 1805 version, 12:298-312. The corresponding passage in the 1850 version is 13:299-312. As Read's probable source, see William Wordsworth, *The Prelude, or Growth of a Poet's Mind*, ed. Ernest de Selincourt (Oxford: At the Clarendon Press, 1926).

10. On the development of Keats's sensibility and vision see also Read, pp. 55-75 ("The True Voice of Feeling: John Keats"); Aileen Ward, *John Keats: The Making of a Poet* (New York: Viking, 1963); on his affinity with Hölderlin, see Paul de Man, "Keats and Hölderlin," *CL* 8 (1956): 28-45.

11. The original text is a late fragment by Hölderlin to which Beissner assigns the title "Im Walde" (2:325). Read's note on the translation reads: "Trans. by Douglas Scott, from Martin Heidegger's essay on 'Hölderlin and the Essence of Poetry' included in the volume *Existence and Being*, London (Vision), 1949. The fragment, which was written in 1800, comes from Vol. IV, 246, of Hölderlin's *Werke*, ed. Norbert von Hellingrath, Berlin, 1914" (p. 54).

12. At the very least, there are differences of opinion about the precipitating cause of Hölderlin's madness; Edwin Muir, for instance, tracing the course of Hölderlin's life in the essay in *New Verse* referred to in note 2, says: "Then came his insanity: grief for the loss of Susette Gontard devastated his mind, smashing his classical world to pieces ...." (A slightly revised version of this essay on Hölderlin has also been available in Edwin Muir's volume *Essays on Literature and Society* [London: The Hogarth Press, 1949], pp. 83-89.) There are differences in the degree of knowledge in these matters, too, and diagnosis should surely be in the hands of experts.

13. See the article on *Romanticismo*, by Professor Ugo Dettore, in the opening section ("Movimenti spirituali") of the *Dizionario letterario Bompiani delle opere e dei personaggi di tutti i tempi e di tutte le letterature*, vol. 1 (Milan: Bompiani, 1949). It should

be mentioned that Professor Dettore, whose description of romanticism is fully international in scope, does not mention Hölderlin: in fact, Hölderlin has no entry in Bompiani's *Dizionario*.

14. Italic volume and page alone refer to the first printing of
Hyperion; see the general statement heading the notes.

15. See note 2.

16. Peacock, p. 20. For a comment on the poem that shows sensitivity to Keats's capacity for mystery, see Ward, pp. 321-22.

17. Peacock, p. 21.

Ingo Seidler

1. Stefan George, *Werke*, ed. Robert Boehringer, 2 vols. (Munich and
Düsseldorf: Küpper [Bondi], 1958), 1:520. This statement by
George is part of a *Lobrede* on Hölderlin originally printed in
Blätter für die Kunst, 11th and 12th ser. (1919), pp. 11-13.

2. Theodor Adorno, "Parataxis: Zur späten Lyrik Hölderlins," in
idem, *Noten zur Literatur*, 3 (Frankfurt am Main: Suhrkamp, 1965):
156-209, esp. pp. 188-89. The essay is reprinted in Jochen
Schmidt, ed., *Über Hölderlin* (Frankfurt am Main: Insel, 1970),
pp. 339-78.

3. Walther Killy, *Wandlungen des lyrischen Bildes*, 3d ed. (Göttingen:
Vandenhoeck und Ruprecht, 1961), p. 44.

4. Friedrich Nietzsche, *Werke*, ed. Karl Schlechta, 3 vols. (Munich:
Hanser, 1954-56), 3:95-98.

5. Werner Volke, *Hugo von Hofmannsthal in Selbstzeugnissen und
Bilddokumenten* (Reinbek bei Hamburg: Rowohlt, 1967) contains
a letter to the poet's father, in which the young Hofmannsthal
reports on his reading *"die schönen ernsten Gedichte von Hölderlin"* (the beautiful serious poems of Hölderlin [p. 54]).

6. George, *Werke*, 1:519-21.

7. Robert Boehringer's Hölderlin poem was printed in *Blätter für
die Kunst*, 10th ser. (1914), pp. 134-35.

8. Friedrich Gundolf, *Stefan George* (Berlin: Küpper Bondi , 1920),
here quoted from the catalogue of the centennial George exhibit
held in 1968 at the Schiller-Nationalmuseum, Marbach am Neckar:
Bernhard Zeller, comp., *Stefan George 1868-1968: Der Dichter und
sein Kreis*, 2d ed.(Munich: Kösel,1968), p. 279.

9. Edgar Salin, *Hölderlin im George-Kreis* (Bad Godesberg: Küpper,
1950), p. 29.

10. A more critical, and less prejudiced, discussion of George's relationship to Hölderlin will be found in the article by Hans-Georg Gadamer, "Hölderlin und George," *HöJb* 15 (1967-68): 75-91.

11. Reference to George's prose homage to Hölderlin of 1919 is made in note 1. The sequence of three verse monologues involving Hyperion, the protagonist of Hölderlin's only novel ("Hyperion I, II, III"), are printed in George, *Werke*, 1:404-6. Clearly, the Hyperion monologues can also be interpreted as poems in homage to Hölderlin.

12. This passage is a quotation from an unidentified letter by Karoline von Woltmann, used as a display quotation at the beginning of Alexander Jung, *Friedrich Hölderlin und seine Werke, mit besonderer Beziehung auf die Gegenwart* (Stuttgart and Tübingen: Cotta, 1848).

13. Friedrich Beissner, "Rilkes Begegnung mit Hölderlin," *DuV* 37 (1936): 36-50; Werner Günther, "Rilke und Hölderlin," *HöJb* 5 (1951): 12--57; Herbert Singer, *Rilke und Hölderlin* (Cologne and Graz, 1957).

14. Rilke's "Fünf Gesänge, August 1914" are printed in R 2:86-93, immediately preceding the poem "An Hölderlin" (ibid., pp. 93-95). (Rilke's works are referred to by R; his letters, by RB: see the general statement and list of abbreviations heading the notes.)

15. The first letter quoted, dated November 6, 1914, is to Karl and Elisabeth von der Heydt; the second, dated August 29, 1914, to Anna Freifrau von Münchhausen.

16. A pinpointing of the primacy of Klopstock's influence over Hölderlin's on aspects of Rilke's style is included in Singer, pp. 85-90.

17. Eugen Gottlob Winkler, "Der späte Hölderlin," in Walter Jens, ed., *Eugen Gottlob Winkler* (Frankfurt am Main: Fischer, 1960), p. 152. Winkler's Hölderlin essay is also available in Alfred Kelletat, ed., *Hölderlin: Beiträge zu seinem Verständnis in unserm Jahrhundert*, Schriften der Hölderlin-Gesellschaft, vol. 3 (Tübingen: Mohr [Siebeck], 1961), pp. 371-91.

18. The passage pertaining to Hölderlin will be found in Hugo von Hofmannsthal, *Aufzeichnungen*, ed. Herbert Steiner (Frankfurt am Main: Fischer, 1959), p. 314.

19. Walter Muschg, *Von Trakl zu Brecht: Dichter des Expressionismus* (Munich: Piper, 1961), pp. 45, 83, 171, 293.

20. Studies on expressionism that make no mention of Hölderlin include: Armin Arnold, *Die Literatur des Expressionismus: Sprachliche und thematische Quellen* (Stuttgart: Kohlhammer, 1966); Richard Brinkmann, *Expressionismus: Forschungsprobleme 1952-60* (Stuttgart: Metzler, 1961); Wolfgang Paulsen, ed., *Aspekte des Expressionismus: Periodisierung, Stil, Gedankenwelt* (Heidelberg: Stiehm, 1968). The Marbach exhibition catalogue

on expressionism: Bernhard Zeller, comp., *Expressionismus: Literatur und Kunst 1910-1923* (Marbach, 1960) contains one short reference to Hölderlin: Kurt Pinthus is quoted as having written on the poems of Wilhelm Klemm that *"über ihnen schimmert der feierliche Stern Hölderlins"* (over them there shines the festive star of Hölderlin [p. 129]).

21. Gottfried Benn, *Werke,* ed. Dieter Wellershoff, 4 vols. (Wiesbaden: Limes, 1958-61), 1:244.

22. The Josef Weinheber quotation is here translated from Werner Bartscher, *Hölderlin und die deutsche Nation: Versuch einer Wirkungsgeschichte Hölderlins* (Berlin: Triltsch, 1942), p. 220.

23. Hermann Pongs, "Einwirkungen Hölderlins auf die deutsche Dichtung seit der Jahrhundertwende," *Iduna (= HöJb)* 1 (1944): 114-59. Pongs's opinion concerning Weinheber's importance on the contemporary scene is shared, among others, by Harry Bergholz in his "A Note on Josef Weinheber," *Poetry* 85 (October 1954): 42-47, which Professor George brought to my attention. After looking for "the greatest poet of the generation to which, in Anglo-Saxon letters, T. S. Eliot corresponds" and considering such candidates as Trakl, Carossa (!), Werfel (!), and Benn, Bergholz suggests that "as the years go by, however, it appears that something like a general consensus is evolving, which concedes the first rank to Josef Weinheber" (p. 42). And Bergholz seems to suspect of nonliterary motives anyone who dares call Weinheber's stature as a poet into doubt. By contrast, I feel that it is precisely on literary grounds that Weinheber disqualifies himself, both as a great poet and as a respectable follower of Hölderlin. By the same token, comparison of Weinheber with T. S. Eliot is embarrassingly out of place.

24. Josef Nadler, *Josef Weinheber: Geschichte seines Lebens und seiner Dichtung* (Salzburg: Otto Müller, 1952), p. 120.

25. W 4:56-57. (Weinheber's works are quoted by W, volume, and page; see the list of abbreviations heading the notes.)

26. This passage is from Weinheber's "Wiener Poetik-Vorlesung" of 1944, quoted in Clemens Heselhaus, *Deutsche Lyrik der Moderne von Nietzsche bis Yvan Goll* (Düsseldorf: Bagel, 1961), p. 397.

27. Peter Demetz, *Postwar German Literature: A Critical Introduction* (New York: Pegasus, 1970), pp. 49, 73.

28. Günter Eich's "Latrine" is printed in Horst Bingel, ed., *Deutsche Lyrik: Gedichte seit 1945* (Stuttgart: Deutsche Verlags-Anstalt, 1961), p. 61.

29. Bertolt Brecht, *Gesammelte Werke,* ed. Elisabeth Hauptmann, 20 vols. (Frankfurt am Main: Suhrkamp, 1967), 2:767.

30. Hans Magnus Enzensberger, *Verteidigung der Wölfe* (Frankfurt am Main: Suhrkamp, 1957), p. 89.

31. Hans Magnus Enzensberger, *Landessprache* (Frankfurt am Main: Suhrkamp, 1960), p. 12.

32. Peter Rühmkorf, *Kunststücke: Fünfzig Gedichte nebst einer Anleitung zum Widerspruch* (Reinbek bei Hamburg: Rowohlt, 1962), pp. 79-81.

33. Götz Wienold, "Paul Celans Hölderlin-Widerruf," *Poetica* 2 (1968): 216-28. Paul Celan's poem "Tenebrae" is printed in his volume of poems *Sprachgitter* (Frankfurt am Main: Fischer, 1959), pp. 23-24; Celan's "Tübingen, Jänner" first appeared in his collection of verse *Die Niemandsrose* (Frankfurt am Main: Fischer, 1963), p. 24.
    The poems by George, Rilke, Weinheber, Eich, Rühmkorf, and Celan referred to in this study may also be found in: Dierk Rodewald, ed., *Insel Almanach auf das Jahr 1970: An Friedrich Hölderlin, Gedichte aus 180 Jahren deutsch- und fremdsprachiger Autoren* (Frankfurt am Main: Insel, 1969). In this anthology sixty poems to and on Hölderlin are gathered in one volume: thirty-eight in German, nine in English, four in Swedish, three in French, and one each in Croatian, Czech, Hungarian, Lachic, Latin, and Polish. The non-German originals appear with German translations.

34. Pierre Bertaux, "Ist Hölderlin heute noch aktuell?" *Die Welt* (supp. *Die geistige Welt)*, March 21, 1970, p. 1.

Theodore Fiedler

1. Past discussions of Trakl's relationship to Hölderlin have ignored the crucial question of how much of Hölderlin's poetry was available to the Austrian poet. A survey of the relevant evidence suggests that Trakl used one or more of the following editions of Hölderlin's works: Hölderlin, *Gesammelte Werke*, ed. Wilhelm Böhm and Paul Ernst, 3 vols. (Jena: Diederichs, 1905); Hölderlin, *Werke*, ed. Marie Joachimi-Dege, 2 vols. (Berlin: Bong, n.d. [1908]) (H; see the list of abbreviations); Hölderlin, *Gesammelte Werke*, ed. Wilhelm Böhm, 3 vols. (Jena: Diederichs, 1909-11). All three editions contain, in some form, all of the elegies, most of the odes, and six of the late hymns ("Der Rhein," "Germanien," "Die Wanderung," "Der Einzige," "Patmos," "Andenken") that appear in the *Grosse Stuttgarter Ausgabe*. In all probability, Trakl never saw the early impression of the famous fourth volume of Norbert v. Hellingrath's critical edition, which unearthed the rest, or very nearly the rest, of the late hymns and hymnic fragments. Hellingrath began sending copies of this early impression to his friends on June 6, 1914. Nothing indicates that anyone in the circle of the journal *Der Brenner*, to which Trakl himself belonged, received a copy. For a comprehensive discussion of the issue of Hölderlin editions available to Trakl, see the appendix on that subject in my "Trakl and Hölderlin: A Study in Influence" (Ph.D. diss., Washington University, 1969), pp. 196-208.

2. In citing Hölderlin's poetry, I have with few exceptions employed

the Joachimi-Dege edition of the *Werke* (H). In all probability
this edition was in Ludwig von Ficker's library by mid-1912 when
Ficker's friendship with Trakl began. During the next two years,
but especially in 1914 when he was nearly destitute, Trakl was
a frequent house guest at the Ficker residence and had access
to the library. He had liquidated his own small library in 1912.
Trakl's works are cited according to the new critical edition of
the *Dichtungen und Briefe*, ed. Walther Killy and Hans Szklenar
(T; see the list of abbreviations).

3. Attributing a word such as *Geschlecht* to a specific modern source
   will always remain problematical given its biblical origins, but
   it should be noted that it appears here in conjunction with other
   reminiscences of Hölderlin.

4. Cf. the first nine lines of "Brod und Wein" (H 1:193):

   Ringsum ruhet die Stadt; still wird die erleuchtete Gasse,
   Und mit Fackeln geschmückt rauschen die Wagen *hinweg.*
   Satt gehn heim von Freuden des Tags zu ruhen die Menschen,
   Und Gewinn und Verlust wäget ein sinniges Haupt
   Wohl zufrieden zu Haus; leer steht von Trauben und Blumen,
   Und von Werken der Hand ruht der geschäftige Markt.
   Aber das Saitenspiel tönt fern aus Gärten--*vielleicht dass*
   Dort ein Liebendes *spielt oder ein einsamer Mann*
   Ferner Freunde gedenkt und der Jugendzeit ....

   (Round us the town is at rest; the street, in pale lamplight,
        grows quiet
    And, their torches ablaze, *coaches rush* through and away.
   People go home to rest, replete with the day and its pleasures,
        There to weigh up in their heads, pensive, the gain and the loss,
   Finding the balance good; *stripped bare now of grapes and of*
        flowers,
        As of their hand-made goods, quiet *the market stalls lie.*
   But faint music of strings comes drifting from gardens; it could be
        Someone in love who plays there, could be a man all alone
   Thinking of distant friends, the days of his youth ....)

   with stanzas 2, 3, and 5 of "Träumerei am Abend" (T 1:290):

   Der Markt ist leer von roten Früchten und Gewinden.
   Einträchtig stimmt der Kirche schwärzliches Gepränge,
   In einem Garten tönen sanften Spieles Klänge,
   Wo Müde nach dem Mahle sich zusammenfinden.

   Ein Wagen rauscht, *ein Quell sehr fern durch grüne Pfühle.*
   Da zeigt sich eine Kindheit traumhaft und verflossen,
   Angelens Sterne, fromm zum mystischen Bild geschlossen,
   Und ruhig rundet sich die abendliche Kühle.

   Gezweige stiessen flüsternd ins verlassne Zimmer
   Und Liebendes *und kleiner Abendblumen Beben.*
   Der Menschen Stätte gürten Korn und goldne Reben,
   Den Toten aber *sinnet nach ein mondner Schimmer.*

   (The market is empty of red fruits and garlands,
   Uniformly, the church's congregation darkens,
   The sounds of soft playing are heard in a garden,
   Where after supper there congregate the tired ones.

8. In this and the following quotations from the "Anmerkungen zur Antigonae" the emphasis, represented by roman type in the German original and by italics in the English translations, is Hölderlin's own.

     For assistance with the final shaping of this paper, the author is indebted to the editor.

                         Lawrence O. Frye

1. Italic volume and page reference alone is to the *editio princeps* of *Hyperion;* see the prefatory statement to the notes.

2. The application of the astronomical figure to a presumable mental process in *Hyperion* is treated in detail by Wolfgang Schadewaldt in his article "Das Bild der exzentrischen Bahn bei Hölderlin," *HöJb* 6 (1952): 1-16. I am referring to the critique of Schadewaldt's work in Lawrence Ryan, *Hölderlins "Hyperion": Exzentrische Bahn und Dichterberuf* (Stuttgart: Metzler, 1965), pp. 11-12. I agree with Ryan's objections, but because of the way the concept is applied, not to the concept itself.

3. Usually the seasonal context is explicit (and will not be cited in this paper), even if mention is sometimes delayed so that it must be applied in retrospect. In other cases circumstantial evidence is usually adequate, such as battle dates for volume 2, book 1; or, in some difficult instances, deductions to be made from the stage of growth of vegetation mentioned. In most cases allusions are not to specific dates but to the seasonal periods of the year.

4. Plato *Politikos* 272e-273a. The English translation of this and subsequent passages from the *Politikos* is that found in J. B. Skemp, ed. and trans., *Plato's Statesman: A Translation of the "Politicus" of Plato* (New Haven: Yale University Press, 1952).

5. Beissner has cited the myth in the *Politikos* as the probable source for this allusion (3:450).

6. See Erwin Panofsky and Fritz Saxl, *Dürers "Melencolia I,"* Studien der Bibliothek Warburg, no. 2 (Leipzig and Berlin: Teubner, 1923), pp. 19, 46.

7. Ibid., pp. 57-58.

8. Ibid., p. 10.

9. Cf. Ryan, *Hölderlins "Hyperion,"* pp, 95-98. While Ryan applies the phrase *"in Ausflug und in Rückkehr zu sich selbst"* (in excursion and return to oneself) solely to nature's cycles at this point, the aborted attempt at self-regeneration in the boat scene is not mentioned by him. In general, Ryan does not undertake a closer study of seasonal features in the temporal structure of the novel.

10. There are various allusions in the text which convey the titan-like birth of Alabanda. The narrator's words allow for some ambiguity as to the direction of growth, although rejuvenation is in any case the result. A comparable interpretation of man returning to the cradle of life and time also applies to the line in the ode "Natur und Kunst oder Saturn und Jupiter," quoted from Beissner's variant apparatus (2:459):

> *und war In Wonne mir in ihrer*
> *Wiege, die wandelnde Zeit entschw⟨unden⟩*

> (and pleasurably for me in her
> Cradle, the wandering time had vanished .)

11. For a discussion of the titan in this vein see Emil Staiger, "Natur und Kunst oder Saturn und Jupiter," in idem, *Meisterwerke deutscher Sprache aus dem neunzehnten Jahrhundert*, 4th ed. rev. (Zürich: Atlantis, 1961), pp. 27, 30-31; also Staiger's study on the ode "Chiron," ibid., p. 52.

12. See also Ryan, *Hölderlins "Hyperion,"* p. 111.

13. Cf. a passage highly similar in wording--although not identical--much earlier in the novel: *"Du bist der Göttersohn, und teilst mit deinem sterblichen Kastor deine Unsterblichkeit"* (you are the son of a god, and share with your mortal Kastor your immortality *[1:61]*).

14. The whole series of Diotima-Hyperion letters from the book exhibits an interesting structure in which, among other things, they encompass a complete winter-to-winter cycle within half a year: from natural winter to Hyperion's psychic winter. One might say that this attempt to die and reenter the earth is an offense against nature, coming as it does so out of tune with nature's own rhythm. We observe in the autonomous cycle of Hyperion another expression, in temporal terms, for the reversal of orbital direction which characterizes the second volume: although the season and Hyperion's experience of time mesh for a while in the spring, the phases of his psychic year unfold in a contrasting relationship to the natural phases--until his ultimate decline which, in seeking death, polarizes the summer season. This is one of the more extreme instances of many that distinguish the temporal complexities of Hölderlin's novel from the plan of Goethe's first novel, *Die Leiden des jungen Werthers*. For an analysis of the latter, see Frank G. Ryder, "Season, Day, and Hour--Time as Metaphor in Goethe's *Werther*," *JEGP* 63 (1964): 389-407, especially the statement: "It is abundantly clear that the whole story of Werther moves in accord with the progression of the seasons" (p. 400).

15. It was written perhaps in June, judging by the reference in the letter preceding to Hyperion's having joined the Russian fleet (for the battle of July 5); this short letter Diotima says she received by May *(2:67)*. The silence in not having received Hyperion's letters during the summer is for Diotima another variation on the eclipse experience of the preceding summer.

16. Alabanda feels that his temporal cycle is being altered: *"Meine Seele wallt mir über von selbst und hält im alten Kreise nicht mehr. ... Wenn der Baum zu welken anfängt, tragen nicht alle seine Blätter die Farbe des Morgenrots?"* (My soul boils over by itself and will no longer be contained in its old circle. ... If the tree starts to turn, don't all its leaves bear the color of dawn? *[2:88-89]*). The titan in Alabanda is at the end of his era, but the spirit--still held to be free and self-determining by Alabanda--is rejuvenated through union with the spirit of natural regeneration. Diotima expresses comparable feelings of a time when *"die überwallende Seele auszugiessen wünschte"* (the spirit, boiling over, wanted to spill out *[2:98]*), so that it would no longer be in its old earthbound orbit: *"Du entzogst mein Leben der Erde"* (You deprived earth of my life *[2: 100]*). But death also is new life, where the world is *"wie ein wandelnder Triumphzug, wo die Natur den ewigen Sieg über alle Verderbniss feiert"* (like a wandering triumphal procession in which nature celebrates its eternal victory over all ruin *[2: 103-4]*).

17. She thereupon gives her *"schönster Traum"* (loveliest dream) of a renewed communal life of man and nature.

18. I refer to Ryan, *Hölderlins "Hyperion."*

Lawrence Ryan

1. In an early letter to Neuffer Hölderlin devotes a great deal of space to the development of *Hyperion* in his mind; the pertinent passage reads: *"Was zu so schön von der terra incognita im Reiche der Poesie sagst, trifft ganz genau besonders be einem Romane zu"* (What you so beautifully express concerning the *terra incognita* in the realm of poetry, applies quite accurately to a novel in particular *[6:87; No. 60]*).

2. Hans Heinrich Borcherdt, "Hölderlins *Hyperion,*" in idem, *Der Roman der Goethezeit* (Urach and Stuttgart: Port, 1949), p. 348.

3. Fritz Martini, "Der Bildungsroman: Zur Geschichte des Wortes und der Theorie," *DVLG* 35 (1961): 62.

4. Friedrich Schlegel, "Über Goethes Meister," *Athenaeum: Eine Zeitschrift,* ed. August Wilhelm Schlegel and Friedrich Schlegel, 1 (Berlin: Vieweg, 1798): 323-54. Reference to specific passages from Schlegel's review will be to this first printing, in conjunction with Wolfdietrich Rasch's edition of the *Kritische Schriften* (S; see the list of abbreviations).

5. The wording of the pertinent passage at the end of the novel is: *"Auch wir, auch wir sind nicht geschieden, Diotima, ... Lebendige Töne sind wir, stimmen zusammen in deinem Wohllaut, Natur!"* (We, we are not separated, either, Diotima, ... We are live tones, and harmonize, O nature, in your euphony *[2:124]*).

6. The most important of several Hölderlin passages referring to this unique astronomical metaphor for man's existence will be found in the preface to the "Thalia-Fragment" of *Hyperion* (3:163):

   Die exzentrische Bahn, die der Mensch, im Allgemeinen und Einzelnen, von einem Punkte (der mehr oder weniger reinen Einfalt) zum andern (der mehr oder weniger vollendeten Bildung) durchläuft, scheint sich, nach ihren wesentlichen Richtungen, *immer gleich zu sein.*

   (The eccentric path which man, in general as in particular, traverses from the one point [innocence more or less pure] to the other [culture more or less perfected] seems, *in point of its basic directions,* always to equal itself.)

7. S, p. 27.

8. *Athenaeum* 1:350 (S, p. 469).

9. *Athenaeum* 1:350; ibid., p. 348 (S, pp. 469, 468).

10. ibid., p. 348 (S, p. 468).

11. *Athenaeum* 1:204-6. (S, pp. 38-39).

12. S, pp. 20-21.

13. *Athenaeum* 1:334 (S, p. 459).

14. From a letter by Novalis to Karoline Schlegel of February 27, 1799. Quoted from: Novalis, *Briefe und Dokumente,* ed. Ewald Wasmuth (Heidelberg: Schneider, 1954), p. 459.

15. Friedrich Schlegel, *Literary Notebooks 1797-1801,* ed. Hans Eichner (Toronto: University of Toronto Press, 1957), no. 289. Cf. Hans Eichner, "Friedrich Schlegel's Theory of Romantic Poetry," *PMLA* 71 (1956): 1018-41.

Helm Stierlin

1. Two of the most representative collections of essays on Hölderlin by writers and critics of diverse backgrounds are: Alfred Kelletat, ed., *Hölderlin: Beiträge zu seinem Verständnis in unserm Jahrhundert,* Schriften der Hölderlin-Gesellschaft, vol. 3 (Tübingen: Mohr [Siebeck], 1961), and Jochen Schmidt, ed., *Über Hölderlin* (Frankfurt am Main: Insel, 1970).

2. Sigmund Freud, "Eine Kindheitserinnerung des Leonardo da Vinci," F 8:128-211.

3. See especially Wilhelm Lange, *Hölderlin: Eine Pathographie* (Stuttgart: Enke, 1909); Rudolf Treichler, "Die seelische Erkrankung Friedrich Hölderlins in ihren Beziehungen zu seinem dichterischen Schaffen," *ZfgNP* 155 (1936): 40-144.

4. The nonschizophrenic co-twin may or may not have a spectrum disorder, as just described.

5. L. Heston, "Psychiatric Disorders in Foster Home Reared Children of Schizophrenic Mothers," *British Journal of Psychiatry* 112 (1966): 819–25.

6. 6:52–53; No. 32. The letter seems to have been written under considerable emotional stress, and relies heavily, both on innuendo and on allusion to letters by Hölderlin's mother to her son, which are not preserved. For the one exception see her letter to Hölderlin dated October 29, 1805, quoted in this study.

7. Letter to Immanuel Nast, 6:8–9, No. 5, is only one good example of a number of letters from the Denkendorf-Maulbronn period (1784–88) in which similar sentiments are expressed.

8. See Philip Weissman, "Theoretical Considerations of Ego Regression and Ego Functions in Creativity," *Psychoanalytical Quarterly* 36 (1967): 37–50.

9. The present theory is not intended to slight, or even to de-emphasize, the importance to Hölderlin's fate·of unalterable external circumstances. Thus, for example, it is only sensible to note that the failure of the planned journal *Iduna* was in good measure the outcome of the inability, or even outright refusal, of distinguished writers like Schiller to collaborate. On the plans for *Iduna* see, in particular, Hölderlin's letter to Schiller of July 5, 1799 (6:342–43; No. 184) and Schiller's answer of August 24, 1799 (HW 6:326–27).

10. Eugen Bleuler, *Dementia praecox oder Gruppe der Schizophrenien* (Leipzig and Vienna: Denticke, 1911).

11. Friedrich Beissner, "Hölderlins letzte Hymne," in idem, *Hölderlin: Reden und Aufsätze* (Weimar: Böhlau, 1961), pp. 211–46; Hölderlin, *Selected Verse*, trans. Michael Hamburger (Baltimore: Penguin, 1961), pp. xxv–xxvi. Most recently this studied confusion in Hölderlin's latest fragments has been investigated sensitively from the point of view of a presumable language loss in Winfried Kudszus, *Sprachverlust und Sinnwandel: Zur späten und spätesten Lyrik Hölderlins* (Stuttgart: Metzler, 1969).

12. Pierre Bertaux, *Hölderlin und die französische Revolution* (Frankfurt am Main: Suhrkamp, 1969), p. 120.

13. Frida Arnold and Carl Viëtor, eds., *Die Briefe der Diotima* (Leipzig: Insel, 1921), p. 48.

14. In March 1799 Hölderlin sends Susette volume 2 of *Hyperion* enclosed with these lines: *"Hier unsern Hyperion, Liebe! ... Verzeih mirs, dass Diotima stirbt. Du erinnerst Dich, wir haben uns ehmals nicht ganz darüber vereinigen können"* (Here is our *Hyperion*, dear one! ... Forgive me that Diotima dies. You will recall, back then we were not quite able to agree on this point [ibid., p. 57]).

15. See especially Beissner, "Hölderlins letzte Hymne," pp. 239-46.

Emery E. George

1. These late odes—in almost every instance reworkings of earlier versions—are printed in 2:56-68. Together with the three strange short poems "Lebensalter," "Der Winkel von Hardt," and "Hälfte des Lebens," they constitute the cycle of "Nachtgesänge" published by Friedrich Wilmans in his *Taschenbuch für das Jahr 1805, der Liebe und Freundschaft gewidmet.*

2. Besides Hamburger's four versions or revisions of his translation of "Patmos," three in verse (1943, 1952, 1967) and one in prose (1961), and four unpublished translations by colleagues, I might mention as the most important renditions, complete and fragmentary: R. F. C. Hull, in Angel Flores, ed., *An Anthology of German Poetry from Hölderlin to Rilke* (Garden City, N. Y.: Doubleday, Anchor Books, 1960), pp. 34-40; K. W. Maurer, in *Universitas*, Quarterly English Language Edition, 4 (1961): 389; Frederic Prokosch, in *Some Poems of Friedrich Hölderlin*, trans. Frederic Prokosch (Norfolk, Conn.: New Directions, 1943), unnumbered pp. 23-29; Vernon Watkins, in *QRL* 10 (1959): 57-63.

3. Friedrich Hölderlin, *Gedichte, Hyperion*, ed. Kurt Waselowsky, Goldmanns Gelbe Taschenbücher, vol. 429 (Munich: Goldmann, 1957).

4. Edwin Muir, "Hölderlin's *Patmos*," in idem, *Essays on Literature and Society* (London: Hogarth, 1949), pp. 90-102; Alice Gladstone, "Hölderlin's 'Patmos': Voyage as Homecoming," *QRL* 10:64-76.

5. See especially the perceptive essay by Robert L. Beare, "Patmos, Dem Landgrafen von Homburg," *GR* 28 (1953): 5-22.

6. Cf. a closely pertinent passage toward the end of Hölderlin's essay "Über die Verfahrungsweise des poetischen Geistes": *"... und es ist vorzüglich wichtig, dass er in diesem Augenblicke nichts als gegeben annehme, ..., dass die Natur und Kunst, ..., nicht eher spreche, ehe für ihn eine Sprache da ist"* (and it is especially important that in this moment he take nothing for granted, ... that nature and art ... do not speak sooner than a language is there for his use [4:263-64]).

7. Hölderlin's term for the main divisions of the Pindaric hymn is *Parthien,* and understandable doubts have been voiced as to the precise definition of this term in Hölderlin's poetics. See my article "A Family of Disputed Readings in Hölderlin's Hymn 'Der Rhein'," *MLR* 61 (1966): 627, and fn. 4.

8. By this I do not mean to disagree with critics who say that Hölderlin here means the Christ in Glory; my world-mythological view is meant as an *addition to and possible enrichment of* this image.

9. Homer, *The Iliad of Homer*, trans. Richmond Lattimore (Chicago: University of Chicago Press, 1962), p. 7.

Bibliography

The following, strictly select, list of references overlaps with, but makes no attempt to duplicate, the bibliographical information contained in the footnotes. Nor does it list historical-critical editions, or collections of verse by poets represented in part I. The purpose of the bibliography is to orient the reader to the main points of view represented by the essays and commentaries in parts II and III, and to recommend further reading. Material is organized under five headings: (1) secondary readings on Hölderlin, (2) classics, (3) comparative literature (including English, German, and Russian and East European studies) and comparative aesthetics, (4) history, (5) psychiatry. Comparative and psychiatric entries involving Hölderlin will be found under the first heading.

Secondary Readings on Hölderlin

Bartscher, Werner. *Hölderlin und die deutsche Nation: Versuch einer Wirkungsgeschichte Hölderlins*. Berlin, 1942.

Beissner, Friedrich. *Hölderlins Übersetzungen aus dem Griechischen*. 2d ed. Stuttgart, 1961.

_____. "Hölderlins letzte Hymne." *HöJb* 3 (1948-49): 66-102.

Benn, M. B. *Hölderlin and Pindar*. Anglica Germanica, no. 4. The Hague, 1962.

Bertallot, Hans-Werner. *Hölderlin-Nietzsche: Untersuchungen zum hymnischen Stil in Prosa und Vers*. Germanische Studien, no. 141. Berlin, 1933.

Bertaux, Pierre. *Hölderlin und die französische Revolution*. Frankfurt am Main, 1969.

Böhm, Wilhelm. *Hölderlin*. 2 vols. Halle/Saale, 1928-30.

Bowra, C. M. "Hölderlin's Hymns." In *Inspiration and Poetry*, pp. 130-52. London, 1955.

Dilthey, Wilhelm. *Das Erlebnis und die Dichtung: Lessing, Goethe, Novalis, Hölderlin.* 13th ed. Göttingen, 1957.

Gadamer, Hans-Georg. "Hölderlin und George." *HöJb* 15 (1967–68): 75–91.

Guardini, Romano. *Hölderlin: Weltbild und Frömmigkeit.* 2d ed. Munich, 1955.

Heidegger, Martin. *Erläuterungen zu Hölderlins Dichtung.* 2d rev. ed. Frankfurt am Main, 1951.

Hölderlin, Friedrich. *Poems and Fragments.* Translated by Michael Hamburger. Ann Arbor, 1967.

Kelletat, Alfred, ed. *Hölderlin: Beiträge zu seinem Verständnis in unserm Jahrhundert.* Schriften der Hölderlin-Gesellschaft, vol. 3. Tübingen, 1961.

Killy, Walther. *Wandlungen des lyrischen Bildes.* 3d ed. Göttingen, 1961.

Kirchner, Werner. *Der Hochverratsprozess gegen Sinclair: Ein Beitrag zum Leben Hölderlins.* Marburg/Lahn, 1949.

Lange, Wilhelm. *Hölderlin: Eine Pathographie.* Stuttgart, 1909.

Man, Paul de. "Keats and Hölderlin." *CL* 8 (1956): 28–45.

Mason, Eudo C. "Hölderlin and Goethe." *PEGS* n.s. 22 (1953): 64–83.

Michel, Wilhelm. *Das Leben Friedrich Hölderlins.* Frankfurt am Main, 1967.

_____. *Hölderlins abendländische Wendung.* Weimar, 1922.

Muir, Edwin. *Essays on Literature and Society.* 2d rev. ed. London, 1965.

Peacock, Ronald. *Hölderlin.* London, 1938.

Pellegrini, Alessandro. *Hölderlin: Storia della critica.* Florence, 1956.

_____. *Friedrich Hölderlin: Sein Bild in der Forschung.* Translated by Christoph Gassner. Berlin, 1965.

Ryan, Lawrence J. *Hölderlins "Hyperion": Exzentrische Bahn und Dichterberuf.* Stuttgart, 1965.

_____. *Hölderlins Lehre vom Wechsel der Töne.* Stuttgart, 1960.

_____. "Hölderlins prophetische Dichtung." *JDSG* 6 (1962): 194–228.

Schadewaldt, Wolfgang. "Das Bild der exzentrischen Bahn bei Hölderlin." *HöJb* 6 (1952): 1–16.

Schmidt, Jochen, ed. *Über Hölderlin.* Frankfurt am Main, 1970.

Silz, Walter. "Hölderlin and Wordsworth: Bicentenary Reflections." *GR* 45 (1970): 259–72.

_____. *Hölderlin's "Hyperion": A Critical Reading*. University of Pennsylvania Studies in Germanic Languages and Literatures. Philadelphia, 1969.

Stahl, E. L. "Hölderlin's 'Friedensfeier' and the Structure of Mythic Poetry." *OGS* 2 (1967): 55-74.

Treichler, Rudolf. "Die seelische Erkrankung Friedrich Hölderlins in ihren Beziehungen zu seinem dichterischen Schaffen." *ZfgNP* 155 (1936): 40-144.

Wells, F. L. "Hölderlin: Greatest of Schizophrenics?" In *The Literary Imagination: Psychoanalysis and the Genius of the Writer*, edited by Hendrik M. Ruitenbeek, pp. 233-46. Chicago, 1965.

Wienold, Götz. "Paul Celans Hölderlin-Widerruf." *Poetica* 2 (1968): 216-28.

Wöhrmann, Klaus-Rüdiger. *Hölderlins Wille zur Tragödie*. Munich, 1967.

Classics

Bowra, C. M. *Sophoclean Tragedy*. Oxford, 1944.

Kirkwood, G. M. *A Study of Sophoclean Drama*. Ithaca, 1958.

Kitto, H. D. F. *Greek Tragedy: A Literary Study*. 3d ed. New York, 1961.

_____. *Sophocles, Dramatist and Philosopher*. London, 1958.

Lattimore, Richmond. *Story Patterns in Greek Tragedy*. Ann Arbor, 1969.

Lesky, Albin. *Die tragische Dichtung der Hellenen*. 2d rev. ed. Studienhefte zur Altertumswissenschaft, no. 2. Göttingen, 1964.

Long, A. A. *Language and Thought in Sophocles: A Study of Abstract Nouns and Poetic Technique*. London, 1968.

Opstelten, J. C. *Sophocles and Greek Pessimism*. Amsterdam, 1952.

Reinhardt, Karl. *Sophokles*. 3d ed. Frankfurt am Main, 1948.

Waldock, A. J. A. *Sophocles the Dramatist*. Cambridge, 1951.

Webster, T. B. L. *An Introduction to Sophocles*. Oxford, 1936.

Weinstock, H. *Sophokles*. 3d ed. Wuppertal, 1948.

Whitman, Cedrick H. *Sophocles: A Study of Heroic Humanism*. Cambridge, Mass., 1951.

Wilamowitz-Moellendorff, Tycho von. *Die dramatische Technik des Sophokles*. Philologische Untersuchungen, no. 22. Berlin, 1917.

Comparative Literature and Comparative Aesthetics

Abrams, M. H. "Coleridge, Baudelaire, and Modernist Poetics." In *Immanente Ästhetik--ästhetische Reflexion: Lyrik als Paradigma der Moderne*, edited by Wolfgang Iser, pp. 113-38. Poetik und Hermeneutik, no. 2. Munich, 1966.

_____. *The Mirror and the Lamp: Romantic Theory and the Critical Tradition*. Oxford, 1953.

Anderson, Warren D. *Matthew Arnold and the Classical Tradition*. Ann Arbor, 1965.

Arrowsmith, William, and Shattuck, Roger, eds. *The Craft and Context of Translation: A Critical Symposium*. Garden City, N. Y., 1964.

Borcherdt, Hans Heinrich. *Der Roman der Goethezeit*. Urach and Stuttgart, 1949.

Brower, Reuben A., ed. *On Translation*. Harvard Studies in Comparative Literature, no. 23. Cambridge, Mass., 1959.

Clark, Robert T., Jr. *Herder: His Life and Thought*. Berkeley and Los Angeles, 1955.

Demetz, Peter. *Postwar German Literature: A Critical Introduction*. New York, 1970.

Frye, Northrop. *Romanticism Reconsidered*. New York, 1963.

Furst, Lilian R. *Romanticism in Perspective: A Comparative Study of Aspects of the Romantic Movements in England, France, and Germany*. New York, 1969.

Gundolf, Friedrich. *Stefan George*. Berlin, 1920.

Hamburger, Käthe. *Von Sophokles zu Sartre: Griechische Dramenfiguren, antik und modern*. Stuttgart, 1962.

Heselhaus, Clemens. *Deutsche Lyrik der Moderne von Nietzsche bis Yvan Goll*. Düsseldorf, 1961.

_____. "Die 'Elis'-Gedichte von Georg Trakl." *DVLG* 28 (1954): 384-413.

Karlinsky, Simon. *Marina Cvetaeva: Her Life and Art*. Berkeley and Los Angeles, 1966.

Miles, Josephine. *Style and Proportion: The Language of Prose and Poetry*. Boston, 1967.

Muschg, Walter. *Von Trakl zu Brecht: Dichter des Expressionismus*. Munich, 1961.

Nadler, Josef. *Josef Weinheber: Geschichte seines Lebens und seiner Dichtung*. Salzburg, 1952.

Oates, Whitney J., ed. *From Sophocles to Picasso: The Present-Day Vitality of the Classical Tradition*. Bloomington, Ind., 1962.

Panofsky, Erwin, and Saxl, Fritz. *Dürers "Melencolia I."* Studien der Bibliothek Warburg, no. 2. Leipzig and Berlin, 1923.

Paulsen, Wolfgang, ed. *Aspekte des Expressionismus: Periodisierung, Stil, Gedankenwelt*. Heidelberg, 1968.

Prawer, Siegbert, ed. *The Romantic Period in Germany*. New York, 1970.

Praz, Mario. *Mnemosyne: The Parallel between Literature and the Visual Arts*. The A. W. Mellon Lectures in the Fine Arts. Bollingen series, vol. 35, no. 16. Princeton, 1970.

Read, Herbert. *The True Voice of Feeling: Studies in English Romantic Poetry*. London, 1953.

———. *The Philosophy of Modern Art*. New York, 1953.

Rubulis, Aleksis. *Baltic Literature: A Survey of Finnish, Estonian, Latvian, and Lithuanian Literatures*. Notre Dame, Ind., 1970.

Schwarz, Egon. "Hermann Hesse, the American Youth Movement, and Problems of Literary Evaluation." *PMLA* 85 (1970): 977-87.

Stepun, Fedor. *Mystische Weltschau: Fünf Gestalten des russischen Symbolismus*. Munich, 1964.

Sypher, Wylie. *Rococo to Cubism in Art and Literature*. New York, 1963.

Tecchi, Bonaventura. *Svevia, terra di poeti*. Rome, 1964.

Walzel, Oskar. *Gehalt und Gestalt im Kunstwerk des Dichters*, Berlin, 1923.

Ward, Aileen. *John Keats: The Making of a Poet*. New York, 1963.

Weissenberger, Klaus. *Formen der Elegie von Goethe bis Celan*. Berne and Munich, 1969.

Wellek, René. *Concepts of Criticism*. Edited by Stephen G. Nichols, Jr. New Haven, 1967.

Willson, A. Leslie. *A Mythical Image: The Ideal of India in German Romanticism*. Durham, N. C., 1964.

Wittkower, Rudolf. *Art and Architecture in Italy: 1600-1750*. 2d rev. ed. Baltimore, 1965.

History

Butler, Elizabeth M. *The Tyranny of Greece over Germany*. Cambridge, 1935.

Dodds, E. R. *The Greeks and the Irrational*. 2d paperbound ed. Berkeley, 1964.

Gay, Peter. *The Enlightenment: An Interpretation*. 2 vols. New York, 1967-69.

Gebhardt, Jürgen. *Die Revolution des Geistes*. Munich, 1968.

Hammond, N. G. L. *A History of Greece to 322 B.C.* 2d ed. Oxford, 1967.

Hatfield, Henry. *Aesthetic Paganism in German Literature*. Cambridge, Mass., 1964.

Hazard, Paul. *The European Mind, 1680-1715*. London, 1953.

_____. *European Thought in the Eighteenth Century, from Montesquieu to Lessing*. London, 1954.

Heer, Friedrich. *The Intellectual History of Europe*. Translated by Jonathan Steinberg. New York, 1968.

Manuel, Frank E. *The Eighteenth Century Confronts the Gods*. Cambridge, Mass., 1959.

Mollenauer, Robert, ed. *Introduction to Modernity: A Symposium on Eighteenth-Century Thought*. Austin, Tex., 1965.

Murray, Gilbert. *Five Stages of Greek Religion*. 3d ed. New York, 1955.

Rehm, Walther. *Griechentum und Goethezeit: Geschichte eines Glaubens*. 4th ed. Berne and Munich, n.d. [1968].

Psychiatry

Bleuler, Eugen. *Dementia praecox oder Gruppe der Schizophrenien*. Leipzig and Vienna, 1911.

Freud, Sigmund. "Eine Kindheitserinnerung des Leonardo da Vinci." F 8:128-211.

_____. "Trauer und Melancholie." F 10:428-46.

Heston, L. "Psychiatric Disorders in Foster Home Reared Children of Schizophrenic Mothers." *British Journal of Psychiatry* 112 (1966): 819-25.

Jaspers, Karl. *Strindberg und Van Gogh: Versuch einer pathographischen Analyse unter vergleichender Heranziehung von Swedenborg und Hölderlin*. 3d ed. Bremen, 1951.

Kringlen, Einar. *Heredity and Environment in the Functional Psychoses: An Epidemiological-Clinical Twin Study*. Oslo, 1967.

Kety, Seymour S., and Rosenthal, David, eds. *The Transmission of Schizophrenia*. London, 1969.

Rosenbaum, C. Peter. *The Meaning of Madness*. New York, 1970.

Stierlin, Helm. "Bleuler's Concept of Schizophrenia: A Confusing Heritage." *American Journal of Psychiatry* 123 (1967): 996-1001.

_____. *Conflict and Reconciliation: A Study in Human Relations and Schizophrenia*. New York, 1969.

Tienari, Pekka. "Psychiatric Illnesses in Identical Twins." *Acta Psychiatrica Scandinavica*, supp. 171, 39 (1963): 9-195.

Weissman, Philip. "Theoretical Considerations of Ego Regression and Ego Functions in Creativity." *Psychoanalytical Quarterly* 36 (1967): 37-50.

Contributors

Herbert Barrows is Professor of English at The University of Michigan. His special interests include English romantic poetry and theory and the study of travel journals of the eighteenth and early nineteenth centuries. He is editor of the travel journal by Hester Lynch Piozzi, *Observations and Reflections Made in the Course of a Journey through France, Italy, and Germany,* published in 1967 by The University of Michigan Press.

Gerald F. Else, Professor of Greek and Latin at The University of Michigan and Director of the University's Center for Coördination of Ancient and Modern Studies, has among his numerous publications two books, *Aristotle's Poetics: The Argument* and *The Origin and Early Form of Greek Tragedy,* both published by Harvard University Press. In 1967 The University of Michigan Press published his translation of Aristotle's *Poetics.*

Theodore Fiedler, Assistant Professor of German at the University of California, Irvine, is especially interested in Hölderlin and Trakl and in the fields of twentieth-century literature and literary theory. He is at work on a book on Roman Ingarden.

Lawrence O. Frye, Associate Professor of German at Indiana University, specializes in Hölderlin, early German romanticism, and Fontane. A volume of essays in progress will treat structural and narrative devices in novels by Hoffmann, Novalis, Friedrich Schlegel, and Tieck.

Emery E. George, Associate Professor of German and Comparative Literature at The University of Michigan, is interested in Hölderlin, twentieth-century poetry, and the application of linguistics to poetics. He has published articles on Hölderlin, Trakl, and Apollinaire, translations of poetry from Estonian, German, Hungarian, and Russian, and poetry in several literary quarterlies.

Michael Hamburger, distinguished poet, critic, and translator, lives in London and is Visiting Professor at the University of Connecticut this year. His numerous books include four collections of poetry and the definitive volume of translations, *Friedrich Hölderlin, Poems and Fragments*. The latter was published in 1967 by The University of Michigan Press. An expanded version of his volume of essays on German literature, *Reason and Energy*, was published by E. P. Dutton & Co. in 1970 under the title *Contraries*.

Cyrus Hamlin is Associate Professor of English and Comparative Literature at the University of Toronto. He has translated Hölderlin's poetry extensively and has contributed studies on Hölderlin to journals and yearbooks published in Canada and in Germany. His deluxe facsimile edition of the London manuscript of Hölderlin's elegy "Stutgard" was published in Stuttgart during the bicentennial year.

Wilfried Malsch is Professor of German at the University of Massachusetts. He specializes in Goethe, Hölderlin, and Novalis, on all of whom he has contributed scholarly articles. His book *"Europa": Poetische Rede des Novalis* was published in Stuttgart in 1965 by J. B. Metzler.

Christopher Middleton is Professor of German at the University of Texas at Austin. He is a distinguished poet, with several books of poetry to his credit. His well-known anthology

Modern German Poetry 1910-1960, which he edited in collaboration
with Michael Hamburger, was published in 1962 by Bobs-Merrill.
His *Selected Poems of Friedrich Hölderlin and Eduard Mörike* is
scheduled for publication by The University of Chicago Press.

Aleksis Rannit, Curator of Russian and East European Collections at Yale University, is a distinguished poet in his
native Estonian and an internationally recognized art critic
and essayist. He has published five volumes of verse in addition to several books on aesthetics and art criticism, both in
this country and abroad. Comparative aesthetics is one of his
central interests.

Lawrence Ryan, Professor of German at the University of
Massachusetts, is one of the most important Hölderlin scholars
living. He is the author of three books on the poet, among
them *Hölderlins "Hyperion": Exzentrische Bahn und Dichterberuf*,
published in 1965 by J. B. Metzler. His critical introduction
Friedrich Hölderlin was published in the Sammlung Metzler
series in 1962. He has also published on Goethe, Hebbel, Rilke,
Kafka, and Brecht.

Ingo Seidler is Professor of German and Comparative Literature at The University of Michigan. He is a specialist in
literary criticism, theory, and aesthetics, and has published
widely on nineteenth- and twentieth-century German writers and
philosophers, especially Hölderlin, Nietzsche, Musil, Mann,
Kafka, and Grass. His studies of contemporary poets have included Rilke, Benn, Brecht, and Huchel. He is also a translator of modern poetry into English and German.

Helm Stierlin is Acting Chief of the Family Studies Section, Adult Psychiatry Branch, at the National Institute of
Mental Health, Bethesda, Maryland. He has to his credit numerous contributions to medical journals and books, as well as
the book *Conflict and Reconciliation: A Study in Human Relations
and Schizophrenia* published in 1969 as a Doubleday Anchor
Original. His studies reflect his combined interest in psy-

chiatry and literature and often involve literary figures such as Hölderlin and Strindberg.

Stephen Tonsor is Professor of History at The University of Michigan. His main fields of interest include nineteenth-century and contemporary European intellectual history, nineteenth-century historiography, and contemporary educational theory. He is the author of a book on National Socialism, published by Holt, Rinehart, and Winston in 1959, and is at work on another to be entitled *"Jugendstil" and "Jugendbewegung."*

ERRATUM

All Roman numerals in this Index
should be one number higher.

Index

The index of names and subjects includes the notes, but not the
bibliography. Italic page references are to unabridged printings or
reprintings of texts in this book.

J